SolidWorks®

FOR

DUMMIES®

2ND EDITION

SolidWorks® FOR DUMMIES®

2ND EDITION

by Greg Jankowski and Richard Doyle

BICENTENNIAL
1807
WILEY
2007
BICENTENNIAL

Wiley Publishing, Inc.

SolidWorks® For Dummies®, 2nd Edition

Published by
Wiley Publishing, Inc.
111 River Street
Hoboken, NJ 07030-5774
www.wiley.com

Copyright © 2008 by Wiley Publishing, Inc., Indianapolis, Indiana

Published by Wiley Publishing, Inc., Indianapolis, Indiana

Published simultaneously in Canada

For general information on our other products and services, please contact our Customer Care Department within the U.S. at 800-762-2974, outside the U.S. at 317-572-3993, or fax 317-572-4002.

For technical support, please visit www.wiley.com/techsupport.

Wiley also publishes its books in a variety of electronic formats. Some content that appears in print may not be available in electronic books.

Library of Congress Control Number: 2007936102
ISBN: 978-0-470-12978-4

Manufactured in the United States of America

10 9 8 7 6 5 4 3 2 1

WILEY

About the Authors

Greg Jankowski is the Customer Satisfaction Manager at SolidWorks corporation. He is a veteran (translation: been doing this longer than he cares to admit) in the CAD industry with experience using SolidWorks, ProEngineer, and Computervision CAD systems in a variety of mechanical design and developmental positions. Greg was the Principal at CIMCO, a SolidWorks Solution Partner since SolidWorks 95.

Greg is the author of the book *SolidWorks for AutoCAD Users* and the e-book *Exploring SolidWorks.* In addition, he authored and developed the SolidWorks workstation benchmark. He is also the author of the *Cadalyst* magazine column "Solid Thinking" and is a regular columnist for the *SolidWorks Express* newsletter.

Richard Doyle is the User Community Coordinator at SolidWorks, responsible for helping SolidWorks user groups grow and thrive. A SolidWorks user since 1997, Richard has 29 years of experience in the field of mechanical drafting and design, including 22 years spent working with CAD. As one of the original founding members of the SolidWorks User Group Network (SWUGN) committee, Richard has spent a good deal of time helping to keep SolidWorks users informed and educated and enjoying the benefits of working with 3D CAD.

Dedications

Greg Jankowski: This book is dedicated to the three women in my life, my wife Sandy and daughters Alexis and Kaitlyn, who continue to put up with me and my crazy projects. I appreciate their patience, love, and understanding.

I also want to dedicate this book to all the hard-working folks at SolidWorks. It continues to be my pleasure to work with some of the best, hardest-working, and brightest folks in the industry.

Richard Doyle: This book is dedicated to the SolidWorks User Group Network (SWUGN) committee and all the SolidWorks user group leaders. These hard-working volunteers spend a lot of their own time making sure that fellow SolidWorks users have an outlet for networking and learning and for sharing information about SolidWorks and mechanical engineering.

Authors' Acknowledgments

Thanks to Ricky Jordan, who did the technical editing for this edition. Ricky's careful attention to detail and vast knowledge of SolidWorks made him the perfect choice.

Thanks to Greg Jankowski, who allowed me the opportunity to update this book for SolidWorks 2008.

Special thanks to Becky Huehls, project editor, who offered encouragement and advice and showed remarkable patience during this entire process.

Publisher's Acknowledgments

We're proud of this book; please send us your comments through our online registration form located at www.dummies.com/register/.

Some of the people who helped bring this book to market include the following:

Acquisitions, Editorial, and Media Development

Project Editor: Rebecca Huehls

Acquisitions Editor: Kyle Looper

Copy Editor: Rebecca Whitney

Technical Editor: Ricky Jordan

Editorial Manager: Leah P. Cameron

Media Project Supervisor:
Laura Moss-Hollister

Editorial Assistant: Amanda Foxworth

Sr. Editorial Assistant: Cherie Case

Cartoons: Rich Tennant
(www.the5thwave.com)

Composition Services

Project Coordinator: Erin Smith

Layout and Graphics: Claudia Bell,
Melissa K. Jester, Stephanie D. Jumper,
Christine Williams

Proofreaders: ConText Editorial Services, Inc.,
John Greenough

Indexer: Sherry Massey

Anniversary Logo Design: Richard Pacifico

Publishing and Editorial for Technology Dummies

Richard Swadley, Vice President and Executive Group Publisher

Andy Cummings, Vice President and Publisher

Mary Bednarek, Executive Acquisitions Director

Mary C. Corder, Editorial Director

Publishing for Consumer Dummies

Diane Graves Steele, Vice President and Publisher

Joyce Pepple, Acquisitions Director

Composition Services

Gerry Fahey, Vice President of Production Services

Debbie Stailey, Director of Composition Services

Contents at a Glance

Table of Contents

Introduction

I started using SolidWorks when the first version, SolidWorks 95, came out on the market. It's amazing to see how far solid modeling has come since then. Working within a 3D environment has transformed the way I create, iterate, and document a design.

One reason I wrote this book is to help boil down much of the material that's out there and focus on not only what I believe to be important from my design experience but also how I think the software should be used.

Although many things are similar to what was done ten years ago, many things have changed. Even some of the saltier veterans out there can gain something from the ideas presented within this book.

SolidWorks is becoming a more mature application, and instead of getting harder to use, it makes modeling easier and, quite frankly, more fun.

One concept that recurs throughout this book is the ability of SolidWorks to reuse design information, saving you from having to do things manually. For example, SolidWorks can use the information in your part or assembly model to create manufacturing drawings automatically.

This way of creating products saves time and produces better results. *SolidWorks For Dummies,* 2nd Edition, shows you how.

Enjoy your journey with SolidWorks. You'll love the experience.

About This Book

This book isn't designed to be read from cover to cover, although it can be. *SolidWorks For Dummies* is designed as a reference book that you can use at any time.

This book isn't meant to be a complete reference for SolidWorks. If it were, you probably wouldn't want to drop it on your foot. Instead, I have focused on the key and commonly used elements of SolidWorks.

Conventions Used in This Book

I use the following conventions throughout this book:

- ✔ I use the term *document* to refer to drawing, part, or assembly files in SolidWorks.
- ✔ The list of items across the top of the SolidWorks interface comprises the main menu. Each item on the main menu also has a hidden list, or *pull-down* menu. Whenever I want you to choose a series of commands from the menu, I use the phrasing "Choose File⇨Save," for example.

What You're Not to Read

Sometimes this book can be a little bit technical. But because I'm a nice guy, I always warn you about the stuff you can skip, by planting a handy Technical Stuff icon nearby. Although the information next to this icon is interesting, you don't have to read it. The same holds true for sidebars, which are the gray boxes that you see scattered throughout the book. Although the information in the sidebars is interesting, it's just extra information that's nonessential to understanding the topic at hand.

Foolish Assumptions

When I wrote *SolidWorks For Dummies,* I assumed very little about you — just that you're somewhat familiar with a computer and the Windows operating system. But I didn't assume that you have any earlier SolidWorks experience.

If you're not comfortable working with your computer, you may want to pick up a copy of *PCs For Dummies,* by Dan Gookin (Wiley), which walks you through the basics.

I also assume that you have a slight CAD system background. I counted on your having a basic knowledge of geometry, lines, circles, and points, for example. I don't, however, assume that you can create these objects.

One other assumption I make is that you have some experience in engineering or design or that you're pursuing a career in a related field.

How This Book Is Organized

This book has five major parts. Each part contains several chapters, and each chapter contains several sections. You can read any section without reading the entire book or even without reading earlier sections within that same chapter. Here's what you find in each part:

Part 1: Beginning the SolidWorks Journey

This part introduces SolidWorks and 3D design. You find out about the user interface, SolidWorks file types, and system setup. I also highlight the new features in SolidWorks 2008.

Part 11: Design Intent and the Virtual Prototype

This part contains the "beef" of the book. In this part, I talk about creating sound, robust 2D sketches and examine design intent. (Do what I mean, not what I sketch!) I also talk about the many ways to design and model a part and the virtual prototype.

Part 111: The Devil's in the "Drawing" Details

Drawings are a necessary part of the manufacturing process. In this part of the book, I talk about how SolidWorks uses information captured in the model to create drawings automatically. I also cover several other SolidWorks drawing features that make your life easier.

Part 1V: Playing Nicely with Others (And Picking Up Your Toys)

If you can't find anything on your desk, this chapter may be a tough read. This part focuses on managing and sharing information with other team members so that your projects are more effective.

Part V: The Part of Tens

The Part of Tens provides examples, tips, and references for SolidWorks. You discover how you can become more proficient in SolidWorks, as well as how you can reuse design information and extend the capabilities of SolidWorks. Lastly, you find out about resources in the vast SolidWorks community.

About the CD

The CD included with *SolidWorks For Dummies* contains a product demo and add-on solutions. For more information on the CD, see the "About the CD" appendix, at the back of this book.

Icons Used in This Book

Throughout this book, I use icons to flag information. Some icons mark topics that are useful down the line, whereas others warn you of geek topics ahead.

Here's what each icon means:

This icon flags useful tips and insight into the current topic. Read these tips carefully because they can save you time and effort.

Think of this icon as a message taped to your forehead. It serves as a gentle reminder to help reinforce a concept or an idea.

This icon says "Beware — potential problems lie ahead." To steer clear of trouble, pay close attention to the text that this icon flags.

This one is for the technogeeks out there. (I number myself as one.) If you get bored easily, skip this text.

Where to Go from Here

If you're ready to get started, turn the page and keep reading or, better yet, review the table of contents or index to find topics that interest you. No matter which approach you choose, you're well on your way to becoming a SolidWorks user. Creating products in 3D is a fun and effective way to design. Enjoy!

Part I

Beginning the SolidWorks Journey

In this part . . .

Beginning the journey into 3D can seem daunting. It's not that bad — honest. In fact, it can be fun. This part introduces you to SolidWorks. You find out about some of the new features in SolidWorks 2008 as well as how to set up SolidWorks before you start your first design project. You also delve into the topics of design layout and intent.

Chapter 1

Getting to Know (And Love) SolidWorks

In This Chapter

▶ Becoming familiar with SolidWorks

▶ Discovering the advantages of the virtual prototype

▶ Figuring out where to start with SolidWorks

▶ Getting acquainted with new features in SolidWorks 2008

SolidWorks is a tool that helps design engineers harness their imaginations and add creativity to their designs. The true mark of a good tool is when it becomes part of your process without getting in your way. When you design, you need to do just that — design!

When SolidWorks was created, the power of 3D wasn't yet widespread. The company's original mission back in 1995 — and a goal it still pursues today — is to bring the power of 3D to every engineer's desktop. Two early quotes of SolidWorks founders that still hold true today are

✔ "No matter how easy it is to use, it is never easy enough."

✔ "No matter how fast we make it, it is never fast enough."

In this chapter, I introduce you to SolidWorks, the wonderful world of 3D, and the virtual prototype. You discover the basic system requirements for SolidWorks and tips to keep the program running smoothly. I also give you the lowdown on the newest features in SolidWorks 2008.

Exploring the SolidWorks Advantage

As a design engineer, you need to be critical about how you work with your craft and to understand how you can do it better. As tools and technology continue to improve, you also need to evolve. That means staying abreast of the latest design tool innovations. In this section, you find out how to take advantage of the benefits that 3D and SolidWorks offer.

Improving the way you work

Designing in SolidWorks may be different from how you designed in the past. My greatest satisfaction in my early days as a designer came from creating a complex assembly on my computer and then watching the darn thing actually come together on the shop floor just the way I designed it.

Without the ability to create 3D solid models and assemblies, however, your goal isn't easily attainable. The following workflow example shows how modeling in SolidWorks enables you to achieve better results:

1. **Design 3D parts (such as the one shown in Figure 1-1) and assemblies.**

   One big advantage to working in 3D is the ability to capture design intent early in the design process. Good designs are built on solid foundations. SolidWorks 3D modeling gives you a better understanding of your design, long before you create the first part.

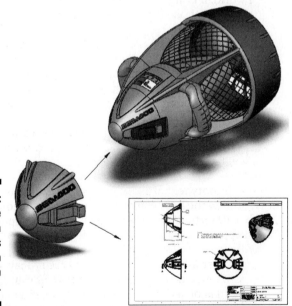

Figure 1-1:
An example of how a part is reused in the design process.

Design intent is an intelligent arrangement of part features and dimensions, or in the case of assemblies, the location of parts and the interaction between them. Starting your designs by building in good design intent makes reacting to future changes or additions easier.

2. **Test your design as a virtual prototype, using advanced features in SolidWorks to test different ideas more quickly and easily than you can with drawings or traditional prototypes.**

   A virtual prototype is such an important idea in using SolidWorks that I discuss it greater detail in the next section.

3. **Generate 2D manufacturing drawings, based on the geometry defined in the original part or assembly.**

   Refer to Figure 1-1 for an example. You can find out more about generating drawings in Chapter 7.

Embracing the virtual prototype

In the old days (more than 25 years ago), designers drew their designs on paper. When a designer was done drawing, he built a physical prototype to test his design ideas in the real world. If things didn't work quite right, he went back to the drawing board. Building all those prototypes was time consuming.

Nowadays, you do all that testing and simulating on a *virtual prototype,* which is a concept I refer to throughout this book. When you design a product in SolidWorks, essentially you create a virtual prototype with all the characteristics of the real thing (dimensions, mass properties, screws, and fittings, for example). Your virtual prototype behaves in the computer realm as it would in the real world.

The power of the virtual prototype is that it allows you to test countless design ideas quickly on your computer. And although the physical prototype hasn't vanished, at least you don't need so many of them.

Figure 1-1 shows a virtual prototype. Imagine if you had to draw this baby from scratch. In a drawing, changing the height from 100mm to 120mm requires major effort. In contrast, with a 3D virtual model, you can modify and update key design attributes with ease.

If you think you can work faster in a 2D environment, you're probably right. But that's only because you can't include the detail required to fully manufacture the part. When I made designs on a drawing board with paper and pencil, I could easily add a radius to any corner because I had my trusty ellipse template. In other words, I would "fudge" the corner geometry and let the toolmaker properly fillet the corner. Sometimes this lack of detail is good, and sometimes it's bad.

People use SolidWorks because they can create 3D parts, place them in assemblies in the same way as though they were assembling physical parts, and then create 2D drawings directly from that information.

Getting Your System Ready for SolidWorks

SolidWorks comes to you on a single DVD. When you're ready to install, put the disc in your DVD drive and follow the instructions provided by the Installation Manager. During installation, you have the opportunity to activate your SolidWorks license automatically over the Internet. (You can also activate your license via e-mail, but that may take a few hours to a few days.) When you first install SolidWorks, you have up to 30 days to activate the license or the software will simply stop working. For more information about activation, or if you experience any difficulties, visit the SolidWorks Customer Portal site at `https://customercenter.solidworks.com`.

The minimum computer requirements boil down to the following:

- **CPU:** Get the fastest one you can afford. The performance of SolidWorks depends on your CPU speed. If you get a CPU that's too slow, you can add a second one later. Although a second CPU adds some performance increase, it doesn't come close to doubling performance, so it's best to start off big.

- **RAM:** Although SolidWorks lists the minimum requirements, a better way to gauge how much RAM you need is to open SolidWorks on your computer along with all the other applications you normally have open at one time, such as the ones you use for e-mail, word processing, and Web browsing. Then open a good sampling of SolidWorks documents. (You can find some in the Tutorials folder in the SolidWorks program folder.) Open Windows Task Manager (press Ctrl+Alt+Delete) and click the Performance tab. Check the amount of available memory in the Physical Memory area. If the amount of available memory isn't greater than 0, you need more RAM.

  RAM is cheap, so make sure that you have plenty. The amount of RAM you have is important. If Windows runs out of physical memory, bad things happen. Your system becomes sluggish and less stable.

- **Graphics card:** Make sure that you have a certified graphics card and driver version. The SolidWorks support Web site lists combinations of certified graphics cards and drivers. For a listing of supported graphics cards and drivers, visit the hardware page of the SolidWorks support site at `https://customercenter.solidworks.com`.

- **Hard drive:** Big and fast is where it's at. These days, folks who use SolidWorks typically have 80 to 120GB hard drives.

Keeping Your Computer Happy

A commonly overlooked means of making sure that your computer stays happy and healthy is regular system maintenance. Just as craftspeople take good care of their tools, you should treat your computer in much the same way. The two most important tasks are making sure you have sufficient disk space and performing routine disk defragmentation.

You should also check the backup settings in SolidWorks by choosing Tools➪Options➪System Options➪Backup/Recover.

The following settings are particularly important to check:

- ✔ **The number of backup copies per document:** If you set the number of backup copies, keep this number low (one or two) because SolidWorks creates a copy of every document that's opened.

- ✔ **The location of the backups:** You should store backups on a different computer or at a different site. Remember to check your backup drive regularly to make sure that you have enough disk space. If you run low on space, clean up your hard drive or buy a bigger one.

Even when you work normally on a computer, the disks become *fragmented,* which means that Windows can't store all of a file in one contiguous spot, so it starts using a number of places on the hard drive to store documents. As you can imagine, fragmentation makes Windows run slower and causes stability issues with the system and the applications running on the computer. To alleviate this problem, use the Windows Disk Defragmenter (choose Start➪All Programs➪Accessories➪System Tools). I run a complete scan weekly. It makes a difference.

For more information on many of these administrative tasks, check out the *SolidWorks Express* archive. *SolidWorks Express* is a bimonthly electronic newsletter for the SolidWorks community. To view technical tips in the archive, go to https://www.customercenter.solidworks.com.

Starting Up SolidWorks the First Time

The first time you run SolidWorks, the Welcome to SolidWorks dialog box appears (see Figure 1-2) and asks how you want to configure the help and workflow customizations. You can set up SolidWorks based on your industry and skill level.

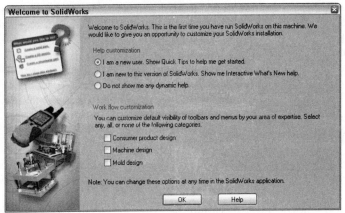

Figure 1-2:
Set up
SolidWorks
according to
how you
work and
what you
know and
don't know.

The first section in the dialog box is labeled Help Customization. If you're a new user, you can activate *Quick Tips,* a set of pop-up messages that appear while you create SolidWorks documents. The messages display hints and options about what to do next. Figure 1-3 shows a Quick Tip that pops up when you create a new part document. The Quick Tip walks you through what is required to perform this task.

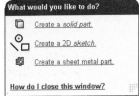

Figure 1-3:
Quick Tips
give you
an idea
of where to
go next.

You can turn on Quick Tips in each type of document (drawing, part, or assembly) by choosing Help➪Quick Tips.

The second section is labeled Work Flow Customization. If you make a selection there, SolidWorks displays toolbars and menus that relate to the type of work you do. The choices are

✔ Consumer Product Design

✔ Machine Design

✔ Mold Design

You can select one, all, or none of these categories.

Based on the type of industry you select, SolidWorks displays a different set of tools in the *CommandManager,* a context-sensitive toolbar that's dynamically updated based on the toolbar you want to access. In Figure 1-4, you see the Surface toolbar.

Figure 1-4:
The Surface
toolbar
appears.

To change the icons shown within the CommandManager, right-click the CommandManager and choose Customize CommandManager. A menu of available CommandManager icons appears. Select the icons that fit the type of work you most commonly perform.

Checking Out the Features

SolidWorks 2008 is the 16th version of SolidWorks to be released since the initial release of SolidWorks 95. Version updates, known as *service packs,* come out about every six weeks, whereas major releases occur typically 10 to 12 months apart.

You can download service packs from the SolidWorks Customer Portal Web site at `https://customercenter.solidworks.com`, or by choosing Help⇨Check for Updates.

Finding help and tips

A couple of resources can help get you started. The SolidWorks Resources tab (look for a house icon on the far right end of the user interface) in the task pane, as shown in Figure 1-5, displays links to these items:

✔ **Tutorials:** Online tutorials offer a group of 30-minute, step-by-step tutorials on a wide variety of topics. The first tutorial, Lesson 1, gives a quick overview of the basic features and functions in SolidWorks and is a good starting point if you haven't ever used the software.

✔ **What's New:** This document describes the new features within the latest version of SolidWorks based on area (features, parts, assemblies, and drawings, for example). You can also access the What's New document (a PDF file) from the Help menu.

✓ **Machine Design, Mold Design, or Consumer Product Design:** The title and contents of this tab relate to the industry type you chose in Workflow Customization. Figure 1-5 shows resources for machine design. If you chose mold design, other resources are displayed. On this tab, you find an overview of the industry and industry-specific tutorials.

✓ **Tip of the Day:** This tip changes each time you open SolidWorks.

Figure 1-5:
Inside the
SolidWorks
Resources
tab in the
task pane,
you find a
plethora of
learning
resources.

You can also find the following references on the Help menu:

✓ **SolidWorks Help:** This option opens the *SolidWorks Online User's Guide.* The guide is organized into chapters with an index you can browse. A search tool guides you to information on just about any feature in SolidWorks.

✓ **Moving from AutoCAD:** This online guide is designed to help you move from AutoCAD, a popular 2D design program, to SolidWorks. Many SolidWorks users come from AutoCAD backgrounds.

Finding out what's new in SolidWorks 2008

 We based this book on SolidWorks 2008. Each version of SolidWorks has updates to accommodate new features and requirements. When you save a file in the newest version, keep in mind that older versions can't read these newer files because the new features weren't available in the older version. However, you can open older versions of documents in the new version.

Here's a taste of what's new inside SolidWorks 2008:

- **Browse Recent Documents:** This new interface feature allows you to select a list of recent documents and see a visual preview in the Recent Document browser. Clicking the preview window opens the document (see Chapter 2).

- **Context Toolbars:** When you select items in the graphics area or FeatureManager design tree geometry, context toolbars appear and provide access to frequently performed actions for that context — for example, editing the sketch of a selected face (see Chapter 5).

- **Instant3D:** Drag geometry and dimension manipulators to resize features and make other modifications (see Chapter 9).

- **AssemblyXpert:** The AssemblyXpert analyzes the performance of assemblies and suggests actions you can take to improve it. This feature is useful when you work with large and complex assemblies (see Chapter 6).

- **DimXpert:** DimXpert for parts is a set of tools that applies dimensions and tolerances to parts according to the requirements of the ASME Y 14.41-2003 standard. Covering the DimXpert is a bit beyond the scope of this book, but you can find more information in the SolidWorks Help.

- **TolAnalyst:** The tolerance analysis application, or TolAnalyst, determines the effects that dimensions and tolerances have on parts and assemblies. The TolAnalyst tools let you perform worst-case tolerance stack-up analysis on parts and assemblies (see Chapter 8).

- **Mates:** Several new mate types have been added, including Screw mates and Universal joint mates (see Chapter 6).

- **Quick View:** Quick View allows you to open assembly models with only selected parts available for viewing and modifying (see Chapter 6).

- **Scenes and Appearances:** Adds photorealistic display of your models and environments. Types of scenes that can be displayed include reflective floors, your own photos, and reflections of backgrounds.

Chapter 2

Taking Control of SolidWorks

*W*hen 3D design programs first hit the market, they were complex to learn and difficult to operate. Then SolidWorks came along and did everything that the other programs did, except that it was less expensive and easier to use, enabling design engineers to get up and running fast. What gives SolidWorks a familiar look and feel is its Windows-like user interface and the use of other standard conventions, such as icon command buttons, menus, and toolbars.

This chapter describes the SolidWorks user interface: how to navigate it and how to personalize it to fit your needs. In this chapter, you discover how to open a new document and how to set up and maintain the SolidWorks program. Whether you work alone or in a group of 50 other engineers, the ability to define, save, and share document templates and common SolidWorks settings makes you more effective in using SolidWorks.

Working with SolidWorks Documents

SolidWorks is a *multidocument system,* which means that it uses different file types for different purposes. Part, drawing, and assembly files are some examples.

Many SolidWorks file types link to other files. A *drawing* references a part to create the detail views. An *assembly* references parts and other assemblies. The different types of documents are fully associative within SolidWorks, so a change to a part propagates to any drawing or assembly that uses the part.

Here's a list of SolidWorks document types that appear throughout this book:

- ✓ **Assembly:** A collection of related parts saved in one document file with the `.sldasm` extension. An assembly can contain from two to more than a thousand components, which can be parts or other assemblies called *subassemblies*.

- ✓ **Block:** A group of 2D entities (such as standard notes, title blocks, and label positions) that you can use in drawing files. *Blocks* can include text, any type of sketch entity, balloons, and imported entities. You can attach blocks to geometry or to drawing views and insert them into sheet formats. Blocks have the extension `.sldblk`.

- ✓ **Drawing:** 2D documents that convey a design to manufacturing. A drawing file consists of one or more sheets that contain different views of the model. SolidWorks gives drawing files the extension `.slddrw`.

- ✓ **Drawing Sheet Format:** You can save a border or a title block (which includes company name, material, sheet size, and other information) of a drawing in the `.slddrt` format to use in creating new drawings.

- ✓ **Library Feature:** A frequently used part feature or combination of part features that you create once and save in a library for future use (and reuse). You can use library features as building blocks to construct a single part to ensure consistency and save time. Library features have the extension `.sldlfp`.

- ✓ **Macro:** A set of keyboard commands that you can record and save in a file to automate redundant or menial tasks in SolidWorks. A macro is saved as a block of Microsoft Visual Basic for Applications (VBA) program code. SolidWorks *macros* have the file extension `.swp`.

- ✓ **Part:** The building block of every SolidWorks model. Each assembly and drawing you create is made from parts. Part files consist of a collection of part features (base, extrude, revolve, and loft, for example). SolidWorks attaches the extension `.sldprt` to part files.

- ✓ **Templates:** Documents that include user-defined parameters. When you open a new part, drawing, or assembly, you select a *template* to use for your new document. Templates have the extensions `.drwdot`, `.prtdot`, and `.asmdot` for drawing, part, and assembly documents.

Be sure to develop for your SolidWorks files a consistent naming method that everyone on your design team can follow. SolidWorks follows the same file-naming conventions as Windows. As you develop your own naming style, here's what to keep in mind:

- ✓ Filenames aren't case sensitive. They can be upper- or lowercase.

- ✓ Filenames can include spaces.

✔ A filename can have up to 256 characters in front of the file extension.

✔ You can't include special characters (*, /, or %, for example) within the filename.

✔ Filenames that you store in the same data directory should be unique so that you don't accidentally choose the wrong file. For example, you don't name a connector part `connector.sldprt` because someone might use the same name for a part on another project. Filenames should include the part number, the project name or number, and then a description.

Creating and Opening a Document

Before you explore the ins and outs of the SolidWorks user interface, you need to understand how to create a new document in SolidWorks. When you create a new part, assembly, or drawing document, you select a template to work with. A *template,* which is the foundation of the SolidWorks document, stores the default document properties for each document. SolidWorks has default part, assembly, and drawing templates, but you can create your own templates, and the next section, "Working with Templates," tells you how.

To create a new SolidWorks document, follow these steps:

1. **Choose File⇨New.**

   The New SolidWorks Document dialog box appears.

   The New SolidWorks Document dialog box has two versions: Novice and Advanced. You can toggle between them by simply clicking the Novice or Advanced button at the bottom of the dialog box.

   - *Novice* is the simplified version of the dialog box. It's also the default. In Novice mode, you have only three document templates (Part, Assembly, and Drawing) to choose from.

   - *Advanced* mode shows the standard templates as well as any custom templates. The template icons appear on various tabs (see Figure 2-1). When you select a document template type in Advanced mode, a preview of the template appears in the Preview box. You can find out how to create custom templates and add new tabs to the New SolidWorks Document dialog box in the next section, "Working with Templates."

2. **In the dialog box, select Part, Assembly, or Drawing.**

3. **Click OK.**

   A new document opens.

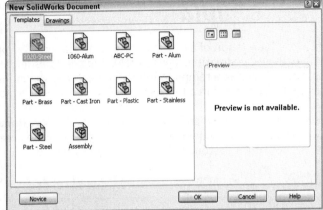

Figure 2-1:
Advanced
mode of the
New
SolidWorks
Document
dialog box
shows
document
templates
on tabs.

To open an existing SolidWorks document, follow these steps:

1. **Choose File⇨Open.**

   The Open dialog box appears.

2. **From the Files of Type drop-down list, select the type of document you want to open (.sldprt, .sldasm, or .slddrw for part, assembly, or drawing or a combination of SolidWorks files).**

3. **In the Look In drop-down list, find the folder that contains the document you want to open.**

   The files of that folder appear as a list in the middle of the dialog box.

4. **Click the file you want to open.**

   A preview of the document appears on the preview screen.

5. **Click Open.**

   The document opens in SolidWorks.

New in SolidWorks 2008 is the Recent Document browser, which is a handy way to open documents you accessed recently. To open an existing document by using the Recent Document browser, follow these steps:

1. **Choose File⇨Browse Recent Documents.**

   The Recent Documents box appears.

2. **In the browser, move the pointer over the preview to display the full path to the document.**

3. **To open the document, click the preview.**

Working with Templates

A *template* is the foundation of a new SolidWorks document. Templates contain basic document information, such as document settings and custom properties. You can create a template from any SolidWorks document by simply saving the document in a template format.

Templates are a good place to store company standards. For example, you can create templates that use inches and millimeters. You can create drawing templates that include a custom Title Block that's ready to go.

When you open a new document, the Advanced version of the New SolidWorks Document dialog box has tabs for templates. The default tab is Templates, but you can create your own tabs where you can add custom templates.

To create a new tab in the Advanced version of the New SolidWorks Document dialog box, follow these steps:

1. **In Windows Explorer, create a new folder.**

   For example, you can put a set of templates in a special folder named `<SolidWorks install directory>\SolidWorks\data\templates\My Special Templates`.

2. **Choose Tools⇨Options.**

   A dialog box appears, with tabs for Systems Options and Document Properties.

3. **Click the Systems Option tab.**

4. **Click File Locations.**

   The File Location options appear.

5. **In Show Folders For, click the arrow and from the drop-down list, click Document Templates.**

   Document Templates appears under Show Folders.

6. **Next to the Folders box, click Add.**

   The Browse for Folder dialog box appears.

7. **Browse for the folder you created in Step 1 and click to select it.**

8. **Click OK.**

   The Browse for Folder dialog box closes, and the new folder is added under Folders.

9. **Click OK again to close the Options dialog box.**

   After you save a template to the new folder, a new tab with the name of the folder you created appears in the Advanced version of the New

SolidWorks Document dialog box. You can add any number of templates to the folder or add more tabs to keep different template sets organized. Keep in mind that empty folders don't appear in the New SolidWorks Document dialog box.

To create a template, follow these steps:

1. **Choose File⇨New.**

   The New SolidWorks Document dialog box appears.

2. **In the dialog box, select Part, Assembly, or Drawing.**

3. **Click OK.**

   A new document opens.

4. **Choose Tools⇨Options.**

   A dialog box appears, with tabs for Systems Options and Document Property.

5. **On the Document Property tab, select the options you want to customize in your new document template.**

   The most important options are described in this list:

   - *Dimensions:* Set options for how you want dimensions handled in documents. Options include Snap to Grid, Arrow Style, and Text Alignment (horizontal or vertical).

   - *Notes:* Select how you want drawing notes to appear. Options include Text Alignment, Leader Anchor, Leader Style, and Border.

   - *Annotation Font:* You can select the type and style of font to show in drawing and model annotations.

   - *Units:* Select the units for the document (IPS or MMGS, for example): Length Units, Dual Units, Angular Units, or Density Units.

6. **Click OK.**

7. **Choose File⇨Save As.**

   The Save As dialog box appears.

8. **In the Save As Type drop-down list, select a template type (`.prtdot`, `.asmdot`, or `.drwdot` for part, assembly, or drawing).**

   You need to select the template type that matches the item you selected in Step 2. Refer to "Working with SolidWorks Documents," earlier in this chapter, for an introduction to the different document types.

9. **In the File Name box, type a name for your new template.**

   SolidWorks adds the extension automatically.

10. **In the Save In box, click the drop-down arrow to browse to the folder where you want to save your template.**

    Save the template in the new template folder if you want the template to appear under a different tab in the Advanced mode of the New SolidWorks Document dialog box.

11. **Click Save.**

    The new template appears in the New SolidWorks Document dialog box, and you can use it the next time you create a new document.

Understanding the User Interface

You don't feel like you're on alien landscape when you open SolidWorks. In fact, if you know how to use Windows, you're well on your way to understanding SolidWorks. SolidWorks has many familiar Windows functions, such as dragging and resizing windows. SolidWorks also uses Windows icons, such as Print, Open, Save, Cut, and Paste.

Touring the document window

When you open a document in SolidWorks, two important panels appear in the user interface. The right panel is the *graphics area,* where your model or drawing appears in all its glory. You can create and manipulate the document in the graphics area. The left panel contains these SolidWorks management tools: FeatureManager, PropertyManager, ConfigurationManager, and DimXpert.

Also in the document window, you can access commands by using menus and toolbars and your mouse. The SolidWorks interface is *dynamic:* Different menus and toolbars appear depending on the active document type. When you open a part, for example, the Feature toolbar appears with commands to build a part. Open an assembly, as shown in Figure 2-2, and you see assembly commands.

The following list offers a more detailed tour of the main elements you see (refer to Figure 2-2 for the corresponding item numbers):

1 Menu bar: Displays the name of the active document and the active document window. Also displays a subset of tools from the standard menu, the SolidWorks menus, the SolidWorks Search Oval, and a flyout menu of Help options. If you haven't saved changes in the document, you see an asterisk (*) after the document name.

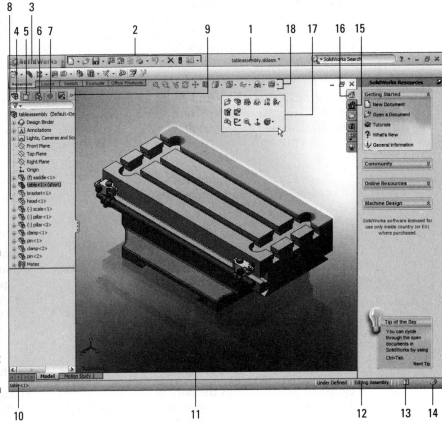

Figure 2-2:
SolidWorks
displays
commands
relevant to
the
document
type.

2 Standard toolbar: Appears next to the SolidWorks logo when the menu bar menus are hidden. These buttons provide quick access to the commands you use most often, such as New (to open a new document), Open (open an existing document), and Print (print the active document).

3 Menu bar menus (hidden by default): A set of items (File, Edit, and View, for example) across the top of the user interface. By default, the menus are hidden. To display them, either move the mouse over the SolidWorks logo or click it. Each menu bar item also has a pull-down menu of functions and commands. The menu bar contents are task-dependent, based on the active document type. You find these functions on SolidWorks toolbars. Whereas the toolbars contain commands that you use more often, though, the menu bar contains the complete set.

4 FeatureManager design tree tab: Displays the FeatureManager design tree, similar to a Windows Explorer tree, where you can navigate the structure of your SolidWorks document. You can expand or collapse the "tree" to see how a model or assembly is constructed or to examine sheets and views in a drawing.

5 PropertyManager tab: Appears in the left panel when you select certain SolidWorks commands, such as sketches, fillet features, and assembly mates. The PropertyManager is a place for you to enter relevant command options, such as design data and parameters. When you click the tab, you can also display the PropertyManager, where you enter the properties and other options for a SolidWorks command.

6 ConfigurationManager tab: Displays the ConfigurationManager design tree, available for only parts and assemblies. You use this tab to create, select, and view multiple configurations, or variations, of parts and assemblies in a document. (You can find out more about how to manage configurations in Chapter 10.)

7 DimXpertManager: New in SolidWorks 2008; applies dimensions in parts, drawings, and assemblies so that manufacturing features are fully defined.

8 FeatureManager design tree: Displays the structure of your drawing, part, or assembly document.

The Feature Manager and CommandManager are such important tools that they get their own sections a little later in this chapter. Flip to the section "Selecting and editing with the FeatureManager design tree" or "Working with the CommandManager" if you're looking for more details about these tools.

9 Show Display pane: Expands or collapses the display pane.

10 Status bar: Gives a more complete explanation of the selected function.

11 Graphics area: Displays the part, assembly, or drawing. Although SolidWorks allows you to open more than one document simultaneously, only one document is active at a time.

12 Status bar: Indicates the drawing, part, or assembly document that you're editing and helps you keep track of where you are.

13 Quick Tips Help: Indicates with a question mark button whether Quick Tips are turned on or off. Click the icon to toggle the state on or off.

14 Tags: Function as keywords you add to SolidWorks documents and features to make them easier to filter and search.

15 Design Library: Opens the Design Library. Inside, you see the Design Library, Toolbox, and 3D Content Central, three resources that contain a plethora of standard design elements that you can drag and drop into your design. (Find out more about the Design Library in Chapter 13.)

16 SolidWorks Resources: Opens the SolidWorks Resources tab, which contains links to resources, tutorials, tips of the day, and also command buttons to open or create SolidWorks documents.

17 CommandManager: A tabbed, dynamic toolbar, located beneath the Standard toolbar, that lists command buttons for the type of document you're working on. (Read more in the upcoming section "Working with the CommandManager.")

> **18 Heads-up View toolbar:** Features a series of commonly used command buttons that allow you to zoom, rotate, and view the part in different orientations. See the later section "Zoom, pan, and rotate" for more details.

TIP

I prefer to maximize the document window so that I get a full view of what I'm working on. To ensure that SolidWorks uses this setting for all documents, choose Tools⇨Options. In the dialog box that appears, click the Systems Options tab, select General, and select the Maximize Document on Open check box.

Selecting and editing with the FeatureManager design tree

The FeatureManager design tree is to the left of the graphics area when you open a document in SolidWorks. You can think of the FeatureManager as command central for your SolidWorks design. The FeatureManager provides selection and editing access, Windows Explorer style, to all entities in your active document:

- ✔ In a part document, the FeatureManager displays part features, such as extrusions, fillets, and the boss.
- ✔ In an assembly, it gives you access to parts and subassembly components.
- ✔ In a drawing, it provides access to drawing views, annotations, and constraints.

The FeatureManager offers several benefits:

- ✔ **Shows the order in which the elements of a document were created:** The oldest element is on the top, and the newest appears on the bottom.
- ✔ **Links to the graphics area:** You can select an object by clicking it in either the FeatureManager design tree or the graphics area, and *dynamic bidirectional highlighting* occurs. That is, as you move the pointer over the members of the tree, the objects are highlighted in the graphics area. Similarly, if you select an object from the graphics area, that item is highlighted in the tree.
- ✔ **Displays graphical feedback that describes feature or component characteristics:** For example, if an assembly component is hidden, its related icon in the FeatureManager tree looks empty. If the component is *suppressed* (selectively removed from memory), it appears in gray.
- ✔ **Allows you to see the contents of folders in the tree:** You can click + or – to maximize or minimize a folder, respectively.
- ✔ **Gives you access to quick functions when you right-click:** The Context Toolbar and menu that appear change based on each type of document and object (part feature, drawing view, or plane, for example).

You can use arrow key navigation to walk through a design step-by-step if you enable this option: Choose Tools➪Options. In the dialog box that appears, click the Systems Options tab, select FeatureManager, and select the Arrow Key Navigation check box.

If you want to understand how a design was built, select the rollback bar (a light blue line that turns dark blue when you select it) in the FeatureManager design tree. A rollback temporarily reverts the model to an earlier state, suppressing recently added features. Drag the bar up or down the FeatureManager design tree to step forward or backward through the regeneration sequence.

If you're using arrow key navigation, the up and down arrows move the rollback bar.

Working with the CommandManager

Located in the upper left corner of the user interface, just below the Standard toolbar, is the *CommandManager,* a smart toolbar that displays the menus you need for the task at hand. If you're editing an assembly, for example, the CommandManager shows the Assembly toolbar but hides the Feature toolbar because you can't edit a part feature until you open a part file.

The CommandManager is an efficient way to display the numerous SolidWorks toolbars, which might otherwise clutter the screen and block the graphics area. When you open a document, the CommandManager appears with default tools for the file type you're working on. Tabs on the left side of the CommandManager let you change the display of these commands.

The CommandManager is divided into two areas: tabs and the expanded toolbar. If you select a tab, the corresponding toolbar is displayed in the toolbar area. For example, when you open a part document, the Features and Sketch tabs and several others appear by default in the control area (see Figure 2-3). If you click the Features tab, the Feature commands (Extruded Boss/Base or Extruded Cut, for example) are displayed in the toolbar area. If you click Sketch, the Sketch commands (Line and Rectangle, for example) appear.

Figure 2-3:
The Command Manager displays the tools you want to see.

The CommandManager offers many benefits:

- ✔ **Reduces toolbar clutter:** Rather than place toolbars on the top, right, and left sides of the user interface, the CommandManager embeds them in a single toolbar and displays only the tools you need for a particular task.

- ✔ **Streamlines the work:** CommandManager keeps your workspace neat and tidy so that you can find what you need fast and work efficiently.

- ✔ **Minimizes mouse movements:** You can move more efficiently across the screen space because the CommandManager is at the top with the standard icons, the PropertyManager and FeatureManager design tree are on the left side, and the rest of the screen is available for the graphics area.

- ✔ **Minimizes the number of menu picks:** CommandManager puts the commands you need at your fingertips so that you don't have to navigate through menus and toolbars to find what you need.

If you find yourself squinting at the SolidWorks interface, try making the command buttons bigger. With a document open, choose Tools➪Customize. In the Customize dialog box, on the Toolbars tab, select Large icons. Click OK.

I also prefer to display the CommandManager without the descriptions below the command buttons, as shown in Figure 2-4. Using plain command buttons gives the CommandManager a cleaner look and allows room for more buttons. To turn off descriptions, right-click anywhere on the CommandManager and deselect the Use Large Buttons with Text check box.

Mousing around

One of your most-used tools when working with SolidWorks is the mouse. SolidWorks uses three mouse buttons to access features, select objects, and perform tasks:

- ✔ **Left:** Selects items on the menu, entities in the graphics area, and objects in the FeatureManager design tree. When you select entities in the graphics area, or a feature from the FeatureManager tree, a context-sensitive toolbar appears, giving you immediate access to frequently performed actions for that context.

- ✔ **Right:** Displays context-sensitive options and shortcut menus so that you don't have to flounder around in a sea of menus looking for the right options.

- ✔ **Middle:** Rotates, pans, and zooms a part or an assembly and scrolls in drawing documents.

If you use a wheel-type mouse, you can push down on the wheel to rotate a part. Scroll the wheel to zoom in on a model. Simply position the pointer on the object that you want a close-up of and spin the mouse wheel toward you to zoom in on the object.

Here are a few notes on selecting objects:

- ✔ **To select a single entity:** Click the entity in the graphics area or in the FeatureManager design tree. Selected objects become highlighted in both the graphics area and FeatureManager tree.

- ✔ **To select a group of objects:** Hold down the left mouse button and drag a window around the objects.

- ✔ **To select more than one object:** Hold down the Ctrl key while clicking each object. If you want to deselect an object, click the object again.

- ✔ **To deselect all selected objects:** Click anywhere in the document window or user interface outside the part or assembly.

Figure 2-4:
The
Command
Manager
without
button
descriptions.

Getting a Better View of Things

 One of the real beauties of SolidWorks is that after you build your model in three dimensions, you can move it around and play with it on-screen to ogle the design from a variety of angles. You can zoom in or out, turn the model upside down, or slice it in half to see what's inside. You can also vary the display state. You can view your model in its wireframe rather than solid form to get a better look at dimensions, for example. The ability to view a model in different ways gives you a better understanding of a design.

You control how a design appears on-screen by using the Heads-up View toolbar, which you find at the top of the graphics area. The Heads-up View toolbar has commands for controlling orientation, display state, and display mode. You also see commands for hiding and showing items such as planes, origins, and sketches. Additional items include commands to set up scenes, shadows, and perspective views.

Zoom, pan, and rotate

The orientation section of the Heads-up View toolbar offers several tools that allow you to move the model around on-screen, zoom in and out, pan, and rotate, for example. These manipulation tools include

- **Previous View:** Switches back to the last view of the model. You can undo the last ten view changes.

- **Zoom to Fit:** Moves in or out so that your model or drawing fits entirely into the graphical display and you can see the whole thing.

- **Zoom to Area:** Lets you zero in on the area you want to see. Click the area you want to view and drag the mouse to create a bounding box around the area. Let go of the mouse, and the area fills the screen.

- **Zoom In/Out:** Lets you move in close or far away. Drag the pointer up (toward the top of the screen) to zoom in or drag down to zoom out.

- **Zoom to Selection:** Zeroes in on a portion of a model or drawing that you select. Select an entity or hold down the Ctrl key to select multiple entities in the FeatureManager design tree and select Zoom to Selection.

- **Rotate View:** Allows you to rotate the model in space. Drag the pointer on the graphical display to rotate to the view you want.

- **Pan:** Scrolls the model or drawing in the document window. Drag the pointer in the direction you want to move the model across the screen.

Standard engineering views

The Standard Views toolbar is a flyout toolbar embedded in the Heads-up View toolbar. (You can find out how to add flyouts to toolbars in the later section "Adding flyout toolbars.") If you click the Standard View button on the View toolbar, you see a pull-down menu of several commands that represent standard engineering views. You can orient your model to one of these views manually by using the orientation tools on the View toolbar, or you can save time and click a Standard View command button.

Standard View commands include Side, Front, Top, Right, and Bottom. You can also choose the following perspectives: Isometric, Trimetric, and Dimetric. The difference between the perspectives is basically the angle of the model. The best way to understand each view is to just click a button and see what happens to your model or drawing.

Display styles

Other commands on the Heads-up View toolbar offer the following display styles for model and drawing views in drawing documents. You can use the display modes to make your model look cool and to get a better understanding of it. These tools include

- ✔ **Wireframe:** Displays all edges of the model.

- ✔ **Hidden Lines Visible:** Displays all edges of the model, but edges that are hidden from the current view are displayed in a different color or font.

- ✔ **Hidden Lines Removed:** Displays only those edges of the model that you can see from the current view orientation.

- ✔ **Shaded View with Edges:** Displays a shaded view of the model with all of its edges.

- ✔ **Shaded:** Displays a shaded view of the model (no edges).

- ✔ **Shadows in Shaded Mode:** Displays a shaded view of the model with a shadow beneath the model.

- ✔ **Section View:** Displays a cutaway of a model using one or more cross-section planes (see Figure 2-5).

 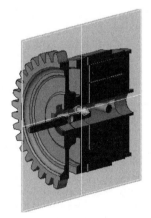

Figure 2-5: Section view displays a cut of the model.

> ✔ **RealView Graphics:** Displays the model hardware accelerator shaders. Available with certain graphics cards, this mode uses realistic textures and highlights. In others words, chrome looks like chrome. (See the Support section of the SolidWorks Web site for details on graphic cards.)

You can set the default display mode of edges in all drawing documents. To do so, choose Tools⇨Options. On the Systems Options tab, under Drawings, select Display Style. From the options that appear, select the check box next to the display mode you want under Display Style for New Views. Click OK.

Exploring the SolidWorks Help Menu

If you get stuck in your quest to master SolidWorks, have no fear. You can check the index of this book for more specific topics or check out the SolidWorks Help menu, which contains a plethora of information to get you back on track or point you in the right direction, at least.

Choose Help from the menu bar menus. A pull-down menu, shown in Figure 2-6, appears with these resources:

Figure 2-6: The SolidWorks Help menu offers a cornucopia of learning tools.

> ✔ **SolidWorks Help:** Takes you to the *SolidWorks Online User's Guide,* which addresses all functions in the SolidWorks software. The guide includes context-sensitive topics, which you access from the PropertyManager, as well as additional topics and graphic examples. You can search the table of contents or the index. A glossary of SolidWorks terminology is also available.
>
> ✔ **SolidWorks Tutorials:** Includes practical, step-by-step examples of more than 20 models you can build. These tutorials cover part creation, assembly operations, drawings, and several of the SolidWorks add-in programs, and are a good starting point for finding out how to use the program.

- ✔ **Quick Reference Guide:** Opens a 4-page guide that provides a handy reference for various program icons and a list of common keyboard shortcuts. Also available is a list of add-on programs and a brief description of their usage.

- ✔ **API Help:** Takes you to an online help resource for the SolidWorks Application Programming Interface (API). The API lets you automate and customize SolidWorks software, and integrate your software with SolidWorks.

- ✔ **Release Notes:** Contains information on new SolidWorks features that weren't available when the documentation was completed. For the most up-to-date information, refer to this document and to online help, which is updated with each SolidWorks service pack. You can find the release notes on the SolidWorks support site at `https://customercenter.solidworks.com`.

- ✔ **What's New:** Opens a printable PDF manual. The manual explains new features and changes in the current version of SolidWorks.

- ✔ **Interactive What's New:** Provides links to topics in the What's New Manual on new menu items and new and changed PropertyManagers. The topics describe functionality added since the previous release of SolidWorks and often include examples with sample files.

- ✔ **Moving from AutoCAD:** Takes you to the online guide *Moving from AutoCAD*. Many new users switch from the 2D AutoCAD program to SolidWorks. This guide shows the differences between the two programs and helps to make the transition easier.

- ✔ **Check for Updates:** Sends a quick ping to the SolidWorks Customer Portal Web site to make sure that you're running the latest and greatest release of SolidWorks. If newer versions are available, you have the opportunity to upgrade.

- ✔ **Activate Licenses:** Launches the SolidWorks Product Activation program, which registers your SolidWorks software online.

- ✔ **Transfer Licenses:** Allows you to immediately deactivate and transfer your SolidWorks licenses for use on another computer. Use this option when you upgrade or replace your existing computer hardware.

- ✔ **Show Licenses:** Shows your currently activated products and the expiration dates.

- ✔ **About SolidWorks:** Displays the version, service pack (minor version), and the serial number of your SolidWorks program. You can also access `solidworks.com` and the license agreement.

SolidWorks also offers context-sensitive help as you're working on documents. When you're working in the PropertyManager, for example, click the question mark in the upper right corner (shown in Figure 2-8, later in this chapter) to link to information about the active command in the *SolidWorks Online User's Guide*.

Another way that SolidWorks walks you through the different program commands is with yellow message boxes, which appear now and then in the PropertyManager (refer to Figure 2-7). These boxes provide information on a particular feature and tell you what to do next.

Figure 2-7:
A context-
sensitive
hint.

Customizing the User Interface

Every user has a preference for how the user interface should look. Fortunately, SolidWorks lets you customize keyboard shortcuts, toolbars, and icons to fit the way you work. In fact, you may notice a couple of our own customizations (large icons and no description for the CommandManager) in screen shots throughout this book.

SolidWorks remembers the way you configure the user interface and saves the settings.(SolidWorks stores these settings in the Windows Registry. I show you how to export and reload these settings in the upcoming section "Defining SolidWorks System Options.")

You can customize the CommandManager by adding or removing tabs and buttons to the CommandManager. But keep in mind that the changes you make stick for only that document type. You have to customize each document type separately.

To add a tab to the SolidWorks CommandManager, follow these steps:

1. **Open a SolidWorks drawing, part, or assembly document.**

2. **Right-click the tabs area of the CommandManager and select Customize CommandManager.**

   A menu of toolbar buttons appears; disregard this box for now.

3. **Right-click the tab that appears to the right of the current tabs and click Rename Tab.**

4. **Type a new name for the tab.**

For example, name your tab something like Custom Commands or My Commands.

5. In the Customize box, click the Commands tab.

A list of categories appears. Selecting one of the categories shows all available toolbar buttons for that category.

6. Drag a toolbar button to the CommandManager area to place that button.

Congratulations! You just created your own, custom CommandManager tab.

7. Click OK in the Customize box to finish.

You can also customize any other toolbar in SolidWorks by adding, deleting, or moving the command buttons. To customize another toolbar (but not CommandManager), follow these steps:

1. With a document open, choose Tools⇨Customize.

The Customize dialog box appears.

2. Select the Commands tab, as shown in Figure 2-8.

3. Under Categories, select the toolbar you want to change.

Figure 2-8:
Drag a command button from the Customize dialog box and place a copy of it on another toolbar in the SolidWorks window.

In the Buttons area, you see all the buttons that appear on the toolbar you selected. If you click a button, a description of what that button does appears in the Description area.

4. **Make your change to the toolbar.**

   What you do in this step depends on what you want to accomplish:

   - *To place a copy of a command button on another toolbar,* in the Customize dialog box, click and drag a command button to another toolbar in the SolidWorks window.

   - *To remove a command button from a toolbar,* in the SolidWorks window, click and drag the button from the toolbar to the graphics area.

   - *To rearrange a command on a toolbar,* in the SolidWorks window, click and drag the button from the toolbar to another area of the toolbar.

   - *To move a command button from one toolbar to another,* in the SolidWorks window, click and drag a button from one toolbar to a different toolbar.

5. **Click OK to close the Customize dialog box.**

Adding flyout toolbars

Another way to save space in the graphics area is with a flyout toolbar, which you can add to any toolbar, including the CommandManager. A *flyout toolbar* makes functions accessible in one button, which takes up minimal space within the user interface and makes commands easy to access. When you click a Flyout button, the toolbar associated with that button appears, allowing you to conveniently scroll down and select the command you need. A good example of a flyout toolbar is the Standard Views flyout (see Figure 2-9), located on the Heads-Up View toolbar, which provides tools (Front, Back, Left, and Right, for example) to rotate the model, assembly, or sketch to a preset standard engineering view.

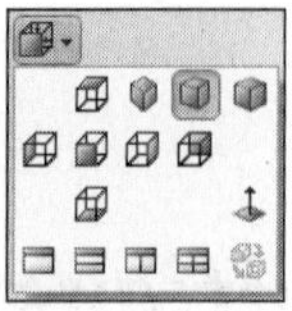

Figure 2-9:
The Standard Views flyout on the View toolbar.

If you want to add a flyout toolbar button to another toolbar, follow these steps:

1. **With a document open, choose Tools⇨Customize.**

    The Customize dialog box appears.

2. **Select the Commands tab.**

3. **Select Flyout Toolbars in the Categories area.**

    You see several buttons appear on the right, under buttons. These buttons are flyout toolbars that you can add to any other toolbar, including the CommandManager. Click a button to see in the Description box a description of what the button does.

4. **In the Buttons area, drag a toolbar button to a toolbar in the SolidWorks window.**

5. **Click OK.**

Taking advantage of single-command mode

By default, when you click a sketch or dimension tool, the command stays active until you click it again, click another command, or press Escape on the keyboard. You can set up SolidWorks to work in what's known as *single-command mode.* This feature ensures that you're not stuck in a command. After a command is set, if you want to keep it active for more than one use, double-click the icon when you select it.

To set single-command mode, follow these steps:

1. **Choose Tools⇨Options⇨Systems Options.**

    The Systems Options dialog box appears.

2. **Select General.**

    The General dialog box appears.

3. **Select the Single Command Per Click check box.**

4. **Click OK.**

Defining SolidWorks System Options

Unlike document properties, the SolidWorks system options relate to the system, not to your document. Throughout this book, you find references on how to change various system options.

1. **Click Tools⇨Options.**

   A dialog box appears with two tabs: System Options and Document Properties. (The Document Properties tab appears only if you have a document open.)

2. **On the System Options tab, select General.**

   Several options become available, as shown in Figure 2-10.

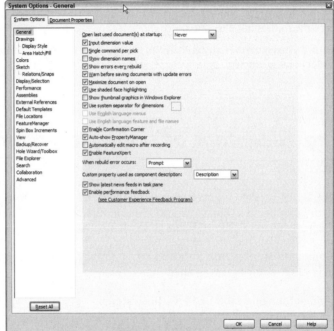

Figure 2-10:
Set the
general
system
options on
the System
Options tab.

The important ones to note are described in this list:

- *Open Last Used Document(s) at Startup:* Lets you select Always or Never. Select Always if you want the documents you used most recently to open automatically when you run SolidWorks again.

- *Input Dimension Value:* Specifies that the Modify dialog box is automatically displayed when you create a new dimension. Otherwise, if you don't check this option, you must double-click the dimension to change its value.

- *Single Command per Pick:* Specifies that sketch and dimension tools are cleared after each use. (Double-clicking a tool causes it to remain selected for additional use.)

- *Show Dimension Names:* Displays the dimension's name as well as its value.

- *Show Errors Every Rebuild:* Displays an error message each time you rebuild the model, if errors are present.

- *Maximize Document on Open:* Opens each document to its largest size within the SolidWorks window.

- *Use Shaded Face Highlighting:* Displays selected faces in a solid color (green by default). To specify a different highlight color, click Tools⇨Options⇨System Options⇨Colors, and then select a different color for Selected Face, Shaded.

Chapter 3

Building Blocks for the Virtual Prototype

*O*ne great strength of SolidWorks is that it gives you the ability to create a complete virtual product on your computer screen. But don't let the word *virtual* fool you. No one will ask you to wear some high-tech headgear or relive an old sci-fi film (although I like doing both).

By *virtual,* we mean that you can build a product in SolidWorks similarly to how you do it in the real world, from drawing an initial sketch to putting together parts and subassemblies to creating the final product. You don't get your hands dirty, and the final product you create looks as it would when rolling off the assembly line. Doing all this work in 3D has many advantages. You can

✔ See how components interact and ensure that parts don't interfere with each other as they move.

✔ Make sure that parts assemble properly on an assembly line and that they disassemble easily for maintenance.

✔ Show customers how final products will look even before they're built.

This chapter covers the plan of your design, the importance of drawing a hand sketch, and the basic building blocks for creating a virtual prototype. As you read the sections on design layout sketches and skeletons, bear in mind that Chapter 4 (sketching) and Chapter 6 (assemblies) cover these topics in greater detail. Here, I introduce them only in the context of building a foundation for what's ahead.

Planning and Capturing Design Intent (Or, Think First and Then Do)

Although throwing ideas onto a computer screen is certainly an easy way to start a project, starting with a plan is a better idea. The concept of "think first and then design" is the key to building successful, reusable designs. Applying some discipline to the design process is a good thing. A clearly defined, well-communicated *design intent* — what you want a design to do, how you want it to move, and how you want it to update when you make changes — results not only in a better design but also one that, in our experience, gets out the door faster.

Some designers may argue that planning *is* extra work. They would rather plunge into the hands-on work and complete the job as soon as possible. I would argue that doing a job right the first time is worth the extra work up front. After all, everyone seems to make time to do the job right the second time! Just think how many times a design changes, during not only its initial development but also the life of the product. The ability to easily understand and change the important elements of the design makes "getting on with it" easier.

So think first and then do. But thinking can be hard work. To make this part of the job a bit easier, we came up with a handy list of tools to use whenever you set out to build the foundation of a design you're working on:

- A hand sketch of your design intent
- An engineering journal
- Early brainstorm sessions
- Design reviews and checklists

These tools allow you to create a consistent and reusable design process, which helps you to define and document the key aspects of the initial design and to modify and create new versions of the product. They also can help you identify what you need to change and how the design will update as a result.

Starting the design with a hand sketch

When you start work on a design, you generally bump into more questions than answers, particularly when you're working on an all-new product as opposed to an improved version of an existing one, about which you likely have information. So, assuming that you're not clairvoyant, how do you create and document a design so that you can easily modify it when new information becomes available? The answer: Simply grab a pencil and paper (or marker and whiteboard) and start sketching. When — and only when — you complete an initial hand sketch should you refer to Chapter 4 to find out how to turn that sketch into a SolidWorks model.

A simple hand sketch allows you to try different ideas and quickly document what you know. Believe it or not, you can capture even fairly complex systems in a design sketch. Sketching allows you to focus on the key elements of design intent rather than on hefty details that you have to address later. The key here is that the sketch should capture the essence of the design and not every minute detail.

Figure 3-1 shows a hand sketch of a machine design with motor and belts, key interface planes, and mounting hole locations. Similarly, your initial hand sketch should include the key functional areas of your design.

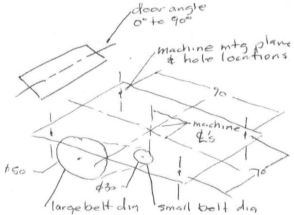

Figure 3-1:
An initial hand sketch covers major design elements.

You want to make sure to cover these key design issues:

- ✔ **Designed versus standard:** How many new versus existing or standard parts do you need for the design?

- ✔ **Major interfaces:** What are the interfaces between major design elements? This information comes in handy when you create the assembly structure.

- ✔ **Collaboration:** How many different people will work on the design? Are they in different locations? The logistics help determine who works on which parts.

- ✔ **Design reuse:** Will you base this design on an existing one? If so, update the old design to meet current standards so that you can reuse it.

- ✔ **Orientation:** Which orientation depicts how you plan to manufacture or use the product in real life? It can be misleading, for instance, if you send your manufacturer a file that shows your assembly upside down. Be sure that front is front and back is back, for example.

- ✔ **Specifications:** What information exists for the design? How big should it be? What is it made of? Are any important elements missing?

- ✔ **Manufacturing:** Include any additional design accommodations that need to be made for assembly fixtures, manufacturing, and tooling, for example.

- ✔ **Design notes and issues:** What additional notes, comments, or issues might the design group bring up? Be sure to capture and track these items.

- ✔ **Product life cycle:** How long do you plan to sell and maintain the product? If the design has a long life cycle, it may undergo a number of revisions in its lifetime, making design documents especially important.

Using an engineering journal and the SolidWorks Design Binder

As your design progresses, you need to answer several questions and make many decisions. In the old days, before computers existed, engineers kept their thoughts and notes and other scribbles in a spiral notebook, or *engineering journal.*

Nowadays, an engineering journal can be a Microsoft Word or Excel document. In SolidWorks, you have something even better, the *Design Binder* virtual design folder, where you can store links to documents that relate to the project. You can never misplace your Design Binder because it's attached to your SolidWorks drawing, part, or assembly file — right in the FeatureManager design tree. To link or attach a document to the Design Binder, follow these steps:

1. **Open the SolidWorks drawing, part, or assembly document.**

2. **In the FeatureManager design tree, right-click Design Binder and choose Add Attachment.**

   The Add Attachment dialog box appears.

   By default, the Design Binder is hidden in the FeatureManager tree. To show the Design Binder, right-click the item at the top of the tree and select Hidden Tree Items⇨Design Binder. The Design Binder can also be shown permanently by choosing Tools⇨Options⇨System Options⇨ FeatureManager and changing the Design Binder option to Show.

3. **In the Add Attachment dialog box, type a path and filename or click the Browse button to navigate to the file you want to link or attach.**

4. **To link the file, select the Link check box.**

   This option allows you to include a link to a document. If you want to attach the physical document, leave this option blank.

5. **Click OK.**

   Your file or a link to your file shows up in the Design Binder. You can see what's inside the Design Binder by clicking the + sign to the left of the Design Binder in the FeatureManager design tree.

By default, the Design Binder also contains the Design Journal, a Microsoft Word document that helps to automate the journaling process. You can use the Design Journal to type notes and other thoughts on the design process. The document resembles an engineering journal with headings for File Name, Description, and Material. These fields link to the SolidWorks document properties and update whenever you open the journal. You can type text, paste images, and format text in the Design Journal just as you do in any Word document. When you open the Design Journal, SolidWorks captures a screen image of your design and attaches it to the Clipboard so that you can conveniently paste the image into the document to help describe what's going on.

To make an entry into the Design Journal, follow these steps:

1. **Click the + sign to the left of the Design Binder icon (see Figure 3-2) within the FeatureManager design tree.**

   The folder maximizes to display its contents, which include the Design Journal and any other documents you add.

Figure 3-2: Design Binder holds project documents and files.

2. **Double-click the Design Journal to open the document in Microsoft Word.**

3. **Make your entries in the Design Journal.**

4. **Paste (Ctrl+V) an image of your design into the Design Journal.**

   SolidWorks takes a snapshot of the design and puts it in the Clipboard each time you open Design Journal, so you can paste it in the journal.

5. **Choose File➪Exit.**

   Your document is updated, Microsoft Word closes, and you return to SolidWorks.

You can use the Design Binder tool consistently throughout the design process to capture ideas, issues, and decisions. You also may want to store engineering notes the old-fashioned way, in a good old spiral notebook. Find the option that fits your requirements and working style.

Capturing design intent: Brainstorming

Brainstorming is a fruitful approach when you need collective ideas from your design team. Have a meeting early in the design process and map out the design intent — including all the big elements of your product design — on a large whiteboard. Write down the ideas and functions that the design should include. Document how the product should move. Make notes on potential issues and risks and include any other information that may be helpful.

These meetings are a great way to document some of the "tribal information" that lives quietly in everyone's head. Get everyone's ideas in writing. This review provides a consistent foundation for the design. The more you can identify before charging forward, the better.

By the way, don't count on everyone to remember exactly what was said in the meeting. If you're using an electronic whiteboard, write a date over the top and print a copy. Otherwise, take a picture with your digital camera and pop the image into your Design Binder.

Making a list and checking it twice

Checklists are valuable tools in the design process. After all, if a checklist works for Santa Claus, why not for a design team? The purpose of the checklist is to provide a consistent basis or foundation for your design project and to reduce those (avoidable) simple mistakes.

Your checklist should list common questions that the design team needs to address early in the design process, such as these:

- ✔ Has anyone approved or sourced the material you want to use?
- ✔ Have you added engineering requirements to the request for quotation (RFQ)?
- ✔ Has your purchasing department submitted an RFQ?
- ✔ Have you completed and documented the design review?
- ✔ Have you checked design standards?
- ✔ Have you checked the assembly to ensure that the parts fit together properly and do not clash, or interfere, with one another when they move?

✔ Are you using standard hardware for all fasteners? (If not, you should be, unless you want to design them all yourself.)

✔ Have you completed the drawing title block and revision block? You should include blocks in the drawing templates:

- *Blocks* include standard information that you insert into drawings.

- A *title block* lists your company name and other basic information about the project.

- A *revision block* includes the revision number of the document.

(See Chapter 7 for more information on blocks.)

✔ Have you added custom properties to the document? *Custom properties* include information that identifies the project and the document. You can link custom property fields to the drawing title block so that information is consistent in both areas. (You can find more information on custom properties in Chapter 10.)

✔ Is your testing and validation plan complete? This process should include a schedule of how and when you plan to optimize the design by using analysis software or physical prototypes or a combination of both.

Quite often, you can use the same checklist from design to design. In fact, having a standard checklist ensures consistency throughout your design processes and makes documenting the design easier. ***Remember:*** A pilot has good reason to go over a checklist every time he flies a plane, so why not review a checklist every time you design?

The process for starting and documenting a design should be a well-worn and familiar path, not something you think up out of the blue each time you design a new product. Build reviews (like the design intent brainstorm listed in the preceding section) into your design process and subsequent design meetings. Planning for success is the best way to ensure that it happens.

Applying Layouts and Design Skeletons

After you come up with a hand sketch (see the section "Starting the design with a hand sketch," earlier in this chapter), you're ready to translate it into a design layout sketch. The design layout sketch is related to — and often a subset of — the design skeleton.

Here are a few working definitions:

✔ **Assembly:** A collection of parts and other assemblies, known as *sub-assemblies*. A SolidWorks assembly file has the .sldasm extension.

✓ **Design skeleton:** A simple framework made up of design layout sketches and simple reference geometry (planes and axes) that document the important elements of the design.

✓ **Design layout:** A 3D sketch that defines the key elements of the design.

This chapter describes how to create a framework for your SolidWorks *assembly* (your virtual prototype) using a design layout sketch or a skeleton. (For more information on layouts and skeletons, see Chapter 6.)

Your assembly can have anywhere from 2 to 1,000 or more components, which can be parts or other assemblies called *subassemblies*. Depending on how complex your assembly is, your skeleton may include one or more layout sketches.

The advantages of the skeleton include the ones in this list:

✓ **It gives you a better grasp of the design you're about to build.** You can create and modify the assembly before you design any parts. Determining the most important aspects of the design early in the design process makes for a better design. The skeleton is the electronic version of the hand sketch discussed early in this chapter. (See the section "Starting the design with a hand sketch.")

✓ **You can capture design intent in the design layout sketch so that you can collaborate better with team members.** Then the designer who works on this assembly can immediately see how parts fit together.

✓ **You can automatically update your design by using references.** As you create components for your assembly, you can design them so that they reference geometry in the layout sketch. If you change the layout sketch, the components that reference it update accordingly. A reference to geometry within the assembly (an *in-context reference*) is a way of making sure that parts fit together correctly.

Designing top down versus bottom up

You can design an assembly in two ways: top down or bottom up. In *top-down design*, you build parts in the assembly, using the geometry of one part to design the others. In other words, top-down design relies on in-context references. *Bottom-up design* is the opposite: You design each part individually and then assemble the components to make the assembly.

Which method is better — top-down or bottom-up design? In reality, a combination of both methods works best. By creating a skeleton first, you can design parts to reference the skeleton rather than have them reference other parts, thereby giving you more control over the design. Other benefits include these:

✔ The assembly components reference the simple skeleton rather than complex parts or subassemblies.

✔ You can select a project leader to control important features. (Too many cooks spoil the soup.) I have worked on a complex design where a skeleton controlled the interaction and location of the major subassemblies. It was too risky to allow just anyone to change the skeleton, which controlled the top-down design. Limiting the number of people responsible for the health of the skeleton works very well.

✔ The entire assembly framework is collected into one skeleton, so even if you work on just the left widget assembly, you can see other important aspects of the design without having to look at the entire assembly.

Although the in-context reference is a powerful feature, it's a stick with a sharp end. Too many external references affect performance because SolidWorks needs to look at the original reference document to determine whether anything has changed. (For more information, see Chapter 6.)

The bottom line: Design top down using a design layout and design skeleton for essential design features. But when you get into the design detail, a bottom-up approach can minimize clutter and avoid a significant performance loss caused by the memory required in order to maintain references.

Creating a design layout

Figure 3-3 shows a design layout that controls the size, location, and design intent for two major sections (each section has its own, separate components) within a larger assembly. The design layout captures only essential design features. Too much detail can clutter the design layout and make it confusing. (Don't forget that all that clutter can make SolidWorks run slower, which can eat into your efficiency ratings.)

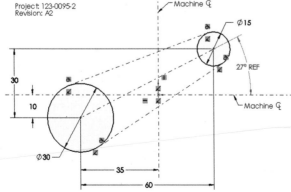

Figure 3-3:
A layout of a belt assembly captures major design elements.

You can find more information about the icons and toolbars that this section describes on the Cheat Sheet in the front of this book or in Chapter 2.

Here's how to create a design layout in SolidWorks:

1. **Choose File⇨New from the main menu.**

   The New SolidWorks Document dialog box appears (see Figure 3-4). You can choose to open a part, assembly, or drawing template.

   SolidWorks uses a *template* to begin a new document. You can modify templates or create new ones based on your needs. If you want to see other available templates, click Advanced in the New SolidWorks Document dialog box. The SolidWorks interface switches to Advanced mode. To toggle to a simpler version of the dialog box, click Novice.

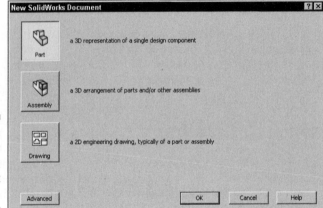

Figure 3-4:
The New
SolidWorks
Document
dialog box.

2. **Select Assembly and click OK.**

   A new SolidWorks assembly window appears, as shown in Figure 3-5.

3. **Click Create Layout.**

   A layout feature is created in the FeatureManager design tree. The command places you in 3D sketch mode, and you can begin creating your layout.

4. **Create your design layout using the sketch tools.**

   Create the 3D sketch of your original hand sketch, making sure that you capture the important elements and design intent. (If you want to find out more about sketching, read Chapter 4.) When you want to use one of the sketch tools in the following list, just choose a command and follow the instructions next to it:

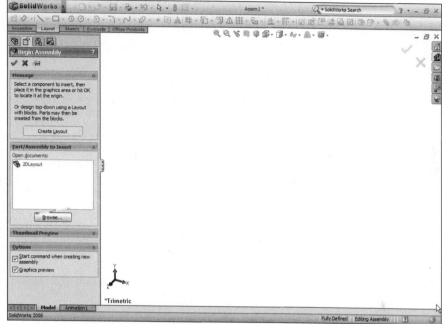

Figure 3-5:
The
SolidWorks
interface
appears
when
starting a
new part.

- *Line:* Sketch a horizontal or vertical line or an angle. Select its orientation in the Insert Line PropertyManager. In the graphics area, click to begin the line, and double-click to end it. Click OK in the Line PropertyManager to accept the line.

- *Rectangle:* Create rectangles whose sides are horizontal or vertical with respect to the sketch grid. Click and place the first corner of the rectangle. Drag and release when the rectangle is the correct size. Other rectangle options include center point rectangles and three-point rectangles.

- *Parallelogram:* Draw rectangles whose sides are at an orientation other than horizontal or vertical with respect to the grid. Click and place the first corner of the parallelogram. Drag and release when the rectangle is the correct size.

- *Polygon:* Create equilateral polygons with 3 to 40 sides. Select the Polygon command. Set properties in the Polygon PropertyManager. In the graphics area, click to place the center and drag out the polygon. Click OK.

- *Circle:* Sketch a center-based circle with this tool. Select the center or perimeter orientation in the Circle PropertyManager. Click the graphics area to place the center, move the point, and then click to set the radius. Click OK in the Circle PropertyManager.

- *Partial Ellipse:* Create a partial ellipse from a center point, a start point, and an end point. Click in the graphics area to place the center point. Drag and click to define one axis of the ellipse. Drag and click to define the second axis. Drag the pointer around the circumference to define the extent of the ellipse and then click to complete the ellipse.

- *Parabola:* Create a parabolic curve. Click to place the focus of the parabola, and drag to enlarge the parabola, which outlines the parabola. Click the parabola to define the extent of the curve.

- *Spline:* Create a series of curves that run through points. Click to place the first point and drag out the first segment. Click to the end point and drag out the second segment. Keep going until the spline is complete. Click OK.

- *Point:* Insert points into your sketch. Click in the graphics area to place the point.

- *Centerline:* Create symmetrical sketch elements. Click to start the centerline. Drag the pointer and click to set the end.

- *Sketch Fillet:* Trim away the corner at an intersection of two sketch entities to create a tangent arc. Click the Sketch Fillet tool and set the properties in the PropertyManager. Select two sketch entities or select a corner. Click OK to accept the fillet.

- *Sketch Chamfer:* Apply a chamfer to adjacent sketch entities in sketches. Click the chamfer tool. Set chamfer parameters in the PropertyManager. Select two sketch entities to chamfer, or select a vertex. Click OK to accept the chamfer.

5. **Click the Layout button on the Layout toolbar to close the layout and the sketch.**

6. **Choose File⇨Save to save the assembly.**

   Don't forget to save your work. SolidWorks also asks whether you want to save any work in progress before you close down the program.

The preceding method creates the design layout within the assembly, but that's not the only way to go. You can also create a design layout sketch in a part file and add the part to the assembly later. I cover this method in Chapter 6.

Creating in-context parts in the assembly

Assembly components can reference information (size or location) in the design layout or in the skeleton, as described in the next section. In both these examples of in-context references, when you change the design layout or the skeleton, you change the geometry that references those updates accordingly.

To reference parts to other parts, use design layouts as in-context relations. Follow these steps:

1. **Open the assembly file that contains the part to edit.**

2. **Click the part to edit within the FeatureManager design tree or in the graphics area.**

3. **Click the Edit Component icon on the Assembly toolbar.**

   The part you select appears normally; the other assembly components are transparent.

4. **Edit the part.**

   Make changes to the parts design. You can reference the assembly components to drive in-context relations.

5. **Click the Edit Component icon within the Assembly toolbar to return to the original assembly.**

Thinking about skeletons you want in your closet

No, this section doesn't talk about Uncle Bob at last year's Christmas party, but rather about a SolidWorks feature you can use to depict and document the major design elements of the assembly.

Although a design layout works well, sometimes you want to use a *skeleton* when creating a large and complex element, such as a lawnmower. Similar to a sketch, a skeleton is saved as a SolidWorks part document (`.sldprt`). However, a skeleton incorporates several design sketches and uses other elements (such as planes and axes) that allow you to simulate the location, the important interfaces where parts fit together, and the motion of the assembly components. Figure 3-6 shows an example of how you can extend 2D layout sketches into a 3D design skeleton.

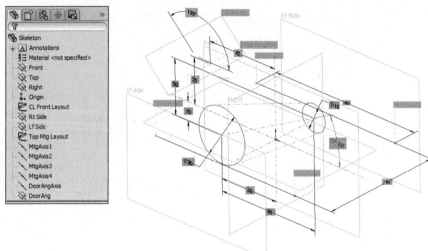

Figure 3-6:
You can
reference
parts and
subassem-
blies to the
skeleton.

You may opt to use a skeleton for several reasons:

- ✔ You can add more than one design layout sketch to the assembly. You may need a number of different orientations and functional design layout sketches to document the design intent for the assembly.

- ✔ You can add reference geometry (for example, 2D planes and axes) to the assembly to document other elements of the design that a layout design sketch cannot describe.

- ✔ Reference geometry can allow your virtual assembly to move or rotate as the real assembly would. If you designed your assembly so that it moves or rotates, you can use the design skeleton to analyze how the assembly works in real life.

If working with a skeleton sounds intriguing, you may want to check out Chapter 6, which delves into the whole concept of design skeletons.

Part II
Design Intent and the Virtual Prototype

The 5th Wave   By Rich Tennant

With Dad's SolidWorks rendering of forest trolls, his campfire stories achieve new heights in realism.

In this part . . .

Easy-to-modify, or *robust,* designs provide a strong foundation for the design because you can create parts that are easy to understand and modify. You then use these parts to build functional assemblies. This design food chain is an effective means to build parts and assemblies.

It's the small things that count during the design process. This part builds on two main ideas: design intent (fit, form, and function) and the virtual prototype. SolidWorks creates the parts in 3D, which helps you get a better understanding of your design, long before you ever manufacture the first part.

Chapter 4

Do What I Mean, Not What I Sketch

*J*ust like building a house, your design needs to start with a sound and sturdy foundation. Sketches are the building blocks for your design. Before you start to build parts and assemblies, you need to know how to create a good sketch and to understand how a sketch affects the rest of the design.

You may think it strange to talk about sketches before creating parts, but the ability to create sketches that capture design intent makes it easier to create the part. In other words, you need to walk before you run, so be sure that these concepts are clear before you go to other chapters in the book. Each step in the sketch process helps you think about how to create a better design and take full advantage of the SolidWorks 3D modeling system.

In this chapter, we introduce what makes up a sketch: sketch entities (lines and arcs, for example) and reference geometry (axes and planes). We also examine how part features use these objects.

Making and Editing a Sketch

A *sketch* is a collection of simple elements, such as lines, rectangles, and circles. Sketches can be 2D or 3D and serve a number of uses within SolidWorks; most important, they're the basis for sketched features. *Features* (extruded bosses and cuts, for example) are the geometrical shapes you use to build parts. A model includes one or more sketches as well as one or more features (unless the part was created from imported geometry). This section focuses on how to create 2D sketches to use as the bases of part features. Chapter 5 goes into detail on all the part features.

Follow this order when you make a sketch:

1. Draw the sketch geometry.

2. Add relations.

3. Dimension the sketch.

Identifying the elements of a sketch

Before you find out how to draw the sketch, you should first become familiar with the sketch lingo that appears throughout this chapter. Refer to the following list of terms whenever you need to:

- **Origin:** Marks the center of the document. When a sketch is active, two red arrows appear in the middle of the graphical display and mark the (0,0,0) coordinate of the sketch. When you're working on a part, the arrows are blue. When a sketch is active, the origin is red. Each part and assembly has its own origin. You can't delete the origin of a part or assembly.

- **Construction geometry:** Assists you in creating the sketch entities and geometry that you ultimately incorporate into a part. Points and centerlines are always construction geometry, but you can convert any other sketch entity into a construction geometry. Construction geometry appears as a dashed line. SolidWorks doesn't look at construction geometry when it creates part features.

- **Reference geometry:** Defines the shape or form of a surface or solid in the model. SolidWorks uses reference geometry (planes, axes, coordinate systems, and points) as the basis for creating part features.

- **Plane:** Refers to flat reference geometry. In a part or an assembly document, SolidWorks provides three default planes (front, top, and right). You can create your own reference planes as well. You must begin a 2D sketch on either a plane or the flat, planar face of a part.

- **Axis:** Refers to an infinite straight dashed line that you use to create model geometry, features, or patterns. You can create an axis in a number of different ways, including by creating a line or a construction line, or by intersecting two planes.

- **Driving dimension (or *model dimension*):** Defines the size of a sketch, which drives the shape of the model. When you change a sketch dimension, the rest of the sketch updates accordingly. (Chapter 3 covers design intent in detail.)

✔ **Driven dimension (or *reference dimension*):** Shows the measurements of a model but doesn't drive the model, and you can't change it. You can add driven dimensions to sketches and drawings.

✔ **Sketch entity:** Simple objects, such as lines, points, and circles, that make up a sketch.

✔ **Relations:** Establish geometric relations for a single sketch entity and between sketch entities. For example, a parallel relation makes two lines parallel to each other, and a tangent relation makes two lines tangent. Relations are an important method for capturing design intent.

Origins and orientation

How you kick off a sketch varies depending on how you want your design to look and the type and order of the design's features. Before you begin a sketch, you want to decide on these elements:

✔ The reference plane or part face that you want to sketch on

✔ The origin of the sketch

✔ The relationships between the sketch entities

✔ The dimensions you need for the drawing

Every time you draw a sketch, you must first select a plane or a part face (such as the left side of a cube) to draw it on. The plane determines the orientation of your sketch. If you sketch on the front plane, you're sketching the front of a part. You don't want to end up with a part that's upside down or sideways, so choosing the right plane or surface is important.

The *origin* is where you start your sketch. In most cases, the origin of the sketch coincides with the origin of the document. The origin anchors yoursketch. Centers of mounting holes, axes of rotation, and the mounting face are also good choices for an origin. Figure 4-1 shows examples of parts with origins defined with design intent in mind.

You can use the following list to determine the orientation or origin of your sketch:

✔ **Part origin:** Parts in an assembly can share a common origin. Parts are built with this common assembly location in mind.

✔ **Final assembly orientation:** You can position a part based on how it fits into the assembly.

✔ **Design layout:** You can position a part based on a design layout sketch or a skeleton.

✔ **Drawing views to create:** You can design a part based on how you want it projected in the drawing.

Origin

Sketching with entities

After you ponder over origins and orientation, you're ready to take your mouse in hand and draw. You begin a sketch in a part document by activating Sketch mode. You can switch back into Solid Modeling mode by exiting Sketch mode. You use sketch entities to build the sketch. The sketch entity commands are located on the Sketch toolbar, which appears by default in the CommandManager when you begin a sketch.

Here's how to start a sketch:

1. **Open a new part document in SolidWorks.**

   The origin appears in blue in the graphics area.

2. **Choose Insert⇨Sketch.**

   The Edit Sketch PropertyManager appears in the left pane. Three default planes (Front, Top, and Right) appear in the graphics area. If you place the pointer over a plane, the plane's edges are highlighted in red.

3. **Click an edge of a plane or anywhere on a part face to sketch in the graphics area.**

   You can begin a sketch on a plane or a part face. You can select a default plane, or you can create your own. (See the section "Adding reference

geometry," later in this chapter.) When you select a plane, the Edit
Sketch PropertyManager disappears, and the plane turns to face you.

4. **Create your sketch using the sketch entities described in Table 4-1.**

5. **Choose Insert⇨Exit Sketch.**

You exit Sketch mode and return to the part. The origin turns blue. Your
sketch is saved with the part document.

When you finish creating a sketch entity, the sketch command is still active,
and you just keep drawings circles and lines, for example. Right click and
choose Select or press Esc to place the entity and exit the command.

Table 4-1	Sketch Entities
Entity	*Function*
Centerline	A straight line that is construction geometry. Click Centerline on the Sketch toolbar and click the start and endpoints to define the line within the graphics area.
Centerpoint Arc	A partial circle defined by three points. Click Centerpoint Arc on the Sketch toolbar and click the origin, start, and end radius locations within the graphics area.
Circle	A full circle. Click Circle on the Sketch toolbar and click the origin and radius locations within the graphics area.
Line	A straight segment. Click Line on the Sketch toolbar and click the start and endpoints to define the line within the graphics area. Additional clicks create a series of connected lines.
Point	An entity that defines a single location in space. Click Point on the Sketch toolbar and click the location for the sketch point within the graphics area.
Rectangle	A box that consists of four lines. Click Rectangle on the Sketch toolbar and then, in the graphics area, click to place the first corner of the rectangle, drag to size the rectangle, and click again. Options are available for center point rectangles and for three-point rectangles.

(continued)

Table 4-1 (continued)

Entity	Function
Sketch Fillet	A tangent arc between two intersecting entities. Click Sketch Fillet on the Sketch toolbar and set properties in the PropertyManager. Hold down the Ctrl key and select two sketch entities to fillet and select a corner.
Spline	A curvy line defined by a set of points. Click Spline on the Sketch toolbar and click the point locations within the graphics area to define the spline.
Tangent Arc	An arc tangent to a sketch entity. Click Tangent Arc on the Sketch toolbar and click the endpoint of an existing tangent entity (line, arc, ellipse, or spline) and the endpoint for the arc within the graphics area.
Three Point Arc	A partial circle. Click Three Point Arc on the Sketch toolbar and click the three points on the arc within the graphics area.

Modifying sketch entities

Several additional commands on the Sketch toolbar allow you to make changes to your sketch, if needed. For example, the Construction command turns any sketch entity into construction geometry.

You create your sketch in a part or an assembly document. When you open a document to edit a sketch, you need to switch back into Sketch mode. To turn on sketching, choose Insert➪Sketch. When you want to go back to solid modeling to create part features, choose Insert➪Exit Sketch. If the sketch already exists, select the sketch in the FeatureManager design tree, right-click, and choose the Edit Sketch icon.

The following sections cover the sketch modification commands (see Figure 4-2), which are on the right side of the Sketch toolbar.

Figure 4-2:
Sketch
modification
commands.

Mirror entities

When you create mirror entities, SolidWorks mirrors the entities that you select about a centerline or line. If that sounds confusing, imagine that you're standing on the edge of a pond. You see a reflection of yourself in the water. The reflection is your mirror image, and the centerline, which you *mirror about,* is the edge of the pond. In SolidWorks, if you change a mirrored entity, its mirror image also changes.

To mirror one or more existing sketch entities in a sketch:

1. **Click Mirror Entities on the Sketch toolbar.**

   The Mirror PropertyManager appears, with the Entities to Mirror field active.

2. **In the graphics area, click the entities you want to mirror.**

   The entities are displayed in the Entities to Mirror field. If you want to remove an entity, select it in the field and press Delete on the keyboard.

3. **Click inside the Mirror About field.**

   The field is highlighted, indicating that the next entity you select goes in this field.

4. **Select the Copy check box to include both the mirrored copy and the original sketch entities. Clear the Copy check box to add a mirror copy of the selected entities and to remove the original sketch.**

   If you remove the original sketch, it's like removing the original object in a mirror and leaving only a reflection.

5. **Click the edge or line that you want to mirror about the centerline.**

   The edge or line appears in the Mirror About field.

6. **Click OK.**

   A mirror image of the entities you selected appears on the other side of the line or edge.

Convert entities

You can create one or more curves in a sketch by projecting an edge, a loop, a face, a curve, an external sketch contour, a set of edges, or set of sketch curves onto an existing sketch plane.

To convert sketch entities in an open sketch:

1. **Click a model edge, loop, face, curve, external sketch contour, set of edges, or set of curves.**

2. **Click Convert Entities on the Sketch toolbar.**

   The new sketch entities appear on the sketch plane.

3. **Click OK.**

Offset entities

You can make a copy of a sketch entity so that the copy appears a specified distance on the sketch plane from the original object. To offset one or more sketch entities in an open sketch, follow these steps:

1. **Click Offset Entities on the Sketch toolbar.**

   The Offset Entities PropertyManager appears.

2. **In the Parameters section of the PropertyManager, type a value for the offset distance.**

3. **In the graphics area, click the entity or entities to offset.**

   To see a dynamic preview, hold down the mouse button and drag the pointer in the graphics area. As you drag the pointer, the size of the offset changes. When you release the mouse button, the Offset Entity is complete.

4. **Click OK.**

Trim entities

You can trim entities to your liking with the Trim Entities command. The command allows you to create unusual shapes. For example, you can sketch a large circle with two small circles intersecting it at the top. You can then trim away the crisscrossing arcs of the three circles to end up with a shape that looks like Mickey Mouse. The Trim Property Manager has several options: The Power Trim option is a quick way to trim or delete any sketch entity, and the Corner option lets you trim two entities to the nearest intersection. Both options allow you to "clean up" a sketch.

To trim sketch entities by using the Power Trim option, follow these steps:

1. **Right-click the sketch and choose Edit Sketch.**

   (For a new sketch, choose Insert⇨Sketch.)

2. **Click Trim Entities on the Sketch toolbar.**

   The Trim PropertyManager appears.

3. **In the Options section of the PropertyManager, click the Power Trim button.**

4. Click and drag your cursor across the entities you want to trim.

The sketch entity trims the portion of the sketch you drag over. If there's no intersecting entity, the entity you select to trim is deleted.

5. Click OK.

To trim sketch entities using the Corner option, follow these steps:

1. Right-click the sketch and choose Edit Sketch.

(For a new sketch, choose Insert⇨Sketch.)

2. Click Trim Entities on the Sketch toolbar.

The Trim PropertyManager appears.

3. In the Options section of the PropertyManager, select Corner.

This option trims two sketch entities to their intersection.

4. Click two entities to trim in the graphics area.

Click the portion you want to keep.

5. Click OK.

The two entities trim to the nearest corner.

Construction geometry

You can change any sketch geometry to construction geometry by using the Construction Geometry command. Construction geometry serves as a guideline for creating the rest of the sketch and doesn't show up in a part feature.

To change sketch geometry to construction geometry, follow these steps:

1. Click the sketch entity that you want to change to construction geometry.

To select multiple entities, hold Ctrl and click. A sketch entity turns green when it's selected.

2. Click Construction Geometry on the Sketch toolbar (or choose Insert⇨Reference Geometry).

The selected entities appear with a dashed line to indicate that they're construction geometry. You can toggle back to sketch geometry by repeating these two steps.

Move entities

You can move any sketch entity to a new location by using the Move or Copy Entities command.

To reposition sketch geometry, follow these steps:

1. **Click Move Entities on the Sketch toolbar.**

   The Move PropertyManager appears, with the Sketch Items or Annotations field active.

2. **Select the entities to move within the graphics area.**

   The entity names appear in the Sketch Items or Annotations field.

3. **Click the From/To or X/Y option from the Parameters field.**

   The base point (From/To) or delta x/delta y (X/Y) fields, based on this selection, appear.

4. **Click inside the Base Point field (From/To) or enter the change in X and Y coordinates (X/Y).**

5. **Click the start point for the move in the graphics area for the From/To option.**

   The entity is highlighted in green, and two green arrows indicating the base point X, Y coordinates appear near the pointer. As you move the pointer, the entities move with it.

6. **Drag the pointer and click to place the entity in its new location for the X/Y option.**

7. **Click OK.**

Adding reference geometry

When you sketch, axes and planes serve as reference geometry for the part you're about to build. *Planes* are flat surfaces on which you draw your sketch. *Axes* are straight lines that serve as the center of rotation for some shapes. You can create axes in many ways. For example, you can create an axis from a centerline or the intersection of two planes.

SolidWorks also creates temporary axes for cones and cylinders in the model. Sometimes confusion occurs about the difference between centerlines and axes. The difference is that a centerline is contained in a sketch, and an axis is in a part.

Here are a few other important aspects of reference geometry:

✔ **To control the visibility for reference planes, axes, and temporary axes:** Choose View from the main menu and select the reference type (Axes or Origin, for example) that you want to turn on or off. A check mark next to a reference means that it's turned on.

✔ **To hide all types of reference geometry with a single selection:** From the main menu, choose View and select Hide All Types. To turn on the display of all reference geometry, just deselect this option. A check mark next to Hide All Types means that all types are hidden. You can also use the Hide/Show buttons on the Heads-Up View toolbar.

✔ **To name a sketch entity:** In the FeatureManager design tree, click the entity, press F2, and type a name. (When you create a plane or an axis, you should name it in the FeatureManager design tree to document how you intend to use it.) Naming items in the FeatureManager design tree is a key concept of capturing design intent.

Creating planes

In a part or assembly document, SolidWorks gives you three default planes to work with: front, top, and right. You can create additional planes to serve as the sketch planes or to create a section view of a model.

To create a reference plane, follow these steps:

1. **Open a part or an assembly document.**

2. **Choose Insert⇨Reference Geometry⇨Plane.**

   The Plane PropertyManager appears, with the Reference Entities field active.

3. **In the PropertyManager, select the type of plane you want to create.**

   You have several options, as shown in Figure 4-3:

   - *Through Lines/Points:* Creates a plane through a point and an edge, an axis, or a sketch line or through three points.

   - *Parallel Plane at Point:* Creates a plane through a point parallel to a plane or face.

   - *At Angle:* Creates a plane through an edge, an axis, or a sketch line at an angle that you specify to a face or plane. (If you choose this plane, enter the angle value into the spin box.)

   - *Offset Distance:* Creates a plane parallel to a plane or a face, offset by a distance you specify. This option is the default plane. (If you choose this plane, enter the offset value in the spin box.)

   - *Normal to Curve:* Creates a plane through a point and makes it perpendicular to an edge or a curve.

   - *On Surface:* Creates a plane on a nonplanar face or an angular surface.

4. **Click the items in the graphics area that you want to use to create the plane.**

   The items appear in the Reference Entities field. You must select valid entities. For example, if you choose Normal to Curve, you must select a point and an edge or a curve. If you want to remove a selection, select the item and press the Delete key.

   A preview of the new plane appears in the graphics area.

5. **Click OK.**

   The PropertyManager closes, and your new plane appears in the graphics area.

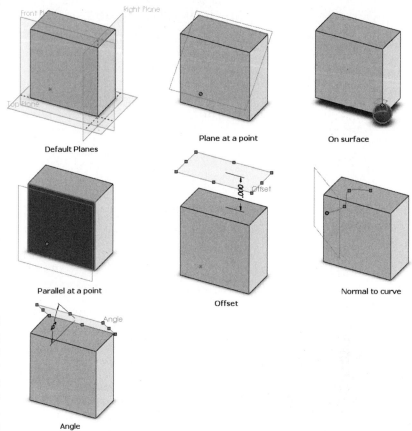

Default Planes

Plane at a point

On surface

Parallel at a point

Offset

Normal to curve

Figure 4-3:
You can
create your
own
reference
planes.

Angle

You can also copy planes offset at a distance. Select the plane in the graphics area by holding down the mouse button and the Ctrl key on the keyboard and then moving the pointer to a new location and releasing the mouse button.

Working with axes

An *axis* is a type of reference geometry that you use to create a part feature. You can create an axis in a number of different ways by selecting different part geometry. Figure 4-4 shows the different axis types and the geometry required to create the axis.

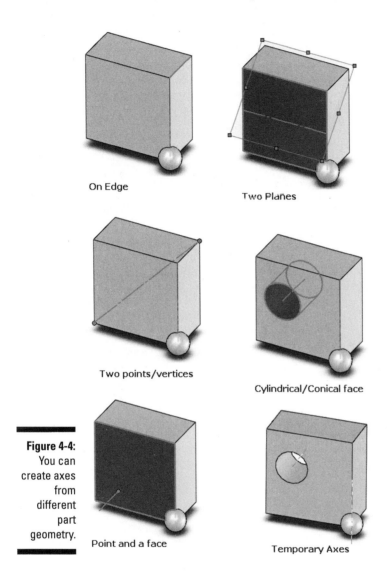

On Edge

Two Planes

Two points/vertices

Cylindrical/Conical face

Figure 4-4:
You can
create axes
from
different
part
geometry.

Point and a face

Temporary Axes

To create a reference axis, follow these steps:

1. **Open a part or an assembly document.**

2. **Choose Insert⇨Reference Geometry⇨Axis.**

   The Axis PropertyManager appears with the Reference Entities field active.

3. **Choose the type of axis to create.**

   Your choices are described in this list:

   - *One Line/Edge/Axis:* Creates an axis through a line, an edge, or a temporary axis. Select a sketch line or an edge or choose View⇨Temporary Axes and select the axis in the graphics area.

   - *Two Planes:* Creates an axis at the intersection of two planes. Select two planar faces or choose View⇨Planes and then select two planes in the graphics area.

   - *Two Points/Vertices:* Creates an axis through two points or part vertices. Select two vertices, points, or midpoints.

   - *Cylindrical/Conical Face:* Creates an axis based on an existing hole or cylindrical feature. Select a cylindrical or conical face.

   - *Point and Face/Plane:* Creates an axis that's normal (perpendicular) to a face or plane through an existing point. Select two entities: a surface or a plane *and* a vertex point or midpoint. The resultant axis is normal to the selected surface or plane through the selected vertex, point, or midpoint. If the surface is nonplanar, the point must be on the surface.

4. **In the graphics area, select the reference entities to create the axis.**

   The reference entities you select appear in the Reference Entity field. If you want to clear a selection, click it in the Reference Entity field and press Delete.

5. **Click OK.**

   The axis appears in the graphics area.

Defining the Sketch

A good sketch captures design intent. *Design intent* is all about how you want your model to behave when you make a change.

Say that you make a part with two holes. You want the holes to have the same diameter and to stay symmetric around the centerline of the part, even when you change the length of the part. You need to capture your intent in your sketches. The way to capture design intent is to *constrain* (define) the design.

SolidWorks offers two types of constraints:

- ✔ **Relations** establish geometric relationships (equal or tangent, for example) between sketch entities.

REMEMBER

✔ **Dimensions** constrain the length, width, or angle of a sketch entity so that it stays constant.

A sketch can by fully defined, underdefined, or overdefined:

✔ A **fully defined sketch entity** is fully constrained. Dimensions or relations (or both) describe the value and position of every line and curve in the sketch. In SolidWorks, fully constrained entities appear in black. A fully defined sketch ensures that your part is updated more predictably.

✔ An **underdefined sketch entity** doesn't have enough geometric relations or dimension constraints to fully define its position and location. An underdefined sketch is okay if you plan to use it to create a feature, but you should fully define a sketch to complete a part. In SolidWorks, underdefined sketch entities appear in blue.

✔ An **overdefined sketch entity** has geometric relations and dimensional constraints that constrain it in more than one way, which creates a conflict. Overdefined entities appear in red or yellow.

Figure 4-5 shows an example of a sketch that's underdefined. Because this sketch isn't fully constrained and dimensioned, it isn't modified predictably when you change a dimension value.

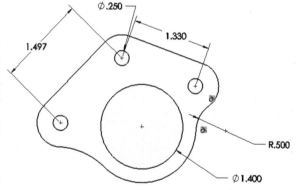

Figure 4-5:
An underdefined sketch, such as this one, is updated unpredictably.

In contrast, Figure 4-6 shows the same sketch fully constrained, which makes the design easy to modify. If you need to change the spacing or angle between the holes, you change a single dimension, and the sketch is updated as intended.

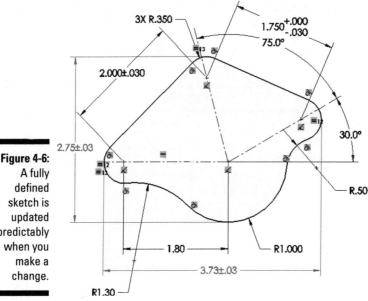

Figure 4-6:
A fully
defined
sketch is
updated
predictably
when you
make a
change.

The example shown in the figure conveys the designer's intent as described in this list:

✔ The overall length and width are driven from other design elements, but are shown on the drawing with a tolerance of ±.030.

✔ All three smaller arcs are the same diameter.

✔ Tolerance between the two smaller arcs is ±.030. The tolerance between the other one is +.000–.030.

✔ The two arcs on the bottom line up horizontally.

✔ The angle between the top two mounting holes is 75 degrees.

✔ The angle between the horizontal mounting hole and the right mounting hole is 30 degrees.

✔ The origin of the sketch is at the center of a bottom mounting hole.

✔ The designer added three small mounting holes and one large one as additional hole features after this sketch was complete, so they're easier to modify.

Working with relations

Relations define how two sketch entities relate to each other. Relations are either inferred or added. SolidWorks infers relations as you sketch (see the upcoming section "Speeding sketch creation by using inferencing") and adds relations automatically, but you can also add your own relations.

Table 4-2 describes the major relation types.

Table 4-2	Relation Types
Relation Type	*Description*
Coincident	A point lies on a line, arc, or ellipse.
Collinear	Two or more lines are linear.
Concentric	Two or more arcs or a point and an arc share the same centerpoint.
Coradial	Two or more arcs share the same center point and radius.
Equal	Two entities remain of equal length or radius.
Horizontal/vertical	One or more lines or two or more points are horizontal or vertical.
Intersection	A point remains at the intersection of two lines.
Merge points	Two sketch points merge into one.
Midpoint	The point or vertex (end of a line) remains at the midpoint of the line.
Parallel	The entities are parallel to one another.
Perpendicular	The items are at 90 degrees to one another.
Tangent	Two items remain tangent — for example, a line that intersects a circle or arc at a single point.

Adding a relation

To add a new relation to sketch entities in an open sketch, follow these steps:

1. **Click the Display/Delete Relations button on the Sketch toolbar and select Add Relation.**

   The Add Relations PropertyManager appears, with the Selected Entities field active.

2. **In the graphics area, select the entity or entities you want to relate.**

   The entities appear in the Selected Entities field. The Existing Relations field shows any relations that already exist for those entities. The Add Relations section shows only the relation types that are valid for the entity or entities you selected.

3. **To delete an existing relation, select the relation in the Existing Relations field and press Delete.**

   Use Display/Delete Relations to see all relations.

4. **To add a new relation, select one of the relation types that appear in the Add Relations box.**

5. **Click OK.**

   SolidWorks adds the relation to the entities.

SolidWorks places tiny icons in the graphics area to let you know which type of relation exists between sketch entities. For example, if two arcs have an equal radial value, SolidWorks puts an equal sign next to them. If a sketch entity has more than one set of equal constraints, SolidWorks places an instance number to the right side of the relation icon. The corresponding relation displays the same number on the right side of the relation tag.

Using relation filters

It's useful to look at a sketch and tell at a glance which relations are where, especially when you need to edit a sketch that's overdefined. But things can get crowded, especially when working on a large sketch, and that's when you want to use a relation filter. A *relation filter* shows only certain types of relations. The Display/Delete Relations command on the Sketch toolbar, shown in Figure 4-7, lets you choose the relations types you want to see and makes it easy to delete relations you don't want.

To set a relations filter in a sketch, follow these steps:

1. **Choose Tools⇨Relations⇨Display/Delete.**

   The Display/Delete Relations PropertyManager appears.

2. **In the Filter area, select a relation to display in the drop-down list.**

   When you select a relation from the list, the appropriate sketch entities are highlighted in the graphics area. The options are described in this list:

   • *All in This Sketch:* (Default) Displays all relations defined within the sketch. This list can be large based on the size and complexity of the sketch.

   • *Selected Entities:* Displays relations for only the selected entities. This filter is the most commonly used.

   • *Dangling:* Occurs when one of the references originally used to create the relation is missing (deleted entity).

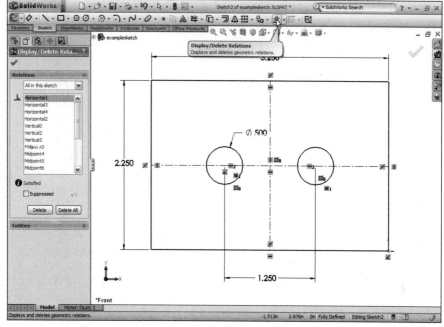

Figure 4-7:
The Display/
Delete
Relations
command
lets you
display only
the relations
you want
to see.

- *Overdefined/Not Solved:* Indicates a redundant dimension or unnecessary relation.

- *External:* Displays relations created externally to the current sketch. Referencing existing part geometry is often useful.

- *Defined in Content:* Displays relations defined in the context of the assembly. This powerful feature has a number of performance considerations.

- *Locked:* Displays relations to locked external features or components. A locked external reference can no longer automatically update. Although not updating automatically can give you a performance gain, you still need to ensure that changes are made correctly.

- *Broken:* Displays relations with broken external references.

3. **To delete a relation, highlight the entity in the graphics area and click Delete in the PropertyManager.**

   The relation changes to green in the graphics area.

4. **Click OK.**

   The PropertyManager closes.

Using Quick Snaps to create relations

When Quick Snaps are enabled, SolidWorks creates a relation (Nearest Snap, Tangent Snap, Perpendicular Snap, or Parallel Snap, for example) as you create the sketch geometry. SolidWorks creates relations automatically when sketching, but Quick Snaps give you more options and control.

For example, you may want a line to be as close as possible to another line. The nearest snap completes the line based on the closest distance to the selected line. Quick Snaps help you better define the attributes, or behaviors, of a sketch entity.

Available Quick Snaps are Point, Center (Arc/Circle), Mid-Points, Quadrants (circle), Intersection, Nearest, Tangent, Perpendicular, Parallel, Horizontal or Vertical Lock, Horizontal or Vertical Point Snap, Length Snap, Grid Snap, and Angle Snap.

To create a sketch line by using a Quick Snap, follow these steps:

1. **Open or create a sketch.**

2. **To display the Quick Snap toolbar, choose View➪Toolbars➪Quick Snaps.**

   The Quick Snap toolbar appears.

3. **Click Line on the Sketch toolbar.**

   Quick Snap also works with other sketch geometry.

4. **To define the starting point for the line, click the first point.**

5. **Click Tangent on the Quick Snap toolbar.**

   Only tangent selections are shown as the cursor moves within the graphics area. Note that you can't select a Quick Snap until after you click to start sketching a new line, arc, circle, rectangle, spline, or point.

6. **Click the endpoint for the line.**

   The line appears, and the selected relation is added.

Speeding sketch creation by using inferencing

As you sketch, SolidWorks infers and creates certain types of relations between entities in a sketch automatically. For example, when you sketch a horizontal line, SolidWorks adds a relation to keep the line horizontal. With automatic inferencing, inferencing lines work together with pointers, Quick Snaps, and relations to graphically display how sketch entities affect each other and which type of relation SolidWorks will create.

Inferencing lines are dotted lines that appear when you sketch. When your pointer approaches highlighted cues, such as a midpoint, blue dotted lines appear in order to guide you relative to existing sketch entities. In some cases, SolidWorks automatically creates relations.

The pointer display indicates when the pointer is over a geometric relation (such as an intersection), which sketch tool is active, and dimensions. If the pointer displays a relation, such as a horizontal relation, SolidWorks adds the relation automatically to the entity.

TIP

When creating a sketch, you may not want to use the automatically created inference relationships (see Figure 4-8). For example, you may not want SolidWorks to add a horizontal relationship to a line, or a coincident relationship to a line that goes over the top of a circle. To override the creation of these relationships, hold down the Ctrl key while creating the sketch entity.

Figure 4-8:
The pointer
display
changes to
indicate the
type of
relation
SolidWorks
will add.

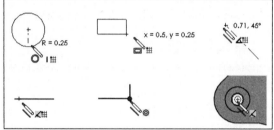

One reason that SolidWorks doesn't create all inferences automatically is that too many extra relations would exist, and the sketch would quickly become overdefined. A sketch entity is *overdefined*, either through dimensions or relations, when it's being told to define something twice. A warning appears whenever a sketch entity is overdefined.

Creating simple dimensions

REMEMBER

You create sketches in three steps: You sketch, add relations, and then add dimensions to size and locate the sketch entities. You can create features without adding dimensions to sketches. However, dimensioning sketches is a good practice. You want to dimension in accordance with the model's design intent. For example, you may want to dimension holes a certain distance from an edge or a certain distance from each other.

You dimension sketch entities and other objects with the Smart Dimension tool. The type of dimension is determined by the items you click. For some types of dimensions (point-to-point, angular, and circular), the location where you place the dimension also affects the type of dimension that SolidWorks adds. You can also drag or delete a dimension while the Smart Dimension tool is active.

To dimension an entity in a sketch, follow these steps:

1. **Click Smart Dimension on the Dimensions/Relations toolbar.**

   The pointer changes to a dimension icon.

2. **Depending on the entity to dimension, select the items as indicated:**

   - *Length of a line or edge:* Click the line.

   - *Angle between two lines:* Click two lines or a line and a model edge. How you place the dimension affects how the angle is measured. It's based on which quadrant of an imaginary circle you place the final dimension text on.

   - *Distance between two lines:* Click two parallel lines or a line and a parallel model edge.

   - *Perpendicular distance from a point to a line:* Click the point and the line or model edge.

   - *Distance between two points:* Click two points. One of the points can be a model vertex.

   - *Radius of an arc:* Click the arc.

   - *True length of an arc:* Click the arc and then the two endpoints.

   - *Diameter of a circle:* Click the circumference. The dimension is displayed as linear or diameter, depending on where you place the pointer.

   A preview of the dimension appears in the graphics area as a blue line with arrows on either end and the measurement value on top. As you move the pointer, the dimension moves with it.

3. **Move the pointer and click to place the dimension.**

   The Modify dialog box appears.

4. **Enter a value for the dimension in the Modify dialog box, as shown in Figure 4-9.**

   You don't have to enter a value; you can accept the existing value.

5. **Click Rebuild in the Modify dialog box to see the model updated with the new value.**

   If the value isn't correct or you want to change it, change the values and click Rebuild in the Modify dialog box again.

6. **Click OK.**

   The Modify dialog box closes, and the dimension appears in the graphics area. The model is updated accordingly.

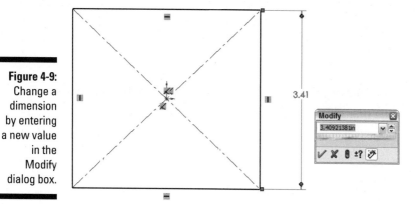

Figure 4-9:
Change a dimension by entering a new value in the Modify dialog box.

Marking a dimension for drawing reuse

When you create dimensions in part sketches, you can specify whether the dimension should be included in the drawing. In the Modify dialog box, after you enter the dimension value, the button Mark Dimension to Be Imported into a Drawing is selected by default, as shown in Figure 4-10. Clicking this option flags the dimension for import into a drawing by using the Insert Model Items feature (see Chapter 8).

Figure 4-10:
A dimension value marked for drawing import.

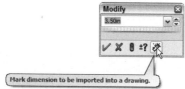

Because the dimensions are reused within your drawing, spend some extra effort positioning the dimensions the way you want to see them in your drawing. You should also add any tolerances, notes, and symbols to the sketch dimensions to eliminate duplicate work on the drawing and to include the information in the part where it belongs. You can read more on how to add annotations to models in Chapter 7.

Before you finish your sketch, give it some exercise. Click and drag entities to see whether the sketch is updated as you intend. If you resize an arc by dragging one of its endpoints, notice whether the attached lines stay tangent. If the sketch doesn't capture design intent, you may want to add constraints.

Chapter 5

Making Better Parts

· ·

In This Chapter

▶ Familiarizing yourself with parts and features

▶ Creating sketched features and applied features

▶ Using pattern and mirror features

▶ Building a part

▶ Naming and organizing features and dimensions

▶ Making parts more robust by using function feature order

▶ Documenting designs by using comments

▶ Knowing what to model

· ·

*P*arts are the basis of drawings and assemblies. Just as assemblies are made from individual parts, parts are made from individual features. This chapter explains how to create a part and introduces the different types of features you can use to construct that part. This chapter doesn't cover every feature type that SolidWorks offers. Instead, it focuses on the most common ones.

Introducing Part Features

Parts consist of features. *Features,* or shapes, are the building blocks of a model. You begin a part with a flat sketch. You dimension the sketch to make sure that it's the proper size and then you create features.

The first feature in a part is the *base feature* because it forms the base of the part. Generally, but not always, the first feature is a *base extrusion.* An *extrude* adds material by pulling the shape out. If you extrude a rectangle, for example, you get a cube. After you have a lump of material to work with, subsequent features add or subtract material by scooping or rounding, for example. Eventually, your part takes shape.

A SolidWorks feature is one of two types:

- A *sketched* feature is based on a 2D sketch.
- An *applied* feature is one that you apply directly to the model.

The following list presents examples of these types of features:

- **Boss/base features (sketched):** Add material to the model (extrude, revolve, sweep, loft). The first feature is a *base,* and subsequent features are *bosses.*
- **Cut features (sketched):** Remove material from the model (extrude, revolve, sweep, loft).
- **Model features (applied):** Perform a specific modeling task (fillet, chamfer, draft, shell, hole, wizard hole, and more). Model features act on existing geometry.
- **Pattern and mirror features (applied):** Act on existing geometry and create copies of existing features. You can create a linear, circular, or sketch-driven pattern. Mirror features create copies of existing features by using planes or faces to create symmetrical copies.

The examples in the figures throughout this chapter are meant to give you some ideas for starting a part and crafting the final part design. Figure 5-1 shows how part features produce a model. You can refine a design by adding, changing, or reordering features.

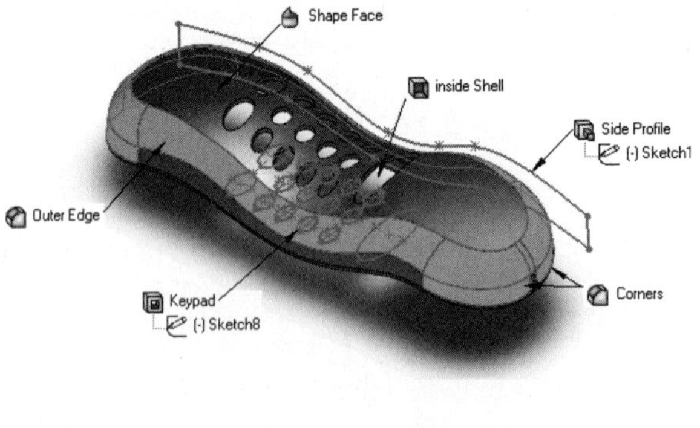

Figure 5-1:
Individual features combine to make a part.

Here are the general steps to create the part example shown in the figure (the feature name is in parentheses):

1. **Create the sketch for the feature (Side Profile/Sketch1) and extrude the profile by using Extruded Boss/Base.**

2. **Shape the profile (Shape Face) by using the Shape feature.**

3. **Round the four corners (Corners) by using a fillet.**

4. **Round the top edge (Outer Edge) by using a fillet.**

5. **Hollow out the part (Inside Shell) by using a shell.**

6. **Create the sketch for the keypad cutout (Keypad/Sketch8) by using an extruded cut.**

As you create a feature, you see a preview of what the model will look like in the graphics area. The absence of a preview is an indication that SolidWorks can't create the feature. If you don't see a preview, change the parameters in the PropertyManager.

Working with the Features Toolbar

A handy tool to have around when working on parts is the Features toolbar. SolidWorks offers an extensive set of feature commands to shape your model, and not all of them show up on the default Features toolbar. You can add or remove command buttons to customize this toolbar to suit your needs. (Chapter 2 explains how to customize toolbars.)

The Features toolbar, shown in Figure 5-2, shows the commonly used feature commands that appear in this chapter. This section assumes that you know how to create a sketch. (If you don't, see Chapter 4.)

Figure 5-2:
The
Features
toolbar.

The following list describes the commands that appear in the Command-Manager, as shown in the figure, when you first open a part document in SolidWorks:

- **Extruded Base/Boss:** Click to start an extruded feature.
- **Extruded Cut:** Click to start an extruded cut feature.
- **Revolved Base/Boss:** Click to start a revolved feature.
- **Revolved Cut:** Click to start a revolved cut feature.
- **Swept Base/Boss:** Click to start a swept feature.
- **Lofted Base/Boss:** Click to start a lofted feature.
- **Fillet:** Click to start a fillet feature.
- **Rib:** Click to start a rib feature (not covered in this chapter).

- ✔ **Shell:** Click to start a shell feature.

- ✔ **Draft:** Click to start a draft feature.

- ✔ **Hole Wizard:** Click to start the Hole Wizard feature.

- ✔ **Linear Pattern:** Click to start a pattern feature.

- ✔ **Circular Pattern:** Click to start a pattern feature.

- ✔ **Mirror:** Click to start a mirror feature.

- ✔ **Reference Geometry:** Click to display a menu of common reference geometry features (not covered in this chapter).

- ✔ **Curve:** Click to display a menu of common curve features (not covered in this chapter).

Creating Sketched Features

You must create a 2D sketch as the basis for a sketched feature (extrude, revolve, sweep, or loft) in SolidWorks. Sketched features can add or remove material from a part. A sketched feature that adds material is a *base* or a *boss*. A sketched feature that removes material is a *cut*.

When you design a part, imagine that you're a machine tool cutting away at a solid hunk of metal. In SolidWorks, a base feature gives you that solid hunk. Pick the most prominent section of the part as a base and choose a shape to best describe it. The most common base feature is a *base extrude,* but you can also create base features with a sweep, revolve, or loft.

Your 2D outline for a sketched feature generally requires a profile. A *profile,* or sketch, is the flat shape that pulls out or revolves about, for example.

If you click a sketched feature before you sketch the profile, SolidWorks puts you in Sketch mode automatically. For example, if you click Extruded Base/Boss before you sketch the extrude, SolidWorks puts you directly in Sketch mode. When you complete the sketch, click the confirmation corner in the upper-right corner of the graphics area. SolidWorks extrudes the part and displays the Extruded Cut PropertyManager.

Pulling and carving out extruded features

Using an *extrusion* is like making a cookie from a cookie press. You place a shape (or profile) in the press, and the dough comes out in that shape. An extruded boss/base adds material; an extruded cut removes material. The material that's added is extruded along a specified direction. SolidWorks bases the direction of the extrusion on a distance normal (perpendicular) to the plane of the 2D sketch or along a selected vector (direction).

The FeatureManager design tree displays the individual features of a part. You may find it easier to select the feature in the FeatureManager design tree rather than in the graphics area, especially if it's a tiny feature that you have to zoom in on to spot. When you select a feature, the feature is highlighted in both the graphics area and the FeatureManager design tree.

In the PropertyManager that appears for sketched features, a field turns light blue to indicate that it's active and waiting for you to select one or more entities in the graphics area. If the field accepts only one entity, the next field is activated automatically after you make a selection.

In some PropertyManagers and dialog boxes that appear when you choose a command, you enter values for a distance or angle, for example, in a spin box. You can click the up arrow or down arrow to increase or decrease the value incrementally. To change the default spin box increments, choose Tools➪Options. On the System Options tab, select Spin Box Increments and enter the new increment values.

To create an extruded-base/boss or cut feature, follow these steps:

1. **Sketch the profile you want to extrude.**

   You can sketch on a plane or the face of a part.

2. **Choose Insert➪Exit Sketch.**

   You exit Sketch mode.

3. **In the FeatureManager design tree, select the sketch to extrude.**

   You can preselect a sketch.

4. **Click either Extruded Boss/Base or Extruded Cut on the Features toolbar.**

   The Extrude PropertyManager appears (see Figure 5-3), and the shape is extruded by the amount that appears in the Depth field. SolidWorks prompts you for the parameters of the extrusion.

5. **In the From pull-down list, select Sketch Plane.**

   The feature extrudes from the sketch plane. You can also set From so that the feature extrudes from a surface, face, or vertex and offset. For a base extrude, extrude from the sketch plane.

6. **Set the End Conditions option to Blind.**

   You use this setting to specify the exact depth of the extrusion. Click the arrows to the left of Blind to change the direction that the part extrudes from. You can also set end conditions so that the feature extrudes up to the vertex or up to the surface, for example (see Figure 5-4).

7. **Specify the width in the Depth field.**

   Enter a parameter for how far you want the shape to extrude.

8. **Click OK.**

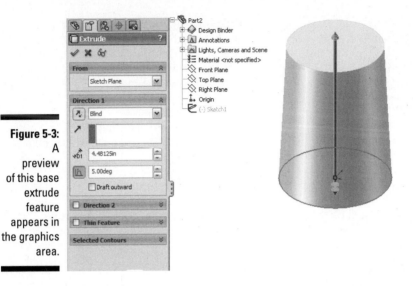

Figure 5-3:
A
preview
of this base
extrude
feature
appears in
the graphics
area.

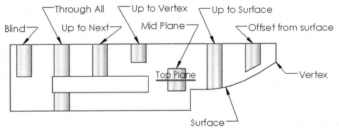

Figure 5-4:
Select
an end
condition
type for
extruded
features.

Revolving features around an axis

A *revolve* rotates a sketch profile around an axis to create a 3D shape. Door knobs and bedposts are shapes you can create with a revolve. You can set the angle of a revolve to 360 degrees for a full revolve or set it to less than that — for example, when you want only a quarter of a door knob.

The sketch you create for a revolve feature must include a centerline. The *centerline* serves as an axis of rotation. (The axis of rotation can be a centerline, a line, an edge, or an axis.) On one side of the centerline, you sketch the profile of the revolve. Don't let your sketch cross the centerline (see Figure 5-5). Otherwise, the profile may self-intersect, and SolidWorks then cannot create the feature.

Figure 5-5:
A simple
semicircle
on one side
of the
centerline is
the profile
for this
revolve.

To create a revolved feature, follow these steps:

1. **Sketch a centerline and a profile.**

   A more complex shape can have one or more profiles and a centerline, a line, or an edge to use as the axis around which the feature revolves.

2. **Choose Insert⇨Exit Sketch.**

   You exit Sketch mode.

3. **On the Features toolbar, click Revolved Boss/Base or Revolved Cut.**

   The Revolve PropertyManager appears, and a preview of the revolve feature appears in the graphics area. The Axis of Revolution field is active.

4. **Select an axis to serve as an axis of revolution.**

   This axis can be the centerline you created in your sketch, a line, or an edge. The name of the axis or sketch appears in the Axis of Revolution field.

5. **In the Revolve Type field, select One-Direction.**

   Your revolve is created in one direction from the sketch. You can also choose one of these other types of revolves:

   • *Mid-Plane:* Creates the revolve in the clockwise and counterclockwise directions, which is located at the middle of the total revolve angle.

   • *Two-Direction:* Creates the revolve in the clockwise and counter-clockwise directions from the sketch plane. You need to set two angles whose total does not exceed 360 degrees.

6. **Enter a value in the Angle field.**

   This step defines the angle covered by the revolve, which can't exceed 360 degrees. If you selected Two-Direction in Step 5, you need to enter values for Direction 1 Angle and Direction 2 Angle.

7. **Click OK.**

Sweeping features along a path

When you create a base extrusion, you extrude a shape straight out so that a circle becomes a cone, for example. In contrast, a sweep extrudes a shape along a *path*. Sweeps create curvy, ergonomic shapes. You need to create a profile and a path to serve as the basis for a swept feature. (In Figure 5-6, a rectangle serves as a profile for the sweep feature.) Because the profile and path must be on different planes, you need to create two sketches.

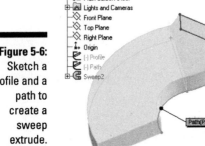

Figure 5-6:
Sketch a profile and a path to create a sweep extrude.

You can also add guide curves to the path to further define the shape of your sweep. Guide curves can be on the same plane as the path.

Your sweep sketch needs to adhere to these rules:

- ✔ If you're adding material (base or boss), the profile must be closed (no gaps in the sketched geometry); the profile can be open or closed for a surface sweep feature.

- ✔ The path may be open or closed.

- ✔ The path may be a set of sketched curves contained in one sketch, a curve, or a set of model edges.

- ✔ The start point of the path must lie on the plane of the profile.

- ✔ Neither the section, the path, nor the resulting solid can be self-intersecting.

To create a swept feature, follow these steps:

1. **Sketch a profile for the sweep.**

   If the sweep is your base feature, sketch on a plane; otherwise, choose a face of the existing part to sketch on. Your profile can be as simple as a square or circle or something more complex.

2. **In a second sketch on a different plane, sketch a path for the sweep.**

   You can add guide curves for a more complex shape. If you add guide curves, you need to create coincident or pierce relations between the guide curves and the profile.

3. **Choose Insert⇨Exit Sketch.**

   You switch to Part mode.

4. **Select Swept Boss/Base or Swept Cut from the Features toolbar.**

   The Sweep PropertyManager appears with the Profile field activated.

5. **Select the sketch to use for the profile.**

   The sketch appears in the Profile field. The Path field is activated.

6. **Click a sketch to use for the path.**

   The sketch name appears in the Path field. A preview of the sweep appears in the graphics area.

7. **If you're using a guide curve, under Guide Curves, click the Guide Curves field.**

   The field is activated, turning light blue. If you're not using a guide curve, skip to Step 9.

8. **In the FeatureManager design tree, select the sketch to use for the guide path curve.**

   The sketch name appears in the Guide Path Curve field.

9. **Click the up or down arrows under guide path curve to indicate the order in which the guide curves are evaluated.**

10. **Click OK.**

Lofted features: A sketch of many profiles

A *loft* feature is similar to a sweep, but rather than a single profile in the sketch, it has two or more profiles, and the loft transitions between them. A loft can add material or take it away. If you want to create a more complex shape, you can include guide curves and end conditions in your sketch.

When you create your sketch for a loft:

✔ Only the first, last, or first and last profiles can be points.

✔ If you create a solid loft, the first and last profiles must be model faces or faces created by split lines, planar profiles, or surfaces.

Consider the following when creating lofts with guide curves:

- ✔ You can use any of the following items as a guide curve: sketched curves, model edges, or curves of any kind.
- ✔ Guide curves must intersect all the profiles.
- ✔ There's no limit to the number of guide curves you can use.
- ✔ Guide curves can intersect at points.

Always select profiles on the same general area. In the example shown in Figure 5-7, the lower-right corner of each profile is selected. Otherwise, the resulting lofted feature twists in a way that you may not want. Always watch the preview in the graphics area and reselect profiles if necessary.

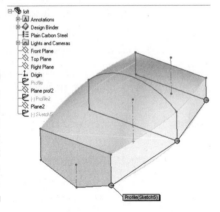

Figure 5-7:
A lofted feature is similar to a sweep but with two profiles.

To create a loft feature, follow these steps:

1. **Sketch two profiles and any guide curves for the feature.**

   Faces, curves, and edges can serve as profiles. You don't need to sketch two or more profiles if one is on the model.

2. **Choose Insert⇨Exit Sketch.**

   You exit Sketch mode and return to Part mode.

3. **Click Lofted Base/Boss or Lofted Cut on the Features toolbar.**

   The Loft PropertyManager appears, with the Profile field active.

4. **Select the two profiles in the graphics area.**

   The items appear in the Profile field. You can use the up and down arrows in the Profile section to switch the profile order.

5. **Select the Guide Curve field.**

   The field is highlighted in light blue.

6. **Select the guide curves in the graphics area.**

   The items appear in the Guide Curves field. A preview of the loft appears in the graphics area. You can use the up and down arrows in the Guide Curves section to change the order of the guide curves.

7. **Click OK.**

Making Applied Features

After you create a base feature, a solid hunk of material sits in your graphics area. You can add some character to this hunk by using applied features (fillet, chamfer, shell, or draft). Unlike sketched features, applied features don't require sketches. You apply them directly to your part.

Imagine that the applied features described in this section are various machine tools drilling away at your part. One tool rounds off the edges, and another scoops out the middle, leaving a hollow shell, for example. Your part is taking shape.

Rounding parts with Fillet

The Fillet command rounds off the sharp corners of a part or adds volume by rounding off an inner corner. You can create many different types of fillets. The most common is the multiple fillet, shown in Figure 5-8.

Fillets aren't functional design elements. Typically, you add them for cosmetic reasons — to "pretty up" the part. Add cosmetic fillets at the end of the modeling process to minimize unwanted parent/child relations and to produce a more robust model. A *parent/child relationship* simply means that a fillet that references an edge is a "child" of that edge. If you remove the edge, the child becomes "homeless" and fails when you rebuild the part.

SolidWorks displays heads-up labels (see Figure 5-8). The heads-up label includes the radius value (Radius: 01.in) and can be edited. Double-click the numeric-text part of it to change the radius value.

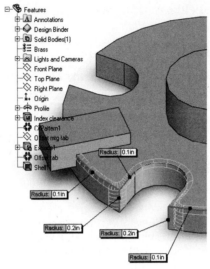

Figure 5-8:
Fillets
primarily
add
cosmetic
appeal to a
part.

To create a fillet feature in a part, follow these steps:

1. **Open a part document.**

2. **Click Fillet on the Features toolbar.**

3. **Select the edges or faces on the part you want to fillet.**

   The Fillet PropertyManager appears, and you see a preview of the fillet in the graphics area (refer to Figure 5-8).

   The order in which you select multiple edges affects the way the fillet *blends* (how it looks when finished) and its *tangent propagation* (how far it goes). For the example shown earlier, in Figure 5-8, the designer selected the larger 0.2 radius first. When the designer chose the smaller radii edges, those edges propagated all the way around the outside edge of the part because they didn't have to stop at the sharp corner.

4. **Select the fillet type.**

   Your options include

   - *Constant Radius:* The fillet has a constant radius for its entire length. After you select Constant Radius, you can set parameters in the PropertyManager to create multiple radius fillets, round corner fillets, or setback fillets.

   - *Variable Radius:* The fillet has variable radius values. Control points allow you to define the fillet.

   - *Face Fillet:* The fillet's nonadjacent, noncontinuous faces are blended.

   - *Full Round Fillet:* The fillet is tangent to three adjacent faces' sets (with one or more faces' tangents.)

5. **Set other options in the PropertyManager.**

Your options include

- *Radius:* Enter the default radius value.

- *Edges:* Select the edges, faces, or loops to fillet.

- *Multiple Radii Fillets:* Select to create multiple radii values (refer to Figure 5-8).

- *Tangent Propagation:* Select to continue the fillet until it runs into a sharp corner.

- *Preview:* Select Full Preview to see a preview of the fillet in the graphics area.

You can select the Preview option in the PropertyManager to get a clear idea of how the radius will look when you change the entities you select, the order of selection, and values. (However, this option can also slow you down, especially if you're using Full Preview.)

6. **Click OK.**

Beveling edges with Chamfer

Chamfer creates a beveled edge on selected edges of a part at a given distance and angle (or two distances). You often use a chamfer to break a sharp edge of a part or to provide a lead-in for mating assembly components. (You can read more about mating assembly parts in Chapter 6.)

To create a chamfer feature, follow these steps:

1. **Open a part document.**

2. **Click Chamfer on the Features toolbar.**

The Chamfer PropertyManager appears with the Edges and Faces or Vertex field active.

3. **In the graphics area, select the edges and faces or vertex to chamfer.**

The selections appear in Edges and Faces and Vertex, and the chamfer is displayed as a preview in the graphics area, as shown in Figure 5-9. In the preview, a tag pointing to the chamfer lists the distance and angle distance.

In the graphics area , you can click the arrow that points to the chamfer to flip the direction of the chamfer. You can do the same by selecting the Flip Direction check box in the Chamfer Parameters section in the Chamfer PropertyManager.

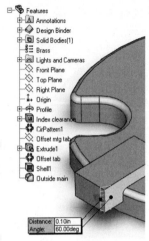

Figure 5-9:
A chamfer
breaks
sharp edges
of a part.

4. **Select other options in the Chamfer Parameters area.**

   Other options include

   - *Chamfer Style:* Select a check box for an angle-distance or distance-distance type chamfer.

   - *Flip Direction:* Select this check box to flip the direction of the chamfer.

   - *Distance:* Enter distance (or distances) values for the chamfer.

   - *Angle:* Enter an angle for the chamfer.

   - *Preview:* Select Full Preview to see how the part looks.

5. **Click OK.**

Angling faces accurately with Draft

You can use the *draft* feature to add an angle to part faces. This feature is useful when designing an injection-molded part. Imagine a cake pan: If the angle of the pan sloped inward, your cake would stay forever stuck in the pan. You would have to cut it in pieces to get it out. It's the same with plastic molds. A proper draft angle, shown in Figure 5-10, ensures that a part easily slips out of a mold.

To create a draft on a neutral plane, follow these steps:

1. **Open a part document.**

2. **Click Draft on the Features toolbar.**

   The Draft PropertyManager appears, with the Neutral Plane field active.

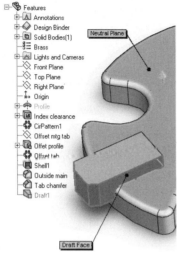

Figure 5-10:
A draft
angle
ensures that
a part will
slip out of its
mold.

3. **Click a face on the part that you want as a neutral plane.**

   The item appears in the Neutral Plane field. (Imagine the neutral plane as the top of the cake pan where the cake slides out.) The Faces to Draft field becomes active.

4. **Click the faces of the part that you want to add a draft angle to.**

   The items appear in the Faces to Draft field. (Imagine that these are the sides of the cake pan.)

5. **In the Type of Draft section, use the pull-down arrow to select Neutral Plane.**

6. **In the Draft Angle section, set a value for the number of degrees.**

   The draft angle is measured perpendicular to the neutral plane.

7. **In the Face section, select a Face Propagation item if you want to propagate the draft across additional faces.**

   Your options include

   - *None:* Drafts only the selected faces

   - *Along Tangent:* Extends the draft to all faces that are tangent to the selected face

   - *All Faces:* Drafts all faces extruded from the neutral plane

   - *Inner Faces:* Drafts all inner faces extruded from the neutral plane

   - *Outer Faces:* Drafts all outer faces next to the neutral plane

8. **Click OK.**

You can select the arrow in the graphics area on the neutral draft plane to flip the direction of the draft angle.

Making parts hollow with Shell

A *shell* feature hollows out a part, leaves out the faces you select, and creates thin-walled features on the remaining faces. If you don't select any face on the model, you can shell a solid part, creating a closed, hollow model. You can shell a model in one thickness, or you can define multiple shell thicknesses.

Before you shell a part, be sure to apply any fillets to the part first. The shell feature uses any existing features in the shell.

To create a shell feature with uniform thickness, follow these steps:

1. **Open a part document.**

2. **Click Shell on the Features toolbar.**

   The Shell PropertyManager, shown in Figure 5-11, appears.

3. **Set the following options in the Parameters section:**

   • *Thickness:* Enter a thickness for the faces you keep.

   • *Faces to Remove:* Select in the graphics area one or more faces that you want to remove when the part is hollowed out.

   • *Shell Outward:* Select the check box for this option to increase the outside dimensions of the part.

   • *Show Preview:* Select the check box for this option to see a wireframe preview of the shell feature in the graphics area.

4. **Click OK.**

Figure 5-11:
Scoop out part innards by using the Shell feature.

If you run into trouble creating a shell, run Error Diagnostics in the Shell PropertyManager to pinpoint problems.

Drilling holes with the Hole Wizard

The Hole Wizard lets you create holes in your part that you can use to insert fasteners. The Hole Wizard can create these hole types: Counterbore, Countersink, Hole (simple holes), Tap, Pipetap, and Legacy.

You don't have to dig out the *Machinery's Handbook* to figure out how big you need to make the holes. The Hole Wizard creates the holes based on the type of fastener you plan to put there.

To add a hole to a part by using the Hole Wizard, follow these steps:

1. **Open a part document.**

2. **Select a face on the part in which you want to insert holes.**

3. **Click Hole Wizard on the Features toolbar.**

   The Hole Definition PropertyManager appears.

   You can preselect or postselect a face when using the Hole Wizard. When you preselect a face and then click Hole Wizard on the Features toolbar, the resulting sketch is a 2D sketch. If you click Hole Wizard and then select a face, the resulting sketch is 3D. Unlike with a 2D sketch, you cannot constrain a 3D sketch to a line. If the start of your hole is going to lie on a planar face, it must be stressed that preselection of that face is *highly recommended.*

4. **Select the Type tab to display the hole options.**

   In the Hole Type section, click the button for the type of hole you want to create. Your choices are Counterbore, Countersink, Hole, Tap, Pipe Tap, and Legacy. (The Legacy option allows you to make holes for files created in older versions of SolidWorks.) You can use pull-down menus to automatically size a hole for a certain type of fastener. Use the Standard pull-down menu to specify your choice of several internationally recognized standards (ANSI inch, ANSI metric, or ISO, for example). Use the Type pull-down menu to choose the type of fastener you're designing the hole to accept.

   Figure 5-12 shows a counterbore hole made for a #10 binding head machine screw.

Figure 5-12:
The Hole
Wizard
creates hole
sizes to
match your
fastener.

5. **Set additional parameters for the type of fastener you chose. The size of the hole is created based on the size of the fastener you select.**

   You can use the pull-down arrows next to the parameters box to select the exact parameters you want.

   For each hole type (except Legacy), you can create and save hole types to include in your favorite property parameters. In the Hole Placement dialog box, after you select the parameters for a fastener, click Select Add in the Favorites area. The next time you want to add holes to a model, click the arrow under Favorites to select the hole type to add.

6. **Click the Positions tab.**

   The Hole Wizard closes, and the Hole Position dialog box appears and prompts you to enter the sketch points in the model where you want to place the holes. (Figure 5-13 shows three points dimensioned to define the three hole locations.) You switch to Sketch mode.

7. **Use the Point tool to mark the spots in the model where you want holes.**

   You're automatically using the Point tool on the Sketch toolbar to add the holes. If you preselected a planar face, the holes must be on the same face.

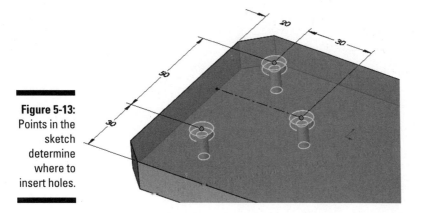

Figure 5-13:
Points in the sketch determine where to insert holes.

8. **Add dimension and relations to locate the hole centers.**

   You can also add sketch geometry to add design intent. See Chapter 4 for more details.

9. **Click OK.**

   The Hole Positions PropertyManager closes. The holes appear in the model and in the FeatureManager design tree.

SolidWorks uses two sketches to define Hole Wizard features. You can view the sketches in the FeatureManager design tree by clicking the plus sign to the left of the hole feature. The first sketch defines the centers of the hole. You can edit the first sketch to move holes. Simply right-click the sketch and choose Edit Sketch. You should not edit the second sketch. The second sketch is the profile for the hole defined by the Hole Wizard.

Designing Pattern and Mirror Features

Pattern and mirror features are applied features, in that you can apply them directly to the part geometry. But they're unique types of applied features, so I put them in their own section. Pattern and mirror features allow you to create a pattern of features in a model, such as a pattern of teeth in a gear.

Linear patterns

A *linear pattern* creates features along a straight line, and a *circular pattern* creates features around a circle.

To create a linear pattern feature, follow these steps:

1. **Open a part document.**

2. **Click Linear Pattern on the Features toolbar.**

   The Linear Pattern PropertyManager, shown in Figure 5-14, appears with the Pattern Direction selection field active.

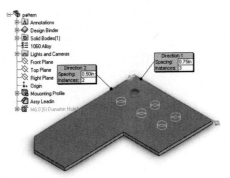

Figure 5-14:
Linear
patterns
repeat
shapes
along a
straight line.

3. **Select an edge to define Direction 1.**

   The edge appears in Direction 1, and the Direction 2 box is active.

4. **If needed, select an edge to define Direction 2.**

   The edge appears in Direction 2.

5. **Set the remaining options in the PropertyManager.**

   Here's what you do to select each option:

   - *Pattern Direction:* If you want to change the direction of the pattern, select the Reverse Direction arrow next to the direction box.

   - *Spacing:* Enter the distance between the pattern instances.

   - *Instances:* Type the total number of pattern features, including the original feature.

   - *Pattern Seed Only:* Pattern only the original feature in the second direction.

   - *Features to Pattern:* Choose the feature or features that you want to pattern.

   - *Faces to Pattern:* Choose to pattern selected faces or a combination of features and faces.

   - *Bodies to Pattern:* In some cases, you may want to pattern only individual bodies.

- *Instances to Skip:* You can select individual instances to leave out of a pattern.

   6. **Click OK.**

Circular patterns

A circular pattern (see Figure 5-15) is similar to a linear pattern with the exception that you need to select geometry that will serve as a basis for rotation. Construction geometry, such as an axis or temporary axis, can be used. You can also use a circular edge or a cylindrical face. Angular dimensions and linear edges are also candidates for specifying the direction of the circular pattern.

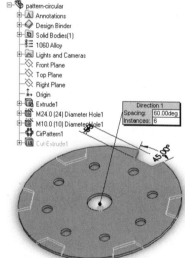

Figure 5-15: The Circular Pattern feature repeats a shape in a circle.

To create a circular pattern feature, follow these steps:

   1. **Open a part document.**

   2. **Click Circular Pattern on the Features toolbar.**

   The Circular PropertyManager appears, with the Pattern Axis field active.

   3. **Select an axis, a model edge, or an angular dimension in the graphics area.**

   The item appears in the Pattern Axis field. The Feature to Pattern field becomes active.

If you're using an axis or a temporary axis, you must remember to display them first. From the main menu, choose View and then select Axes and Temporary Axes from the list. A check mark next to an item indicates that it's already visible.

4. **Select one or more features to pattern in the graphics area.**

   The features appear in the Feature to Pattern field. You can also repeat faces or bodies. If you choose to repeat one of these, you can highlight fields for Faces to Pattern and Bodies to Pattern and click the graphical image to enter the items in those fields.

5. **In the Parameters section, enter values for these two options:**

   - *Number of Instances:* Enter the number of times to repeat the pattern.

   - *Angle:* Indicate the angle of the features.

   Select the Equal Spacing check box to save time when creating a pattern that goes all the way around the part. This option automatically sets the angle based on the number of instances you select.

6. **Click OK.**

You can use the Geometry Pattern option in the Options section to create the pattern using only the geometry rather than the complete feature. The Pattern feature contains only the geometric representation of the feature (faces and edges). In most cases, this option speeds up the rebuilding of the pattern feature.

Mirror features

You can use the Mirror feature to create a copy of a feature (or a group of features) and mirror it around a plane or a part face. The advantage to mirroring an object is that you can create symmetrically similar features. You can manipulate the features by changing the original (or parent) feature.

You can mirror the body of a part so that you don't have to select individual features or faces to mirror. A *body* is the entire solid body. In other words, Bodies to Mirror is used to mirror the part. Click the plus sign (+) next to the Bodies folder to expand it within the FeatureManager design tree to see the body or bodies within the part.

To create a mirror feature, follow these steps:

1. **Open a part document.**

2. **Click Mirror on the Features toolbar.**

   The Mirror PropertyManager, shown in Figure 5-16, appears, with the Mirror Face/Plane feature active.

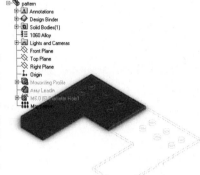

Figure 5-16:
Mirror
feature
example
and
Property-
Manager.

3. **In the graphics area, select the face or plane to mirror on.**

   The item appears in the Mirror Face/Plane feature. The Features to Mirror field becomes active.

4. **Select in the graphics area a feature that you want to mirror.**

   The feature appears in the Features to Mirror field.

   Try to create a mirror pattern with the Geometry Pattern option in the PropertyManager selected first. With this option selected, SolidWorks mirrors only the faces and edges of the features rather than the whole - feature, speeding up the creation of the pattern. If SolidWorks can't solve the geometry pattern version, deselect this option. In some cases, a geometry pattern may be required in order to solve the cases that non-geometry pattern features cannot solve. Either way, if the feature can't be built with the options selected, SolidWorks explains the problem in the What's Wrong dialog box.

5. **Click OK.**

Building a Part

You construct a part in SolidWorks much like you do in the real world. Here are the steps to follow when making a part:

1. **Select a plane and orientation for your part.**

   You don't want your part to appear upside down or sideways. Typically, you begin your part by using one of the default planes (front, top, or right).

2. **Draw a sketch on the plane.**

   This sketch is the basis of the first feature in your part, so be sure to give it an appropriate shape. You want to fully dimension your sketch so that all the lines appear in black.

3. **Create a base feature.**

   Use one of the sketched boss features (extrude, revolve, sweep, or loft) to create the first feature in your part based on your sketch. The base feature is the solid hunk of material that all the other features go on top of.

4. **Add sketched and applied features.**

5. **Add rounds and fillets and other cosmetic features last.**

Always try to break a design into definable segments. I recall many times in my "design youth" when I had no idea about how I could solve a complex design problem. Here's the secret: Start with what's important and with what you know about the design. "Keep it simple, stupid" (KISS) is an adage that applies well. Even the most complex part is manageable when you break down the job into simple steps.

To get a visual grasp on how to build a part, peruse the following part examples. Each part uses a different sketched feature as its base. You can follow the feature-creation order of each part by studying the FeatureManager design tree. The base feature is on the top, and the most recently created feature is on the bottom.

Part example 1

For the part example shown in Figure 5-17, the base feature is a revolve because the original profile is circular.

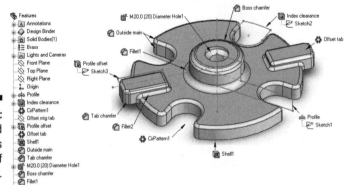

Figure 5-17: A revolved base/boss is the heart of this part.

Part example 2

The part shown in Figure 5-18 found its beginnings with an extrusion feature because the original profile was a planar extruded profile.

Figure 5-18:
An extrusion marked the birth of this model.

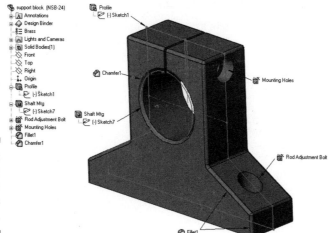

Part example 3

The little darling shown in Figure 5-19 began life as a sweep. The sweep feature sweeps the original sketch profile (Sketch2) along a profile helix (3DSketch2), which formed the basis for the path.

Figure 5-19:
A sweep marked the early life of this part.

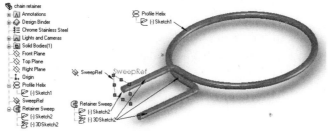

Part example 4

This art piece, shown in Figure 5-20, began as a loft feature because the part shape was created from several 2D sections. This example shows only a portion of the design. Lofts created the handle portion of the drill body.

Building a Better Part

Although you can build your model in numerous ways, no matter how you put it all together, you can do certain consistent things to make your model more readable and easier to modify. This section includes tips on ways you can make your part model even better.

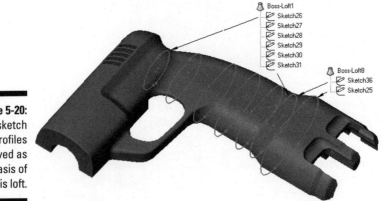

Naming features (Or, you call it tomato, I call it tomato)

After you make your part, you may want to rename some of its features in the FeatureManager design tree. SolidWorks gives features default names, such as Extrude1 and Extrude2, but these names don't offer much of a clue to what a feature does — not to mention that this naming scheme can get messy if your part has 100 features. To find the meaning behind Extrude20, you would have to review the sketch and features in addition to the part geometry. On the other hand, a feature with a name like Upper Boss Relief may give some idea of its purpose.

Relevant names make a feature easier to find in the FeatureManager design tree. But you need to be sure that the name relates to what the feature does. (Names such as Gandalf and the Big Pookie aren't helpful.) A good naming system makes design intent clearer and parts easier to modify.

Be especially sure to name a feature that is an important design element that you're likely to change later. You should name fillets and chamfers only when you use them for noncosmetic purposes.

SolidWorks offers a couple of different ways to rename features:

✔ **To name the feature when you create it,** choose Tools➪Options. On the Systems Options tab, select FeatureManager. In the options that appear on the right, select the Name Feature on Creation check box. This method is my preference because I would rather name the feature as I create it than to have to go back and rename it later.

✔ **To rename the feature within the FeatureManager design tree,** double-click the feature in the FeatureManager design tree and type a new name. You can also right-click the feature in the tree and choose Feature Properties from the menu that appears. This command gets you to the Properties dialog box, where the name is highlighted, and you can change the name of the feature.

The best time to name a feature is right after you create it. If you don't name a feature, most likely no one will do it for you when the project is complete. Make it a habit to name features and reinforce the habit by checking names in the FeatureManager design tree at design checks.

Naming features is a way to organize a design. The example in Figure 5-21 shows two versions of a FeatureManager design tree from the same part. One part (the left side) uses the default feature names, and the other (the right side) uses the named features. Which design would you rather work on when your boss comes in and tells you to modify a design immediately?

Figure 5-21: You can easily locate and modify named features.

In addition to naming features, you should name some dimensions. If you use a dimension in a design table or if an equation references that dimension, give the dimension a meaningful name. To change the name of a sketch dimension, first make the dimension visible. In the FeatureManager design tree, right-click the feature and choose Edit Sketch. Then right-click the dimension you want to rename and choose Properties. In the Name field of the Properties dialog box, type a name for the dimension. The full dimension name appears as *<dimension name@feature name>*. Rather than name a dimension D2@Cut-Extrude1, you can rename the dimension outside and rename the feature MtgBoss so that the new dimension name is outsideDia @MtgBoss.

Thinking about feature order

Another method of documenting a design is feature order. The FeatureManager design tree shows features in the order in which they were made. The feature on the bottom is the newest. The order of features in the FeatureManager design tree should communicate your design intent.

When you change a sketch, you need to rebuild to see how the change affects the model. You can press Ctrl+Q to completely rebuild all features in the model. Click Rebuild on the Standard toolbar or press Ctrl+B to rebuild only new or changed features and their children.

You can change the order in which features are rebuilt by dragging them in the FeatureManager design tree. Place the pointer on a feature name, press the left mouse button, and drag the feature to a new position in the list. (As you drag up or down the tree, each item that you drag over is highlighted. The feature name you're moving drops immediately below the highlighted item when you release the mouse button.)

Moving a feature or folder can cause the model to change. If you don't like the results, click the Undo button to return the feature to its original location.

Organizing features with folders

Just as you use folders and file cabinets to organize paperwork, you can use folders in the FeatureManager design tree to organize your SolidWorks part and assembly data. The part features shown in Figure 5-22 are broken into four main functional areas based on their functions: Profile, Mounting, Molding, or Cosmetic. When working on a specific area of the design, you can expand or collapse a folder by clicking the plus symbol to the left of the folder name.

Figure 5-22:
Folders
make a
FeatureMan
ager design
tree more
manageable.

You can drag part features or assembly components in the FeatureManager design tree to group them into functional folders. To add a new folder in the FeatureManager design tree, right-click a feature and choose Add to New Folder. A new folder appears in the FeatureManager design tree. The feature you right-clicked is now in the new folder. You can rename the folder and drag additional features into the folder.

Name a folder according to its function or role in the model. You don't have to put every part feature or assembly component in a folder. If you group features or components into a folder, you can act on them as a group. SolidWorks lets you suppress part feature or assembly components in a folder as a group. In the example shown in Figure 5-22, you can turn off the mounting features by selecting the folder, right-clicking, and choosing Suppress. You can use the Suppress command for multiple versions of the same design or just for visualization purposes.

When you select a folder in the FeatureManager design tree, the features in the folder are highlighted in the graphics area. Similarly, when you select in the graphics area a feature that's in a folder you created, the folder is expanded to show the highlighted feature in the FeatureManager design tree.

Grouping features has a couple of benefits:

✔ **It makes the design easier to read.** You can look at the FeatureManager design tree and find features by how they relate to function (mounting location or profile, for example) because they're in the same area. Using folders also shortens the length of the features listed within the FeatureManager design tree.

✔ **It enhances performance.** When you work on larger parts, feature order can be a performance enhancer. For example, if you're working on a particular functional area, you can move that folder higher in the FeatureManager design tree so that those features are rebuilt first and see the changes in the model sooner.

Using the Rollback feature

The Rollback bar, a yellow-and-black line in the FeatureManager design tree, turns blue when you select it. You can drag the bar up the FeatureManager design tree to suppress features one by one and revert the model to various earlier states.

The example shown in Figure 5-23 shows the part rolled back to show all features up to the inner hinge. You see the model as it looked at the time the designer added the inner hinge. The features created after the inner hinge don't appear in the model. In this case, the designer used the Rollback bar to go back and insert a new feature after the inner hinge.

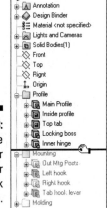

Figure 5-23: The Rollback bar takes your model back in time.

Using comments

You can add comments to the FeatureManager design tree to document design intent. (See Figure 5-24.) These comments appear when you place the cursor over the feature name in the FeatureManager design tree.

Figure 5-24: Using comments is another way to document design intent.

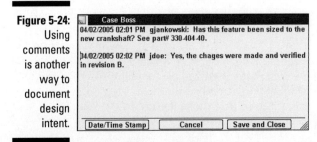

To create and edit a feature comment

1. **Open a part.**

2. **In the FeatureManager design tree, right-click a feature and choose Comment⇨Add Comment, Edit Comment, or Delete Comment.**

   If a comment doesn't already exist, you see Add Comment on the menu. If a comment exists, you see Edit Comment and Delete Comment. Select Delete Comment to delete the existing comment.

   A comment box, which resembles a yellow sticky note, appears. The name of the item is at the top of the note. If you chose Edit Comment, you see the existing comment, and you can change or respond to it.

3. **Click Date/Time Stamp at the bottom of the comment box.**

   The date and time and your name are added to the comment.

4. **Type your comment.**

5. **Click Save and Close.**

   When you roll the pointer over the item in the FeatureManager design tree, the note appears.

Consider adding a comment to a folder so that you know the purpose of the folder. Otherwise, you may have little indication of why the folder exists and what it contains.

Knowing How Much to Model

One question that folks often ask is "How much detail should I include in my model?" For example, if you're making a ruler, do you need to include the metal edge insert and then all the detailed text and ruler markings?

My answer is this: "Just because you can doesn't mean you should." Yes, you can make parts look just like they would in real life, but you pay the piper at some point in terms of assembly performance and the time it takes to maintain that level of detail.

If you need all kinds of tiny details to document or manufacture the part, then by all means add them to the model, particularly if it helps someone else to make the part. However, you don't need as much detail if you plan to make the part yourself.

Use Feature Statistics to determine which features take the most time to open and rebuild. Choose Tools⇨Feature Statistics.

Here's a simple example. Figure 5-25 shows two screws. The screw on the right is loaded with features, including chamfers and fillets on all edges to make it look real. The screw on the left is plain and simple. This screw is a standard part, and the only item that counts is the threaded cut for the screw threads. Even if this part were made in-house, you don't need the detailed geometry to create the screw.

Figure 5-25:
A detailed
screw looks
pretty but is
a waste of
time.

Here's the difference in file size between the simple-versus-detailed version of the screws. Also listed is the effect on a medium assembly (50 fasteners) and a large assembly (250 fasteners):

- ✔ 1 fastener = 115KB versus 470KB (408 percent larger than the simple version)
- ✔ 50 fasteners = 5.7MB versus 23.5 MB (17.8MB difference)
- ✔ 250 fasteners = 28.7MB versus 117.5 MB (88.8MB difference)

Some people may argue that the detailed screw doesn't have enough detail. My response is that unless it's an art project, you should include only the detail that someone really needs. I would rather start simpler and add any needed detail later.

Designing standard parts is a waste of time. The SolidWorks Toolbox includes a library of standard fasteners. You can find other standard part models at www.3dcontentcentral.com.

Chapter 6

Putting It All Together

• •

• •

*O*ne advantage of 3D design is that you can create a complete virtual product that you can assemble and analyze. SolidWorks lets you create a functional assembly so that you can see how your design looks and works before you build a single part. This way, you can quickly identify mistakes before spending time and resources to create the parts.

The SolidWorks virtual assembly mimics the location and movement of the components to determine their fit and function, and it lets you see how the assembly looks in its assembled and exploded states.

Creating and Modifying the Assembly

An *assembly* is a collection of components that consists of parts and other assemblies, called *subassemblies*. You create an assembly in SolidWorks the same way you build a product in the real world. *Mates* position a component in an assembly precisely with respect to each other and define how the components move and rotate together. Assembly reference geometry, such as sketches, planes, and axes, controls the shape and position of components.

Figure 6-1 shows a complete virtual assembly of a personal water propeller in its final stage before going to the manufacturer. In the sections that follow, you find an introduction to the tools used to work with assemblies as well as tips that explain how to plan and design them.

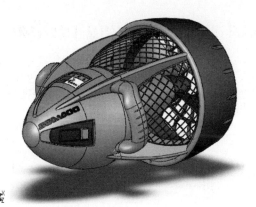

Figure 6-1:
A designer can see how assembly parts in this personal water propeller fit together.

Checking out assembly items

Before you start creating assemblies, it's helpful to understand the various items you can include in one. You use the items in the following list to create an assembly:

- ✔ **Components:** Refer to both parts and subassemblies. You insert components into an assembly to show their orientation and the order in which manufacturing needs to assemble the final product. You can evaluate the form, fit, and function of a component in relation to other components in the assembly.

- ✔ **Mates:** Create geometric relationships between assembly components. When you add mates, you define the linear or rotational motion of the components. You can move a component within its degrees of freedom, to visualize the assembly's behavior. The section "Understanding Your Mates," later in this chapter, explains what you need to know when working with mates.

- ✔ **Planes:** Define the location of an assembly component or provide a construction plane for an assembly object.

- ✔ **Axes:** Define the location of an assembly component or a construction reference for an assembly object.

- ✔ **Layouts:** Control the size and location of assembly components and reference geometry.

When an assembly or part file is open in SolidWorks, the triad (colored X-Y-Z arrows) in the lower-left corner of the graphics area indicates the positive direction of each axis with arrows.

Tooling around the Assembly toolbar

Throughout this chapter, you use the Assembly toolbar, as shown in Figure 6-2. When you're working on an assembly document, the Assembly toolbar appears in the CommandManager by default. (You can read more about the CommandManager in Chapter 2.)

Figure 6-2:
The
Assembly
toolbar.

When active in the CommandManager, the Assembly toolbar includes these functions:

1 Insert Components: Inserts a new component into the current assembly.

2 Hide/Show Components: Turns the display of a component on or off temporarily. Even when you can't see a component, it's still in memory and other assembly components can reference it.

3 Change Suppression State: Allows you to set a component as Suppress, Resolve, or Lightweight. When a component is suppressed, it doesn't load into memory, and other components can't reference it. When a component is lightweight, only a subset of its model data is loaded into memory and the rest is loaded on an as-needed basis. A resolved model loads completely. (Read more on suppression states in Chapter 10.)

4 Show Hidden Components: Shows only components that are hidden in the assembly. Click the Exit Show-Hidden button in the Show Hidden dialog box to return to the previous display state.

5 Edit Component: Allows you to edit a part or a subassembly while the rest of the assembly is visible in an opaque display in the graphics area.

6 No External References: Lets you create a model in an assembly window without creating external references. This chapter covers external references in the later section "In-context assembly modeling."

7 Mate: Adds geometric references between assembly components to position and constrain them.

8 Move/Rotate Component: Allows you to drag an assembly component to a new location or rotates an assembly component.

9 Smart Fastener: Automatically adds fasteners (such as bolts, nuts, and washers) to assembly holes.

10 **Exploded View:** Creates a view of the assembly showing the components pulled apart so that you can see how components fit together. You can use this view in assembly drawings and manuals.

11 **Explode Line Sketch:** Adds lines to components in an exploded view to show the direction and final location of the exploded component.

12 **Interference Detection:** Checks the assembly to ensure that parts don't clash into each other when they move.

13 **Assembly Feature:** Creates assembly-level features, such as Extruded Cut and Hole Wizard. It features a flyout toolbar on the Assembly toolbar that contains only the features you can use in an assembly.

14 **New Motion Study:** Performs a motion study by applying Linear Motor, Rotary Motor, Linear Spring, and Gravity to an assembly and animates the results. Physical Simulation is a flyout toolbar on the Assembly toolbar.

Planning your assembly

A number of factors influence how you go about creating an assembly in SolidWorks. Resist the urge to start modeling immediately. Instead, step back and take time to plan your assembly. Planning pays off later in the design process.

The items in this list, each of which is covered in more detail in this chapter, help define the starting point of an assembly:

✔ **Define what is known.** Every project has certain requirements, such as the product's purpose, size, weight, and cost. Capture these requirements before you start. Where you keep these requirements (for example, in Microsoft Word or Microsoft Excel) doesn't particularly matter, as long as you capture them consistently and store them in a shared location if you're working with other designers.

Well-defined requirements ensure that you go in the right direction. They also save you time and let you know in advance whether you have all the information you need to complete the project.

✔ **Create the structure.** Define the principal components of the assembly and create configurations that show each major subassembly component and suppress everything else. Because a suppressed component doesn't load into memory, these configurations allow other designers to examine the major areas of an assembly without having to resolve the entire kit and kaboodle.

✔ **Collaborate.** Think about how to break up the assembly in order to distribute the workload if you plan to work with several designers on a project.

> ✔ **Review and capture the design intent.** Use a skeleton to capture and control the functions of your design if you plan to create a complex assembly. Test the skeleton before you begin adding components.
>
> ✔ **Review existing information.** Check to see which designs and standard components exist so that you can use them in your assembly design.

You can set document properties (dimensions, standards, text size, and unit of measurement, for example) and custom properties in an assembly template that you can reuse. Defining custom properties in advance helps when you create the drawings. (To find out more about templates, see Chapter 2.)

Designing an assembly

You can use two basic methods to design an assembly: top-down or bottom-up. With either method, your objective is to position and mate the components. Mates position the components and define how they move. (Read more on mates in the "Understanding Your Mates" section, later in this chapter.)

> ✔ In **top-down design,** you start work on the assembly and build parts to fit into the assembly. The geometry of one part defines the geometry of others. You start a top-down design with a skeleton that defines fixed part locations and planes, for example, and then design the parts referencing these positions.
>
> ✔ **Bottom-up design** is a good plan if all parts come from suppliers. You don't need to create references that control the size and shapes of parts because the parts already exist. You simply insert them into the assembly and mate them together. Because components are designed independently, their relationship to each other is simpler than in top-down design.

In most cases, you work with a mix of custom and standard parts, so the best design method is a cross between top-down and bottom-up. Read the sections "Using layouts" and "In-context assembly modeling" for specific techniques on how to design top-down.

The following sections give you three ways to begin work on an assembly. Depending on which documents you have open, one method may be more straightforward than another. In other words, they all work, but the one that works best for you depends on the project you're working on at the time.

Creating an assembly

You can create an assembly by starting with an assembly document and then adding parts one by one. Start with a component that doesn't move with respect to the other components. That way, you can anchor the component to the assembly origin. Anchoring the first component ensures that the planes in both documents are aligned.

To create a new assembly in SolidWorks, follow these steps:

1. **Choose File⇨New.**

   The New SolidWorks Document dialog box appears.

2. **Click Assembly.**

   You select the standard Assembly template. (If you want to select a custom template, click Advanced in the dialog box to display other available templates.)

3. **Click OK.**

   A new assembly document opens. The Begin Assembly PropertyManager appears in the left panel (see Figure 6-3). Any part or assembly files that are already open appear in the Open Documents section.

Figure 6-3: Use the Begin Assembly Property-Manager to insert a part or assembly file into your assembly.

Select the Graphics Preview check box in the Begin Assembly PropertyManager to see a preview of the part you're inserting.

4. **In the Part/Assembly to Insert section, click Browse.**

   The Open dialog box appears.

5. **Navigate to the part or assembly file you want to insert.**

A preview of the model appears in the Preview section of the dialog box. Any configurations appear in the Configurations box.

6. **Select the file and configuration (if one exists) and click Open.**

   The Open dialog box closes, and the model appears in your assembly. The origin of the new component aligns with the assembly origin.

7. **Click View and select the Origins check box to display the assembly origin.**

   The assembly origin appears in blue.

8. **To anchor the part to the assembly origin, click OK.**

   The component anchors to the assembly origin. When you place a component this way, the component origin is located coincident with the assembly origin, and the planes of the part and assembly are aligned, which helps establish an initial orientation for the assembly. An (f) appears next to the component in the FeatureManager design tree to indicate that the component is fixed into place.

Creating an assembly from a part

You don't need to begin an assembly from an assembly document. In many cases, you may want to start building an assembly from an existing part. To create an assembly from a part or assembly:

1. **Open the model to use as the first assembly component.**

2. **Choose File➪Make Assembly from Part.**

   A new assembly document opens, and the Begin Assembly PropertyManager appears.

3. **From the main menu, choose View and select the Origins check box to display the origin in the graphics area.**

   The blue origin appears.

4. **In the PropertyManager, in the Options section, select Graphics Preview.**

   A preview of the model appears in the graphics area.

5. **Move the pointer over the origin in the graphics area.**

   The model moves with your pointer, and the pointer changes to indicate an inference to the assembly origin.

6. **Click to place the component.**

   The component anchors to the assembly origin.

Adding components to an assembly

After you begin building your assembly, you load additional components and position them. You can position components anywhere in the graphics area and then use the Move Components tool to drag each component closer to the first anchored component. You should leave some space between the components to view the relevant component areas. In many instances, you can use the Rotate, View, and Pan tools on the View toolbar to change the orientation of the components, which simplifies selecting the edge, face, or other entity needed to apply mates.

To insert a part or subassembly into an existing assembly, follow these steps:

1. **Click Insert Components on the Assembly toolbar.**

   The Insert Component PropertyManager appears.

2. **In the Part/Assembly to Insert section, click Browse.**

   The Open dialog box appears.

3. **Navigate to the part or assembly file that you want to insert.**

   A preview of the model appears in the Preview section of the Open dialog box. Any configurations appear in the Configurations box.

4. **Select the file and configuration (if one exists) and click Open.**

   The Open dialog box closes, and the model appears in your assembly. The origin of the new component aligns with the assembly origin.

5. **To place the part in the center of the assembly, click OK.**

   The new component aligns with the origins of the assembly and adds a fixed relation. (If you can't see the blue origins, click View and select the Origins check box.)

6. **To place the part in a different location, move the pointer and click.**

   SolidWorks anchors the component into place. The new file appears in the FeatureManager design tree.

If you click the pushpin in the Assembly FeatureManager window, the dialog box stays open and you can add several instances of the component by clicking repeatedly in the graphics window.

After you insert a new component, you mate it to another component. Read the section "Understanding Your Mates," later in this chapter, to find out how to mate two components.

Another way to add components to the assembly is to drag them from File Explorer in the SolidWorks task pane and place them into the assembly. This method allows you to add several components quickly. You can use the Move command to position them later.

Organizing your assembly

When you're creating a large assembly, you want to group components into manageable subassemblies. The many benefits to breaking up the assembly this way include the ones in the following list. Grouping components

✔ **Distributes the work:** Design team members can collaborate on the same design by working on the subassemblies separately. Having a number of designers in the same subassembly would create a huge train wreck.

✔ **Organizes the assembly based on manufacturing considerations:** You may want the components to appear in the bill of materials list in the same order in which you want to build them. (Find out more about inserting a bill or materials table into a drawing in Chapter 8.)

✔ **Minimizes visual clutter:** You can use the Change Suppression State command to display only the subassemblies you're working on in order to minimize the visual clutter and the amount of information loaded into computer memory. Select a part or subassembly in the FeatureManager design tree, and on the Assembly toolbar, click Change Suppression State and select Suppress, Lightweight, or Resolve. A suppressed part doesn't load into memory. Only graphical information loads for a light-weight part, and a resolved part is fully loaded.

✔ **Replaces a subassembly more easily:** A subassembly behaves as a single component. You can replace an entire subassembly with another one and fully constrain it with only three mates, making it easier to deal with than lots of individual parts.

✔ **Limits the number of top-level mates within the assembly:** The more subassemblies in a design, the fewer top-level mates. When SolidWorks opens an assembly, it solves mates at the top level first, so the more top-level mates, the longer it takes to open a file. By default, SolidWorks doesn't solve mates inside the subassemblies.

It takes 3 mates to fully constrain a part, so if you do the math, you need only 15 mates to constrain an assembly of 150 parts, if you break the assembly into 5 subassemblies. In contrast, you need 450 mates to fully constrain that same assembly if it were flat (no subassemblies). You may need to wait a long time for the second one to load.

To illustrate how you can best organize an assembly, I created two design trees for the RC car assembly shown in Figure 6-4.

Figure 6-4:
Breaking a large assembly, such as this RC car assembly, into sub-assemblies makes the assembly easier to work with.

Figure 6-5:
This version of the RC car assembly shows a Feature-Manager design tree using a flat assembly structure.

GTX (Everything<Display State-1>)
- Annotations
- Design Binder
- Lights and Cameras
- Car CL
- Plane2
- Plane3
- Origin
- (f) Chassis<11>
- Idler Arm<6>
- (-) Steering Post<6>
- (-) Steering Post<5>
- Bellcrank<3>
- Steering_Sector_Arm<4>
- Fuel Tank<4>
- Throttle Servo Mnt<1>
- Throttle Servo Mnt<2>
- Throttle Servo<3>
- frt_suspension<8>
- (-) Rear Suspension<6>
- (-) Wheel<11>
- (-) Wheel<12>
- (-) 3-16_ball_stud<12>
- (-) 3-16_ball_stud<10>
- Engine Mount<2>
- (-) Right Spindle<1> ->
- (-) 3-16_ball_stud<13>
- (-) Left Spindle<1>
- (-) 3-16_ball_stud<15>
- (-) PivotRecession2<1>
- (-) PivotRecession2<2>
- (-) axle<1>
- (-) axle<2>
- (-) Wheel<13>
- (-) Wheel<14>
- Body<2>
- (-) Engine<1>
- (f) Servo<1>
- ServoSaver<1>
- (-) 4-Ball Stud<1>
- (-) 4-Ball Stud<2>
- (-) Steering Linkage<1>
- (-) Muffler<1>
- (-) Rubber Tubing<1> ->
- MateGroup1

The following two FeatureManager design trees show different versions of the assembly. The design tree shown in Figure 6-5 shows parts and assemblies at the top level, and the design tree shown in Figure 6-6 shows functionally grouped subassemblies. The second assembly is easier to work on — for example, to work on the front suspension, you need to open only a subassembly rather than the entire assembly.

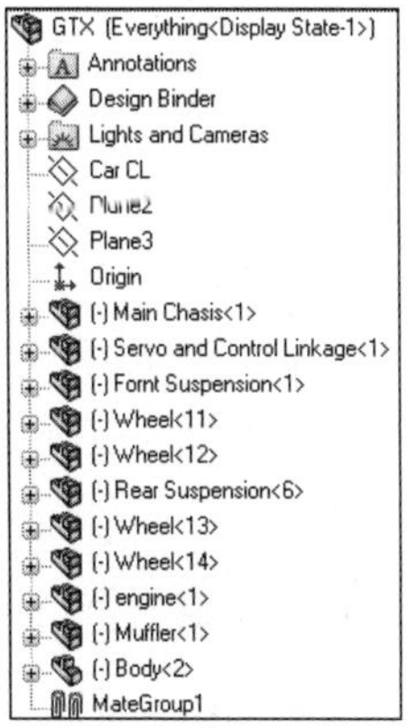

Figure 6-6:
This version of the RC car shows a Feature-Manager design tree broken into functional sub-assemblies.

You can use the following commands to change the level and grouping of assembly components at any time. You can access all these commands by right-clicking a component in the FeatureManager design tree:

- ✔ **Insert New Sub-Assembly:** Creates a new assembly at the level you select. Select the top icon in the FeatureManager design tree, right-click the icon, and choose Insert New Sub-Assembly.

- ✔ **Dissolve Sub-Assembly:** Dissolves the subassembly you select and places the parts individually into the current FeatureManager design tree. Select the subassembly in the FeatureManager design tree, right-click, and choose Dissolve Sub-Assembly.

- ✔ **Add to New Folder:** Creates a new folder within the FeatureManager design tree. To move the assembly component into the new folder, right-click the icon and choose Add to New Folder.

- ✔ **Drag and drop:** Selects parts and subassemblies. Hold down the mouse button and drag the component to the new top-level assembly or assembly location.

Understanding Your Mates

A *mate* is a SolidWorks feature that controls how parts move with respect to each other. Without any connecting mates, a pair of components can move with six unrestricted degrees of freedom relative to one another. (Each mate reduces the degrees of freedom by two. You need only three mates to fully constrain a part so that it can't move.)

Mates also create geometric relations (such as coincident, perpendicular, tangent, angle) between two parts or subassemblies. Mates let components act and react like the ones in a real-world assembly.

For example, if you want a door to open from 0 to 90 degrees within a product (see Figure 6-7), you can add an angular mate that allows a component to open and close within an assembly.

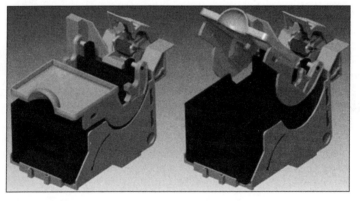

Figure 6-7:
Mates define the movement of the tops of these inkjet cartridges.

Mates allow you to not only review and document fit and form but also simulate how parts function within the assembly. When you design assemblies that move, you can perform fit and interference checks in the open or closed state of a part and at any point between them.

The following concepts make your assemblies more effective and easier to modify:

- ✔ **Make the mate mimic reality.** Mates that mimic the way the part will be assembled in the product ensure realistic motion studies and easier editing later.
- ✔ **Know what you're mating and why.** When you're creating a mate, don't just pick a reference without understanding what you're creating.

Otherwise, you might create a mate reference that doesn't reference what you really want. For example, if you want the top of the ink cartridge holder (refer to Figure 6-7) to open at a specific angle from the ink cartridge itself, place an angle mate by using the two parts that will eventually come together.

✔ **Mate as high as possible in the assembly structure.** Again, try to keep the references between components simple. Choose references for mates that you plan to keep around. If you mate haphazardly, your mates may end up referencing components that don't exist in other configurations of the assembly or that you may remove or change later.

✔ **Name important mates.** Names make mates easier to identify and to change.

✔ **Understand warnings and errors.** The FeatureManager design tree gives you feedback on problems with mates. Figure 6-8 shows examples of a couple of mate issues: A warning icon appears next to Coincident2 and Angle1. To understand a problem, in the FeatureManager design tree, right-click the mate and choose What's Wrong. The What's Wrong dialog box more completely describes the issue and indicates potential sources of the problem.

Figure 6-8:
The
Feature-
Manager
design tree
lists errors
next to the
mates.

✔ **Troubleshoot with Mate Diagnostics.** When problems occur with mates, as just shown in Figure 6-8, use Mate Diagnostics to review the mate errors and warning. To diagnose mate issues, right-click the Mates icon and choose Mate Diagnostics. Click Diagnose and review the mate issues.

✔ **Constrain only the degrees of freedom required.** For example, if you insert a screw, you only need to mate the screw axis and the bottom of the screw head to the assembly component. You can leave the screw free to turn in the hole. The screw appears as underconstrained in the FeatureManager design tree, but that's okay.

Getting familiar with mate types

Each mate is valid for a specific combination of geometry, such as cones, cylinders, planes, and extrusions. For example, you can only use coincident, concentric, and distance to mate a cone to another cone.

The Mate folder in the FeatureManager design tree looks like a pair of paper clips. If you expand the folder, you see a list of all mates in your assembly. Figure 6-9 shows a mate, a pointer indication, and the Mate folder in the FeatureManager design tree.

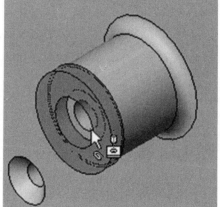

Figure 6-9:
The pointer
changes
when it's
ready to
attach a
mate.

Assemblies created in older versions of SolidWorks refer to Mates as Mategroups.

Mates are broken down into the following three basic categories:

✔ **Geometry-based mates:** When you drag a component into an assembly, you can use the SmartMates command to create mates automatically. SmartMates adds mates according to the type of geometry and references you select.

For example, as just shown in Figure 6-9, I selected the inside edge of the washer in the graphics area and dragged it into the assembly; when the washer passes over the hole on the boss, my pointer changes to indicate the type of mates that will be created. When I drop the washer (by releasing the mouse button), two mates, one concentric to the hole and one coincident to the edges, appear automatically.

✔ **Feature-based mates:** A feature-based mate is created between a boss and a hole. The example just shown in Figure 6-9 is a feature-based mate. (You know this because the pointer is over a cylindrical face.) The pointer gives feedback based on the type of geometry and the reference you select. The pointer type shown in the figure indicates that a feature will be used for the mate.

✔ **Pattern-based mates:** You can also create SmartMates by referencing a circular pattern of holes on a planar face. (These apply to only true pattern features, not those you create manually.) Align the component to the match circular edge. Use the Tab key to align its patterns and release the mouse button to drop the component into place.

For a pattern-based mate, you can create three mates: a concentric mate between the circular edges, a coincident mate between the planar faces, and a concentric mate between the selected part and pattern within the assembly.

You can use feature-based and pattern-based mates to create SmartMates (see the "Working with SmartMates" section, later in this chapter). You use the geometry-based mates to create basic mates. The types of basic mates are shown in this list:

✔ **Coincident:** Places two items (faces, edges, or planes in combination with each other or combined with a single vertex) so that they touch.

✔ **Parallel:** Places two items so that they remain parallel to one another.

✔ **Perpendicular:** Places two items so that they're 90 degrees from one another.

✔ **Tangent:** Places a curve and another item so that they meet at a single point. One of the selected items must be a cylindrical, conical, or spherical face.

✔ **Concentric:** Places two items so that they share the same center axis.

✔ **Distance:** Places two items at a specified distance from one another.

✔ **Angle:** Places two items at a specified angle to one another.

✔ **Lock:** Maintains the position and orientation between two components.

Adding a mate

To add a mate, follow these steps:

1. **Open a SolidWorks assembly document.**

2. **Click Mate in the Assembly toolbar.**

   The Mates PropertyManager, shown in Figure 6-10, appears, with the Mate Selections field active.

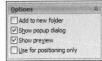

Figure 6-10:
The Mates
Property-
Manager
shows valid
mate types
for the
entities you
select.

3. **In the Options section, select the Show Preview and Show Popup Dialog check boxes (refer to Figure 6-10).**

4. **In the graphics area, click the two faces, edges, vertices (corners or points), or planes that you want to mate together.**

   In the graphics area, the Mate pop-up toolbar (shown in Figure 6-11), appears, with default mates for the entities you selected.

Figure 6-11:
Default
mate types
appear on
the Mate
pop-up
toolbar.

5. **On the toolbar, click the type of mate you want to add.**

   The two components move into place to give you a preview of the mate type.

   In the Mate Alignments section, in the Advanced Mates area of the Mate PropertyManager, you can select Align or Anti-Aligned to switch parts so that the faces of the two parts point together or in opposite directions.

6. **Click OK (the green check mark) on the pop-up toolbar.**

   The Mate pop-up toolbar closes. The Mate PropertyManager stays active so that you can continue adding mates.

7. **Click OK to close the Mate PropertyManager.**

You can test a mate by clicking Move Component on the Assembly toolbar and then clicking and dragging a component to see how it moves. If a component doesn't move, it's fixed or fully constrained. If a component is fixed, it has an (f) before its name in the FeatureManager design tree. A floating, or under-defined, component has a (–). A fully defined component doesn't have a prefix. To fix or float a component, right-click the component in the FeatureManager design tree and choose Fix or Float.

Editing a mate

You can edit an existing mate at any time. To edit an existing mate, follow these steps:

1. **Open an assembly file.**

2. **In the FeatureManager design tree, expand the Mate.**

   You can also select the mate under the Mates folder for the component.

3. **Select the mate to edit.**

   The items (faces and edges, for example) that the mate references are highlighted within the graphics area.

4. **Click the mate.**

   The context toolbar menu appears.

5. **Choose Edit Feature.**

   The Mate PropertyManager appears. The name of the PropertyManager is based on the type of mate.

6. **Edit the mate properties and selections.**

7. **Click OK.**

You can use the middle mouse button to rotate your model to see what you're selecting or working on. If you have a wheel mouse, use the wheel to zoom in and out while you rotate the model. You can use these mouse buttons while using the command without going to another area of the interface.

Working with SmartMates

If you prefer to spend as little time as possible mating components, SmartMates may be your deal. *SmartMates* applies mates automatically when you drag and drop components into an assembly. SmartMates chooses a mate based on the geometry of the part.

SmartMates works with part edges and faces. Depending on what you select, an edge or a face, SolidWorks determines a valid mate type while you drag your pointer over the component or select other geometry.

The example shown in Figure 6-12 shows a washer and a bolt. I selected the washer edge and the edge of the bolt diameter for SmartMates. In this case, SmartMates creates a concentric mate, which constrains the bolt to the washer.

Figure 6-12:
SmartMates
creates a
concentric
and
coincident
mate for this
washer
and bolt.

When working with SmartMates, you still need to watch how the feature is constraining mated items. For example, SmartMates didn't fully constrain the bolt just shown in Figure 6-12; in this case, the constraints are fine, but if you need to fully constrain an assembly component, all six degrees of freedom (front and back, right and left, up and down) must be constrained. You can constrain them by using three mates. In Figure 6-12, the base of the bolt and the top of washer touch, and the hole and bolt diameter align, but a degree or two of movement remains. The bolt head can still spin around its axis. In this case, I wouldn't add another mate to completely fix the component. Why create the last mate if it doesn't make a difference?

You can activate SmartMates when you drop an assembly component into the assembly, in order to eliminate the extra steps of first adding the assembly component and then manually adding more mates.

To activate SmartMates when you pull a component into the assembly, hold down the Alt key and drag a component over potential mate partners. The component becomes transparent, and the pointer changes when it's over a valid mate partner. Drop the component to apply the mate.

To add a SmartMate to an existing assembly component in a SolidWorks assembly, follow these steps:

1. **Click Move Component on the Assembly toolbar.**

   The Move PropertyManager appears.

2. **In the PropertyManager, in the Move area, click SmartMates.**

3. **Double-click a component and then select a valid mate partner.**

   The pointer turns into a paper clip, indicating that SmartMates is active. The Mate pop-up toolbar appears, with the default mate types to fit the geometry you selected.

4. **On the Mate pop-up toolbar, click a mate type.**

5. **Click OK on the Mate toolbar.**

   The components move into place, and the SmartMates PropertyManager stays active for you to add other mates.

6. **To add other mates, repeat Steps 3 through 5.**

7. **Click OK in the PropertyManager.**

   The SmartMates PropertyManager closes.

To add a SmartMate to a new component by dragging and dropping it into an existing assembly, follow these steps:

1. **Open a SolidWorks assembly document.**

2. **Open another SolidWorks part or assembly document.**

3. **Choose Windows⇨Tile Vertical.**

   Both windows appear side by side so that you can see both open files at the same time. You can zoom into either model to get a close look at the areas you want to mate.

4. **Click the model, and drag it into the main assembly document to where you want to mate it.**

   The pointer changes to a mate type when the parts are ready to mate.

5. **Release the mouse button.**

   The Mate pop-up toolbar appears with the default mate types for the two parts.

6. **Click a mate type on the toolbar.**

7. **Click OK.**

   The parts mate, and the toolbar closes.

 After SmartMates mates your two components, you can flip a part if it doesn't point in the right direction, by clicking the part and pressing the Tab key. If the orientation isn't what you want, press the Tab key again to flip the components back around without releasing the left mouse button. If you're mating a pattern feature, clicking the Tab rotates the part about the center of the pattern rather than flips the mate alignment (aligned or anti-aligned).

Working with mate references

Mate references specify one or more entities of a component to use for automatic mating. When you drag a component with a mate reference into an assembly, SolidWorks looks for other combinations of the same mate reference name and mate type. If the name is the same but the type doesn't match, SolidWorks doesn't add the mate.

Here are a few concepts to keep in mind about mate references:

- ✔ **Components:** You can add mate references to parts and subassemblies. In subassemblies, you can select assembly geometry (such as a plane in the assembly) or component geometry (such as the face of a component).

- ✔ **Multiple mate references:** A component can contain more than one mate reference. The MateReferences folder in the FeatureManager design tree holds all mate references. For example, you can have a component in an assembly with two mate references: bolt and washer. When you drag a fastener with a mate reference named `bolt` into the assembly, SolidWorks adds mates between the entities with the same mate reference name.

- ✔ **Multiple mated entities:** Each mate reference can contain as many as three mated entities: primary, secondary, and tertiary reference entities. Each of these entities can have an assigned mate type and alignment. The primary reference entity on one component must mate to the primary reference entity on another. For example, a shaft can have its cylindrical face assigned to a concentric mate and its planar end face assigned to a coincident mate. When you drag that component into an appropriate location in an assembly, SolidWorks adds both mates.

- ✔ **SmartMates:** When the SmartMates PropertyManager is open, SolidWorks adds mates by using mate references before it adds geometric SmartMates.

You have to set up the mate reference in the original document (part or assembly) before you plan to use it in your assemblies. You use mate references mainly in situations where you plan to use a common component often.

In Figure 6-13, the selected face is the primary reference. The axes named Axis1 and Axis2 are the secondary and tertiary references. You can add these three references to the engine so that you can drag new exhaust systems into the assembly and automatically mate them.

Figure 6-13: The muffler assembly shows the three references (primary, secondary, and tertiary) used to mate to the engine assembly.

To define a mate reference, follow these steps:

1. **Open a SolidWorks part or assembly document.**

2. **Choose Insert⇨Reference Geometry⇨Mate Reference.**

   The Mate Reference PropertyManager appears with the Primary Reference Entity field active.

3. **In the Reference Name area, type a name for the mate reference.**

   Always give the mate reference a meaningful name.

4. **Select a face, an edge, a vertex, or a plane for the primary reference entity.**

   The entity appears in the Primary Reference Entity field. Select the most important mate for the primary reference. SolidWorks uses the entity for potential mates when you drag a new component into the assembly.

5. **For the Mate Reference type, use the pull-down menu to select a default mate type for the primary reference.**

6. **In the Mate Reference Alignment area, use the pull-down menu to select the default reference alignment for the primary entity.**

This selection determines which way the part flips or aligns when a mate is applied. The mate reference alignment uses a vector that's perpendicular and pointing away from the face, and this vector helps to determine how to flip the component when it's mated. Your options include the ones in this list:

- *Any:* Positions the components either aligned or anti-aligned based on their current position

- *Aligned:* Positions the components so that the normal vectors of the selected faces point in the same direction

- *Anti-Aligned:* Positions the components so that the normal vectors of the selected faces point toward each other

- *Closest:* Positions the components depending on the condition that can be met, aligned or anti-aligned, with the least amount of movement

 7. **If needed, repeat Steps 3 through 6 to add secondary and tertiary entities.**

    The mate that's referenced appears in the FeatureManager design tree in the MateReferences folder. Each mate can have as many as three reference entities. All three references are required to fully constrain the component within the assembly.

 8. **Click OK.**

After you define the mate references, drag a part or an assembly into the new assembly. If the name and type of the new component match the reference, SolidWorks mates it automatically.

Understanding the FeatureManager design tree Mategroup

The FeatureManager design tree displays a range of information about the assembly components and their status. Figure 6-14 shows an assembly with the Mate and a component expanded to show the mate features.

You can infer the following statements from the display of the FeatureManager design tree objects within the assembly just shown in Figure 6-14:

✔ Some top-level components (such as PSI-DV20-350-46_46 and PSI-DV20-350-46_DV20) are underconstrained as indicated by the (–) next to the component name, indicating that there are still some degrees of movement. You can add more mates to fully define the location of the assembly component.

- ✔ You find only one instance of each component in the top level of the assembly, noted by the <1> after the component name.

- ✔ The mates for each component appear in the FeatureManager design tree below the components. PSI-DV20-350-46_ has two coincident mates (Coincident1 and Coincident2), and one concentric mate (Concentric1).

- ✔ The mate name defaults to the type (Distance or Concentric, for example) followed by [reference 1 (parent), reference 2 (child)]. For example, PSI-DV20-350-46_DV20 has two mates (Coincident1 and Coincident2). The names of these mates define the location of the PSI-DV20-350-46_DV20 (child, reference 2) using PSI-DV20-350-46_705 (parent, reference 1).

- ✔ A total of six mates appear in the assembly, as shown under the Mates folder.

Figure 6-14:
The
Feature-
Manager
design tree
shows the
Mates
component
folder and
Mate.

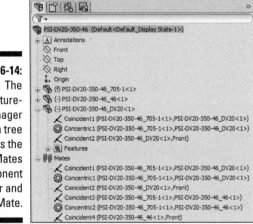

You can click the plus and minus signs on the left side of the object icon in the FeatureManager design tree to expand or collapse a folder.

Working with Your Virtual Prototype

Designing an assembly is a complex task that can involve the work of several designers. SolidWorks offers tools that allow you to plan your design and implement your plan. Layout-based assembly design allows you to switch back and forth between top-down and bottom-up methods. Other tools allow you to build parts inside the assembly window to reference them to other part geometry. And, tools that load only the assemblies you need to see make sharing the workload easy.

Using layouts

You can use layouts to define and control the location and orientation of assembly components. Layouts are made up of 3D sketches and planes. Both are important components in top-down design. (If you're unfamiliar with top-down design, see the section "Designing an assembly," earlier in this chapter.) With layouts, you construct a single 3D sketch to show where each component belongs. Then you can modify the sketch before you add any parts.

The major advantage of designing an assembly by using a layout is that if you change the layout, the assembly and its parts update automatically.

Another benefit is that layouts reduce the amount of parent/child relationships. Components are related by one sketch in the assembly, so parts are more robust and easier to change and redefine.

Creating the layout

To create an assembly layout, follow these steps:

1. **Open a new assembly document by choosing File⇨New⇨Assembly.**

   The Begin Assembly PropertyManager appears.

2. **Press the Create Layout button in the PropertyManager.**

   A 3D sketch opens.

3. **You can begin creating the various parts of your assembly by creating blocks from the sketch geometry (see the next section, "Using blocks in your layout").**

   You use these blocks to create individual parts within the assembly document. These parts can be saved as external files or used as virtual components specific to only the current assembly.

Using blocks in your layout

In SolidWorks 2008, you can create blocks from sketch entities and use them in your layout. *Blocks* let you group sketch geometry. The group updates and behaves as a single entity. The layout sketch must be active in order to create or edit blocks. You save blocks with the .sldblk extension so that you can easily import them into part or assembly or other block files later.

The Blocks toolbar, shown in Figure 6-15, lets you group blocks of sketch entities. To display it, choose View⇨Toolbars⇨Blocks.

The Blocks toolbar includes these functions:

- ✔ **Make Block:** Create a block from selected sketch geometry.
- ✔ **Edit Block:** Change dimensions and relations in a block.
- ✔ **Insert Block:** Insert a saved block into the current sketch.
- ✔ **Save Block:** Save a block to disk for reuse.
- ✔ **Explode Block:** Ungroup a block and convert to regular sketch entities.

You can use blocks to create parts in your assembly layout by selecting one or more blocks and then right-clicking and choosing Make Part from Block. This function takes the sketch block names and creates components for the assembly.

To create an assembly from a layout, follow these steps:

1. **Open an assembly that contains a layout.**

   See the earlier section "Creating the layout."

2. **Create or select existing blocks from the FeatureManager design tree: Right-click and choose Make Part from Block (see Figure 6-16).**

   The Make Part from Block PropertyManager appears, as shown in Figure 6-17.

3. **In the Block to Part Constraint section of the PropertyManager, select a constraint option.**

   The Project Constraint option allows your new part to move in a direction normal to the sketch plane on which the block was created. The On Block constraint restricts all movement of the new part.

4. **Click OK.**

   A part containing the selected block is created and appears in the FeatureManager design tree. The square brackets indicate that it's a virtual component. (It's saved within the assembly file, not in an external part file.) Later, if you want, you can save these virtual components as external files: Right-click the Virtual Component in the FeatureManager design tree and choose Save Part (in External File).

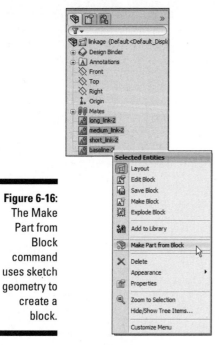

Figure 6-16:
The Make Part from Block command uses sketch geometry to create a block.

Figure 6-17:
The Make Part from Block Property-Manager.

Selecting assembly components

Special selection tools are available in SolidWorks to help you control how components appear in an assembly. The Select Flyout button on the Standard toolbar offers instant access to several criteria you can use to select components. The Advanced Component Selection tool allows you to set special component criteria by specifying categories, conditions, and values.

You can use these tools to create assembly configurations that hide or show components based on the component's mass properties (weight and volume, for example) and custom properties. The ability to control what you can and can't see in an assembly is another example of why custom properties are important to SolidWorks document types.

The example shown in Figure 6-18 indicates how you can use Advanced Component Selection to select all fasteners (nuts, pins, and washers, for example) in an assembly based on the Fastener file type.

SolidWorks defines special properties (SW Special) to use within the selection criteria:

- ✔ **Part Mass:** How much it weighs (numeric)

- ✔ **Part Volume:** How big it is (numeric)

- ✔ **Part Is Interior Detail:** Whether you can see the part or whether it's inside somewhere (Yes or No)

- ✔ **Configuration Name:** Configuration names you have defined (string)

- ✔ **Document Name:** The filename (string)

You can use Advanced Component Selection to specifically hide or show components in an assembly configuration. For example, you may want to create a configuration that doesn't show any of the standard hardware. You can use Advanced Component Selection to select the hardware based on a custom property and then set the components to be hidden or suppressed.

To show or hide components based on advanced selection criteria, follow these steps:

1. **Click the ConfigurationManager tab at the top of the FeatureManager design tree.**

   The FeatureManager design tree disappears, and the Configuration Manager appears in its place. The ConfigurationManager lists the different configurations in the assembly.

2. **Right-click a configuration and choose Advanced Select.**

   The Advanced Component Selection dialog box appears.

3. **Define the Property and Condition values.**

   You can apply more than one condition by using the Boolean values And and Or.

4. **Click Apply to run the query.**

   The components that meet the specified criteria are highlighted in the FeatureManager design tree.

5. **(Optional) Hide, suppress, or even change the display state of the selected items.**

   You can choose these actions even though the Advanced Component Selection dialog box is still displayed.

6. **Click the X Close box in the dialog box to close it.**

You can save a performed search by adding a name in the Name of Search pull-down list and selecting the Save icon. Then switch to the Manage Searches tab and use the Add to Favorites selection. This procedure adds your search to the Select Flyout menu, making it available to you in later searches.

Creating assembly features

SolidWorks allows you to create certain features (Extruded Cut, Revolved Cut, Hole Wizard, and Linear and Circular Patterns) in the assembly.

You can use these features when you're modeling a cut or a hole at the assembly level. For example, in a welded assembly, you may want to add cuts and holes to the assembly after all assembly components are in place.

Assembly features are added at the assembly level, not to the individual components. You add these features the same way you add part features. (You can read about part features in Chapter 5.) You can access the commands on the Features toolbar.

When adding an assembly feature, you can set the feature scope to specify which components should be taken into consideration when creating the assembly feature. So, if you want to cut only certain parts with an assembly cut, you can define the scope to only include those components.

To set the scope for an assembly feature, follow these steps:

1. **In the Cut-Extrude PropertyManager, select the parameters for the cut features (direction and distance, for example).**

2. **In the Feature Scope section of the Cut-Extrude PropertyManager, select either All Components or Selected Components.**

   If you choose Selected Components, deselect the Auto-Select radio button.

3. **In the FeatureManager design tree or in the graphics area, select the components that you want the assembly feature to affect.**

   The selected component names appear in the Feature Scope dialog box.

4. **Click OK.**

   The feature is applied to the selected components. The default feature scope is updated.

In-context assembly modeling

In addition to creating or editing components in their own part windows, you create or edit components in the assembly window. The advantage to this method is that it allows you to build a part that references the geometry of another. If you update one part, the other one updates also, ensuring that the components fit together correctly. This method of design is *in-context* design because you're working in the context of the assembly.

When you create a part in an assembly window, the part appears in the FeatureManager design tree as though you created it in its own window. SolidWorks also adds an item to the FeatureManager design tree that lists information about the part, such as what was used to create it and the referenced assembly component.

Parts created within the context of the assembly contain external references. SolidWorks creates an *external reference* when one document is dependent on another for its solution. The referenced document is the *parent,* and the document that references it is its *child.* If the parent document changes, its children update to reflect that change.

The ability to design in the context of the assembly is a powerful one. But if too many parts are tied to one another, managing the automatic update of changes to the original parts can be harder. I always like having more control over what changes and when.

You can use the following commands to work on parts in the context of an assembly. You can access all these commands when you right-click a component name in the FeatureManager design tree:

- ✔ **Edit Part:** Allows you to edit a part in the assembly window while the assembly geometry is displayed in the background
- ✔ **Edit In-Context:** Recalls the assembly when only the part is active so that you can change, add, or remove references
- ✔ **List External References:** Lists the references of a part and their current state (in or out of context)
- ✔ **Display/Delete Relations:** Allows you to list, review, delete, or replace an external reference

The FeatureManager design tree indicates that a feature has an external reference by appending the -> symbol to the right of the feature name. If the external reference is locked, the symbol changes to ->*.

If you're editing in context of the assembly and you don't want to create external references, click No External References on the Assembly toolbar (see Figure 6-19).

Creating a part in an assembly

To create a part while in the assembly, follow these steps:

1. **Choose Insert⇨Component⇨New Part.**

   A new part appears in the FeatureManager design tree. The new part name is enclosed in brackets, signifying that it's a virtual component.

2. **Click a face or plane to begin sketching geometry for your new part.**

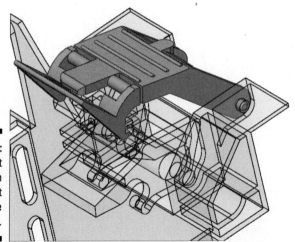

Figure 6-19:
You can edit a part in the context of the assembly.

3. **Construct the part features by using the same techniques you use to build a part on its own by using reference geometry from other components in the assembly as needed.**

   See Chapter 5 to brush up on your part-making skills.

4. **Right-click the new part in the FeatureManager design tree and choose Save Part (in External File).**

   This step saves the part file to your disk.

5. **To return to editing the assembly, right-click anywhere in the graphics area and then choose either Edit Assembly:<*assembly_name*> or Edit Component.**

Editing a part in an assembly

Editing a part while in an assembly allows you to modify a component without leaving the assembly. You can create sketches for the new features that reference an edge or that you dimension to an edge in another part.

When you edit a part in the context of an assembly, the part turns blue and the rest of the assembly turns gray.

To edit a part while in an assembly, follow these steps:

1. **Click the part and then the Edit Part icon.**

   The rest of the assembly becomes transparent in the background.

   You have several options for displaying component transparency when you edit a component in the context of an assembly. These settings affect only the component not being edited. Choose Toolsı̇Options. On the Systems Option tab, select Display/Selection. In the Assembly Transparency for In-Context Edit area, select an option for the type of transparency.

   The title bar shows the name of the part in the assembly that's open for editing as <part_name> in <assembly_name>.sldasm. Note that the message on the status bar indicates that you're now editing the part document even though the entire assembly is visible.

   When you edit a part in the context of an assembly, the referenced configuration in the assembly becomes the active configuration in all open windows (for example, if the part is open in its own window).

2. **Make the necessary changes to the part.**

   You can read more about how to make a part in Chapter 5.

3. **To return to editing the assembly, right-click the assembly name in the FeatureManager design tree, or right-click anywhere in the graphics area and choose Edit Assembly:<*assembly_name*> or click Edit Component.**

Getting information about your assembly

You can squeeze plenty of information out of your solid model. Similar to any real world product, you can measure your model, weigh your model, and examine how parts fit together and come apart — all without getting your hands dirty. Isn't the virtual world grand?

Making sure that everything fits

After you create an assembly, you want to make sure that components interact properly. *Interference checking* in SolidWorks lets you check to see whether any parts clash into one another. Interference checking is an underused feature in SolidWorks, but don't underuse it in your work. Check for interference even after simple design changes. Fixing a virtual model is much easier than fixing than a real one, and you have less explaining to do.

Figure 6-20 shows an assembly where the shaft is too large for the gears and bearing. (Thank goodness that the designer caught it!) Keep in mind, though, that interference isn't always a bad thing. For example, a press fit is a designed interference.

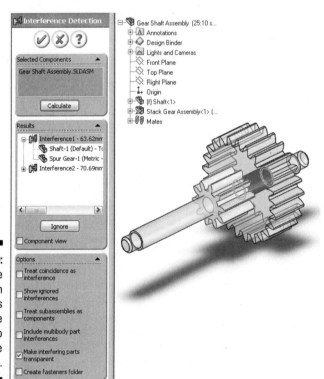

Figure 6-20: Interference detection indicates that the shaft is too large for the gears.

You can see two interferences in Figure 6-20 (Interference1 and Interference2). If you select the interference in the Results field of the Interference Detection PropertyManager, the interference volume is highlighted as shown. The names of the interfering components also appear under the interference.

To check the assembly for interferences, follow these steps:

1. **Open an assembly document.**

2. **Choose Interference Detection on the Evaluate tab.**

   The Interference Detection dialog box appears, with the Selected Components field active. The entire assembly appears in the field by default. You can clear the field and enter any subassemblies individually.

3. **Select (or don't select) the check boxes for these options:**

   - *Treat Coincidence As Interference:* Reports coincident entities as interferences.

   - *Show Ignored Interference:* Shows ignored interferences in the Results list, with a gray icon. When this option is cleared, ignored interferences aren't listed.

   - *Treat Subassemblies As Components:* Treats subassemblies as single components so that interferences between a subassembly's components aren't reported.

   - *Include Multibody Part Interferences:* Reports interferences between bodies within multibody parts. (A *multibody* is a part file with two separate solid bodies that don't touch.)

   - *Make Interfering Parts Transparent:* Displays the components of the selected interference in transparent mode.

   - *Create Fasteners Folder:* Segregates interferences between fasteners (such as a nut and a bolt) into a separate folder in the Results area.

4. **Select Component View in the Results area.**

   Any interferences are highlighted in the model.

5. **Click Calculate.**

   The interference between components is calculated, and the results appear in the Results field.

6. **Click OK.**

Measure your design

Just as with parts, you can measure the assembly by using the Measure tool.

To measure within an assembly, follow these steps:

1. **Open an assembly document.**

2. **Choose Tools⇨Measure.**

   The Measure dialog box, shown in Figure 6-21, appears. The dialog box is a toolbar that you can expand to display the measurement values.

3. **Select the items to measure.**

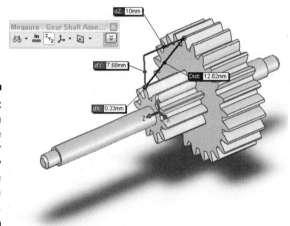

Figure 6-21:
You can
measure
your
assembly
with the
Measure
tool.

   The pointer turns to a ruler to indicate that Measure is active. The items you select are highlighted, and values are displayed in the graphics area. You can expand the Measure box to display values in the box. New measurements are updated dynamically when you change selections.

   While the Measure dialog box is in place, you can switch between different SolidWorks documents without closing the dialog box. The name of the active document is displayed on the title bar of the Measure dialog box. If you activate a document that has items already selected, the measurement information updates automatically.

4. **Click the X Close box to close the dialog box.**

Just the facts, ma'am (Assembly Statistics)

When working with an assembly, especially one that someone else made, you might want to get some of the vital statistics of the assembly. You can quickly determine the number of parts, unique parts (only used once), subassemblies, and mates, for example, by using the Assembly Statistics feature.

For an assembly, the key information to know is the size of the assembly — in other words, the number of components it has. You also need to know how many top-level mates exist. Too many top-level mates creates performance issues.

To determine the assembly statistics, follow these steps:

1. **Open an assembly document.**

2. **Choose Tools⇨AssemblyXpert.**

   The AssemblyXpert dialog box, shown in Figure 6-22, appears. Inside the dialog box, you can see the number of components in the assembly, the types of components, and the number of top-level mates and top-level components, for example.

3. **Review the information.**

4. **Click OK to close the dialog box.**

How big is that breadbasket (Mass Properties)?

Of course, you can use other ways to pry information from an assembly — the Mass Properties tool, for example (see Figure 6-23). You can use Mass Properties to find out your assembly's weight and volume and more. SolidWorks calculates all this information directly on the assembly based on the materials you assign to individual parts.

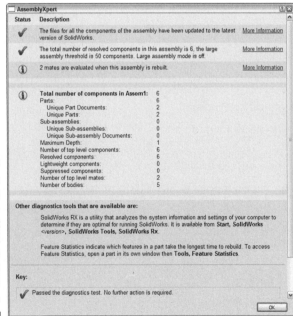

Figure 6-22: The Assembly-Xpert dialog box gives the lowdown on the personal watercraft.

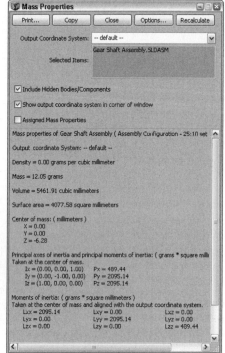

Figure 6-23:
The Mass
Properties
dialog box
indicates
how much
this gear
shaft
weighs.

To calculate the mass properties for an assembly, follow these steps:

1. **Open an assembly document.**

2. **Choose Tools⇨Mass Properties.**

   The Mass Properties dialog box appears. The name of the assembly appears in the Selected Items field.

3. **Select the Include Hidden Bodies/Components check box.**

   Hidden components are included in Mass Properties calculations.

4. **Select components or subassemblies in the FeatureManager design tree to get individual or combined mass properties.**

   By default, the active assembly is shown within the Selected Components field.

5. **Click Close.**

   The Mass Properties dialog box closes.

Part III

The Devil's in the "Drawing" Details

The 5th Wave   By Rich Tennant

It started as a wrap-around porch, and then Stuart started learning SolidWorks.

In this part . . .

After you create the parts and assemblies, you're ready to draw. *Drawings* are the means used to document the design intent and requirements for manufacturing.

You can reuse the information that defines the part or assembly to help produce the drawing. When a change occurs (and it will), you can modify the dimension within the part/assembly or drawings, and both documents are updated. Being able to easily change a design and have your changes updated in a related document illustrates the power of 3D.

Chapter 7

Creating Drawings

In This Chapter

▶ Discovering the elements of a drawing

▶ Setting up and working with drawing formats

▶ Creating drawing views from the 3D model

▶ Making changes and modifying dimensions

▶ Working with annotations and tables

Drawings formally communicate your design to manufacturing. Although technology has come along promising to eliminate the need for drawings, they continue to serve an important purpose in design. Manufacturers need drawings to produce quotes, to determine the proper manufacturing processes, and to inspect parts to ensure that they meet the requirements set forth in the drawings.

SolidWorks offers a number of different tools to automate the drawing process based on information you capture in your 3D design. This chapter focuses on the basics of drawing creation. Chapter 8 expands on these topics and offers some insight on how to automate drawing functions.

Becoming Familiar with Drawing Elements

In essence, *drawings* are large sheets of paper that contain images of your model in various views and orientations along with dimensions, manufacturing symbols, notes, and other annotations.

Back in the good old days, before CAD software, engineers created drawings on drawing boards with paper and pencil. First, they pulled out a preprinted drawing sheet that fit the drawing size they wanted (A, B, or C, for example).

Then they created the drawing views that showed the part as it appeared from different angles (top, front, right, or isometric, for example). Finally, they inserted dimensions, filled in the title and revision blocks, and added notes and other annotations.

SolidWorks follows this same process, only virtually, so that you don't have to physically stand up and sharpen your pencil or fumble with large drawing sheets. The software does the heavy lifting for you.

The best part of SolidWorks is that the drawing file is fully *associative* with the model: If you change the part geometry after the fact, the drawing views are updated automatically so that you don't have to redo them manually. Adding views is simple, and it's all tied together.

The following elements, shown in Figure 7-1, make up a drawing:

1 Drawing sheet format: You can edit the drawing sheet format, which is the predefined background for a drawing, directly. The predefined background for a drawing can also contain title block text and other standard notes. Read the section "Editing the Drawing Sheet Format," later in this chapter, to find out how to change the drawing format.

2 Drawing sheet: A drawing in SolidWorks contains one or more sheets, like a set of drawings, allowing you to keep multisheet drawings in a single file. SolidWorks uses a simple tab organization method for multisheet drawings. You can add sheets at any time, using any format. Select a tab to activate a sheet. To add a new a new sheet, right-click a tab and choose Add Sheet, or simply click the Add Sheet tab.

3 Drawing view (right): This view shows the model from the right.

4 Drawing view (front): This view shows the front of the model.

5 Title block: This area is where the information concerning title, revision, material, drawing size, part number, or drawn by, for example, appears. The title block is contained within the drawing format.

6 Drawing format text (dynamic): This text changes with every drawing. These values are linked to custom properties.

7 Drawing format text (static): Some text notes within the drawing format are static and don't change. The words, such as SIZE and REV, don't change from drawing to drawing.

8 Pointer: Other programs call the pointer a *cursor.* A tag next to the pointer tells you which drawing sheet is active.

9 Drawing view border: When you place a drawing view, a frame appears around the view.

10 Drawing view (isometric): Drawing views on drawing sheets show the model in different orientations and include dimensions and annotations.

This drawing view shows a standard isometric view of the model. This view and the next two are the three standard views you can place on a sheet automatically using the Standard 3 Views command on the Drawings toolbar.

11 Revision table: This special table type also has special functions to add revision marks and new revisions.

12 Surface Finish symbol: This type of annotation indicates the type of surface finish. You can import these annotations directly from the model.

13 Datum annotation: This annotation was created within the part and inserted into the drawing automatically using the Insert Model Items command. (You can read the details of this command in Chapter 8.)

14 Revision annotation: This annotation (or *revision mark*) is tied to the revision table.

15 Dimension: Driven or driving dimensions in SolidWorks. You can insert driving dimensions from the model into the drawing automatically. If you change their values, the changes are updated in the model. Driven dimensions serve only as reference geometry. You can add driven dimensions to a drawing, but they don't change the model.

16 Note: You can create this type of annotation directly in the drawing. Notes can contain text and symbols.

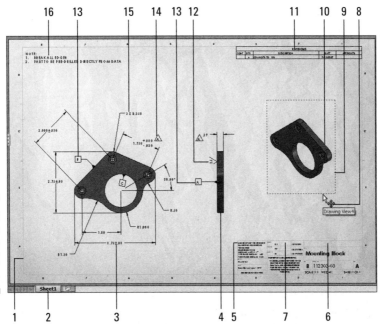

Figure 7-1:
Drawings display your model in all its glory.

SolidWorks supports a number of drawing standards, including ISO, ANSI, DIN, JIS, BSI, GOST, and GB. The standard you choose affects the appearance of drawing views. For example, if you choose ANSI, drawing view projections are third-angle, and the symbols meet the ANSI drafting standard. Likewise, if you choose DIN, the drawing view projections are first-angle, and the symbols comply with the DIN drafting standard. The drawing shown in Figure 7-1 is set to the ANSI standard.

Default values and drawing standards are in the drawing template. You can change the standard template or make your own. Read Chapter 2 for more information on how to define, save, and share drawing templates.

Opening a New Drawing Document

Drawings consist of one or more views generated from a part or an assembly. Views show the model in different orientations. SolidWorks lets you create a drawing from a drawing template or from within a part or assembly document. This chapter shows you how to make a drawing from a model.

Drawing files have the `.slddrw` extension. A new drawing takes the name of the first model you insert into it. The name appears on the menu bar. When you save the drawing, the name of the model appears in the Save As dialog box as the default filename, with the default extension `.slddrw`. You can edit the name before saving the drawing.

You can create a drawing in many ways. The following method is my preference because it's the most straightforward.

To create a new drawing, follow these steps:

1. **Open the part or assembly document you want to use for the drawing.**

2. **Choose File➪Make Drawing from Part or Make Drawing from Assembly.**

   A new SolidWorks drawing document appears. The Sheet/Format Size dialog box appears.

3. **If you don't want to use any sheet format, click Cancel and continue to Step 7.**

   If you click Cancel, the Sheet/Format Size dialog box closes, and the Model View PropertyManager, shown in Figure 7-2, appears in the left pane.

4. **If you want to use a sheet, select the Standard Sheet Size radio button (or Custom Sheet Size if you want to make your own).**

   If you select Standard Sheet Size, the standard sheet sizes become visible. If you select Custom Sheet Size, the Width and Height fields become active, as shown in Figure 7-3).

Figure 7-2:
Select a
single view
orientation
in the
Drawing
View
Property-
Manager.

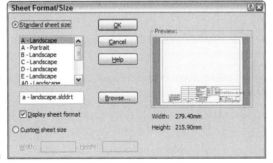

Figure 7-3:
The Sheet
Format/Size
dialog box.

5. **Select a standard sheet size or type a width and height for the custom sheet size.**

6. **Select the Display Sheet Format check box to display a border or title block, for example.**

7. **Click OK.**

A new drawing appears in the graphics area, and the Model View PropertyManager appears.

If you're in a hurry, you may want to place three standard views rather than a single model view. If so, when the Model PropertyManager appears, ignore it and click Standard 3 Views on the Drawings toolbar. The Standard 3 Views PropertyManager appears, and the list of open documents is available. Click an open document, and three standard views (front, right, and isometric) of the model appear on the drawing sheet. You don't need to select any other options.

8. **In the Model View PropertyManager, select a named view under Orientation (Front or Back, for example).**

   If you select the Preview check box, you see a preview of the view next to the pointer.

9. **In the Model View PropertyManager, click a Display Style.**

   You can choose from an assortment of display styles, such as Hidden Lines Removed or Hidden Lines Visible.

10. **Select a scale.**

    You have three options:

    - *Use parent scale:* This option is available only after the first view. When you add views, you can use the parent view parameters to apply the same scale to each child view. If you change the scale of the parent view, the child view updates.

    - *Use sheet scale:* Your model appears scaled to fit the sheet you're using. SolidWorks selects a scale based on the default sheet template and reduces the scale based on the model size.

    - *Use custom scale:* Select a ratio from the drop-down list or enter your own values.

11. **In the Dimension Type section, select either the Projected check box or the True check box.**

    The Projected option shows 2D dimensions, and True displays 3D space dimensions. This option should be used for only isometric drawing views.

12. **Click in the graphics area to place the view on the sheet.**

    As soon as you place the view, the Drawing View PropertyManager replaces the Model View PropertyManager. If you place an orthogonal view orientation, the Projected View PropertyManager appears, and you can place any number of projected views for any orthogonal view. But before you start placing more views, you may want to read the "Placing the Drawing Views" section, later in this chapter.

13. **Click OK in the Model View PropertyManager or in the Drawing View PropertyManager.**

    The PropertyManager closes, and the new drawing appears in the graphics area.

Editing the Drawing Sheet Format

You can think of the drawing sheet format (see Figure 7-4) as letterhead for your drawings. It contains your company name, the size of the sheet, the title of the drawing, and other information that you think is important. You can customize the sheet format to match your company's standard format. The sheet format underlies the drawing sheet and is separate from the drawing sheet. You edit the sheet format directly before you place all the model views.

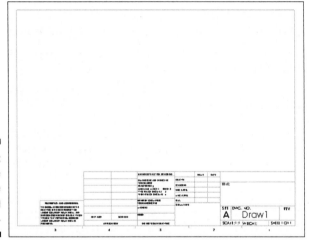

Figure 7-4:
An example
of an A-Size
drawing
format.

Before you get started, you should know the following basic information about drawing sheet formats:

✔ The drawing format has a scale of 1:1. If you use letter-size paper, then that's the true paper size, which makes setting up a drawing format simpler because the drawing formats aren't scaled. Figure 7-4 shows an A-size drawing format.

✔ Standard sheet formats include links to system properties and custom properties. SolidWorks extracts custom properties from the model to use in the drawing.

✔ SolidWorks sheet formats have the file extension .slddrt. You can save sheet formats separately and use them to create future drawings. You can create sheet formats in new drawing documents and in drawing templates.

✔ You can create custom templates to include predefined views or multiple drawing sheets, for example. Drawing templates have the extension .drwdot. A template forms the basis of a new document.

When you open a drawing with an existing drawing sheet format, you can't change the information directly. When you edit the sheet format, the drawing views and other non-drawing format items are no longer visible because you're editing the sheet format (drawing background), not the other drawing information (views, notes, and dimensions, for example).

To edit a drawing sheet format, follow these steps:

1. **Open a drawing file or a drawing template file.**

2. **In the FeatureManager design tree, expand a sheet folder.**

   The sheet format and drawing views become visible.

3. **Right-click the sheet format you want to edit, and choose Edit Sheet Format.**

   You're now in Edit mode.

4. **To edit the title blocks, in the graphics area, right-click the text and choose Edit Text in Window.**

   The Edit Text Window dialog box opens.

5. **Change any items in the Edit Text Window dialog box and then click OK.**

6. **Move, delete, or add lines of text.**

   • *To delete,* click the line of text and press the Delete key.

   • *To move,* click the line of text and drag it to a new location.

   • *To add lines,* click the Line button on the Sketch toolbar.

7. **To add text, click Note on the Annotation toolbar.**

8. **Specify the text properties and then click to place the text in the location you want.**

9. **When you're done editing, in the FeatureManager design tree, right-click the sheet and select Edit Sheet.**

   You return to your drawing default edit sheet.

Placing the Drawing Views

After you edit your sheet format, it's time to place the model views on the drawing sheets. A *drawing view* shows a model in a particular orientation, scale, and display state. Drawing views are important because they convey information about how to build or assemble your model.

Your can create views of one or more parts and assemblies and include them in the same drawing. A perusal of the commands on the Drawings toolbar gives you an idea of the multitude of views you can include on a sheet.

When you open a drawing document in SolidWorks, the Drawings toolbar appears by default in the CommandManager. (You can read more about the CommandManager in Chapter 2.) The Drawings toolbar contains commands that let you add various model views to your drawings.

Your first view must be a standard view, and from there you create other views that are based on the standard views (Section or Detail, for example.) The Model View command allows you to place any single standard view, whereas Standard 3 Views places three standard views automatically.

The following sections explain the Drawings toolbar view commands, including how to place each view. Remember that you need to have a drawing document open to use these commands.

When you place a view, you need to drag it into position. You can see a preview of a model view as you're dragging it by setting this option: Choose Tools⇨ Options. On the Systems Options tab, select Drawings and select the Show Contents While Dragging Drawing View check box. (This option is generally set as a default.)

Model view

You can use the Model View command to place any standard view of your model. Standard views are just that: standard engineering views, such as front, top, and isometric. Item 1 in Figure 7-5 shows an example of this view type.

To insert a model view into your drawing, follow these steps:

1. **Click Model View on the Drawings toolbar, as shown in Item 2 in Figure 7-6.**

   The Model View PropertyManager appears, as shown in Figure 7-7. Any model that is active in SolidWorks appears in the Open Documents section.

2. **Double-click the model listed in the Open Documents section to place a new view, or click Browse to locate a different part or assembly file.**

3. **Select a view (Front or Back, for example) in the Orientation section.**

   Select the Preview check box to see a preview of the model before you place it.

4. **Set the options for display style and scales in the PropertyManager.**

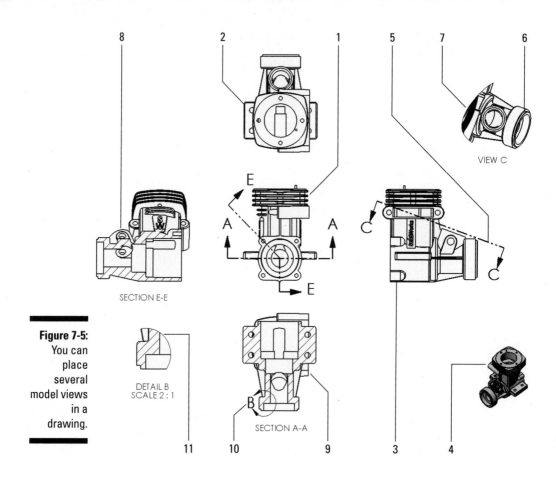

Figure 7-5: You can place several model views in a drawing.

8   2   1   5   7   6

VIEW C

E

A   A

C   C

SECTION E-E

DETAIL B
SCALE 2 : 1

E

B

SECTION A-A

11   10   9   3   4

Figure 7-6: The Drawings toolbar.

(1)
Standard
3 Views

(5)
Section
view

(3)
Projected
view

(7)
Crop
view

(4)
Auxiliary
view

(2)
Model
view

(6)
Detail
view

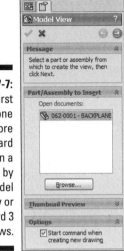

Figure 7-7:
You first place one or more standard views in a drawing by using Model view or Standard 3 Views.

5. **Click in the graphics area to place the view on the sheet.**

   As soon as you place the view, the Drawing View PropertyManager replaces the Model View PropertyManager. If you place an orthogonal view orientation, the Projected View PropertyManager appears, and you can place any number of projected views for any orthogonal view.

6. **Click OK in the Model View PropertyManager or in the Drawing View PropertyManager.**

   The PropertyManager closes, and the new drawing appears in the graphics area.

Standard 3 Views

The Standard 3 Views function creates three views (top, front, and right) and places them on your drawing automatically. This command is a good one to use if you're in a hurry. Standard views are generally the first that you place in a drawing. (Read the section "Opening a New Drawing Document," earlier in this chapter.)

To create three standard drawing views, follow these steps:

1. **Click Standard 3 Views on the Drawings toolbar (Item 1 in Figure 7-6, shown earlier).**

   The Standard 3 Views PropertyManager appears. In the PropertyManager, any open documents are listed in the Open Documents section.

2. **In the PropertyManager, double-click the model in the Open Documents section or choose Browse to locate a different one.**

   The three views appear in the drawing. The alignment of the top and side views is fixed in relation to the front view. You can move the top view vertically and the side view horizontally.

3. **Click OK.**

Projected view

This view allows you to create a new orthographically projected view from an existing, or *parent,* view. Refer to Item 2 in Figure 7-5 to see an example of this view type.

To create a projected view, follow these steps:

1. **Click Projected View on the Drawings toolbar (refer to Item 3 in Figure 7-6).**

   The Projected View PropertyManager appears.

2. **Select an existing view from which to project.**

   The new view is projected as normal (90 degrees) to the selected drawing view.

3. **Click in the graphics area to place the view.**

   The Projected View PropertyManager expands to include several options. You can project the new view in any direction (up, down, right, left, or isometric) from the selected view.

4. **Set options in the PropertyManager.**

   You can set the display style, scale, and dimension type. These options are the same ones covered in the earlier section "Opening a New Drawing Document."

5. **Click OK.**

Auxiliary view

This view is defined by folding the new view perpendicular to an existing view's part or assembly edge. Item 6 in Figure 7-5, shown earlier, shows an example of this view type.

To create an auxiliary view, follow these steps:

1. **Click Auxiliary View on the Drawings toolbar, shown in Item 4 in Figure 7-6, earlier in this chapter .**

   The Auxiliary View PropertyManager appears.

2. **Select a reference edge.**

   Don't select a horizontal or vertical edge, which create a standard Projection view.

   You can use an edge of a part, a silhouette edge, an axis, or a sketched line as a reference. If you sketch a line, activate the drawing view first.

3. **Move the pointer until the view is where you want it, and then click to place the view.**

   The PropertyManager for the drawing view appears.

4. **Set options in the PropertyManager.**

   You can set the display style, scale, and dimension type. These options are the same ones covered in the earlier section "Opening a New Drawing Document."

5. **Click OK.**

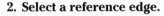

To override the default alignment of any view type, hold down the Ctrl key while placing the view.

Section view

A section view shows the internal details of a part or assembly. Section views make details easier to read than when you use hidden line views. You create a section view by drawing a line through the parent part. Item 9 in Figure 7-5 shows an example of this view type.

To create a section view, follow these steps:

1. **Click Section View on the Drawings toolbar (refer to Item 5 in Figure 7-6).**

   The Section View PropertyManager appears. The Line tool is active, and when you pass the pointer over an existing view, a box appears around the view.

2. **Sketch a section line through an existing view.**

   Draw the section line completely through the box of the model in the view. If the section line doesn't completely cut through the box, you're asked whether you want it to be a partial section cut. If you click Yes, the section view is created as a partial section view. If you click No, a full section view is created for you. After the line is complete, the section view appears as a preview.

3. **Move the pointer until the view is where you want it, and click to place the view.**

   The section view is aligned to the source, so you can only place the new view above or below the section line in the graphics area. After you place the view, the PropertyManager for that view appears.

4. **Set options in the PropertyManager.**

   You can set the display style, scale, and dimension type. These options are the same ones covered in the earlier section "Opening a New Drawing Document."

5. **Click OK.**

Aligned Section view

You create an aligned section view similar to a section view, but rather than sketch a single line, you sketch a section line that consists of two lines connected at an angle. The section view rotates the geometry on the angled segment so that the section can be projected. Item 8 in Figure 7-5 shows an example of this view type.

To create an aligned section view, follow these steps:

1. **Select Aligned Section View from the drop-down icon on the Drawings toolbar (refer to Item 5 in Figure 7-6).**

   The Aligned Section View PropertyManager appears. The Line tool is active, and when you pass the pointer over an existing view, a box appears around the view.

2. **Sketch two lines to define the section cut in a drawing view.**

   The two lines must connect at an angle. After you draw the line, a preview of the section appears in the graphics area near the pointer.

3. **Move the pointer until the view is where you want it, and click to place the view.**

   The view is aligned to the sketch segment you selected when you created the section line; the cut faces from the other segments are projected into the same plane.

4. **Set options in the PropertyManager.**

   You can set the display style, scale, and dimension type. These options are the same ones covered in the earlier section "Opening a New Drawing Document."

5. **Click OK.**

Detail view

A *detail view* is a blown-up portion of a small section of an existing view, which you draw a circle around. Item 11 in Figure 7-5 shows an example of this view type.

To create a detail view, follow these steps:

1. **Click Detail View on the Drawings toolbar (refer to Item 6 in Figure 7-6).**

   The Detail View PropertyManager appears, and the Circle tool is active. When you pass the pointer over a view, a box appears around the view.

2. **Draw a circle around the area you want to blow up.**

   When you complete the circle, a preview of the view appears next to your pointer, and the PropertyManager for the view appears. Click inside the drawing area to place the view.

3. **Set options in the PropertyManager.**

   You can set the display style, scale, and dimension type. These options are the same ones covered in the earlier section "Opening a New Drawing Document."

4. **Click OK.**

Crop view

A *crop view* displays only a portion of an existing view. Cropping a drawing is similar to cropping a photo. If you don't want to look at something in the photo (such as an ex-boyfriend or -girlfriend), you crop a rectangle around the part you want and leave out everything else. SolidWorks lets you crop any drawing view except a detail view, a view from which a detail view was made, or an exploded view. Item 7 in Figure 7-5 shows an example of this view type.

To create a crop view, follow these steps:

1. **Inside one of the drawing views, sketch a closed profile, such as a circle or a rectangle.**

   (You can read more on sketching in Chapter 3.)

   2. **In the graphics pane, select the sketch profile in the view you want to crop.**

      The box is highlighted to show the selected view.

   3. **Click Crop View on the Drawings toolbar (refer to Item 7 in Figure 7-6).**

      The image is cropped. Only the area inside the sketch is displayed. The rest of the view disappears.

Changing View Properties

Setting up drawing views is like arranging your living room: After you get everything in place, it's time to re-cover the sofa and move things around. Luckily, changing drawing views is easier than moving furniture. To edit a drawing view, click the view in the graphics area. The PropertyManager for that drawing view appears, as shown in Figure 7-8.

Figure 7-8:
The
Drawing
View
Property-
Manager.

The PropertyManager for drawing views comes in two versions, and which one you see depends on whether the view is a child or a parent of another view. A child view, such as a detail or section view, references another view that is its parent.

If a view has a parent, the boundary box of the parent view is also highlighted when you select the child view.

The PropertyManager displays only the values you can change, which include the following:

- ✔ **The view's display style (Wireframe or Hidden Lines Removed, for example):** You probably have a favorite display state. Mine is Shaded or Shaded with Edges, which makes the drawing more readable. When you pick a display style, consider who is reading the drawing and the type of printer you're using. Shaded views, for example, look better on higher-definition printers.

- ✔ **The scale of a model:** In the view's PropertyManager, you can select Use Sheet Scale, Use Parent Scale, or Use Custom Scale and then select a default scale or enter your own value.

- ✔ **The placement of the view:** You can move a view by dragging the view border or a model edge. Some limitations exist. If a view is aligned to a parent view, you cannot move it out of alignment.

- ✔ **The size of a drawing sheet:** Right-click the sheet in the FeatureManager design tree and choose Properties. In the Properties dialog box, select a standard size or select a custom sheet size and type the height and width values.

As you're working with view properties, the yellow message box at the top of the PropertyManager and the status window in the lower-left corner of the screen give clues to what is required for the current command.

Creating Drawing Dimensions

Dimensions are important in your drawings because they indicate the size of a part or an assembly and list other critical measurements that the supplier needs to know to make the product. Without dimensions, you don't know whether you're building a model airplane or the kind that people fly around in.

SolidWorks offers two types of dimensions: driving dimensions and driven dimensions. *Driving dimensions,* or model dimensions, control the size and shape of the model. Because *driven dimensions* are reference dimensions, they don't drive the size or location of features but instead help clarify the drawing.

You can change the display of any dimension type in the Dimension Property Manager (see Figure 7-9), which appears when you insert a dimension.

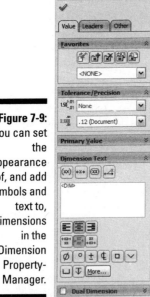

Figure 7-9:
You can set the appearance of, and add symbols and text to, dimensions in the Dimension Property-Manager.

You can set the following options from the Value tab:

- ✔ **Favorites:** You can create and save your favorite dimension styles in this section. Dimension styles save as `.sldfvt` files, and you can add them to your design library. (See Chapter 8 for more info on favorites.)

- ✔ **Tolerance/Precision:** You can change the number of decimal places in the dimension value and change the tolerance type and value in this field. *Tolerance* values determine how precise a manufacturer makes the parts.

- ✔ **Primary Value:** In this field, you can override the value of driving dimensions. Changes to a driving dimension are updated in the model.

- ✔ **Dimension Text:** You can place text and symbols around the dimension value, which is noted as `<DIM>`. Simply type the text. You can left align, center align, or justify the text by clicking the buttons below the text field.

You can insert model dimensions and annotations automatically by choosing Insert⇨Insert Model Items from the main menu. (You can find out more about Insert Model Items and other drawing automations in Chapter 8.)

Smart Dimension

You can add dimensions to drawings in several ways. One way is by using Smart Dimension on the Annotations toolbar. The Annotations toolbar appears by default in the CommandManager when you work on a drawing. You also find Smart Dimension on the Dimension/Relations toolbar.

You can add toolbar buttons to any toolbar. Right-click a tab in the CommandManager and choose Customize CommandManager. In the Customize dialog box, select the Commands tab and then select a category. Drag a command button to any toolbar. Click OK to close the dialog box.

Smart Dimensions knows what type of dimension to add based on the entity you select. If you select a line, Smart Dimension creates a dimension for the length of the line. Likewise, if you select an arc or a circle, Smart Dimensions creates a radial or diameter dimension.

To insert a model dimension in a drawing, follow these steps:

1. **Click Smart Dimension on the Annotations toolbar.**

   The pointer changes to a dimensioning tool icon to let you know that Smart Dimensions is active.

2. **Click the object to dimension.**

   You may need to zoom in on the view first. An object turns red as the pointer moves over it and green when you select it. When you click an entity, the dimension values appear above it in gray.

3. **Drag the dimension text for placement.**

   The dimension text follows the pointer, as shown in Figure 7-10.

4. **Click to place the dimension.**

   The dimension is fixed in place, and the Dimension PropertyManager appears.

5. **Set display options in the PropertyManager.**

   The Smart Dimension tool stays active so that you can continue inserting dimensions.

6. **Repeat Steps 2 through 5 to insert more dimensions.**

7. **Click OK when you're done.**

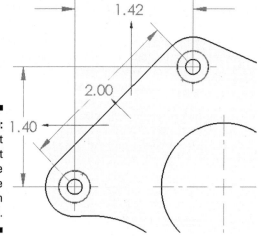

Figure 7-10:
Text
placement
can change
the
dimension
type.

Ordinate and baseline dimensions

Driven dimensions are strictly reference geometry and appear in gray in parentheses by default. You cannot edit the values in reference dimensions.

Two types of driven dimensions that may come in handy as you delve further into the world of drawings are ordinate and baseline dimensions:

  ✔ An *ordinate* set of dimensions is measured from a zero ordinate.

  ✔ A *baseline* set of dimensions is measured from an edge or a vertex.

Both ordinate and baseline dimensions are sets of entities that are grouped. When you drag any member of the group, all the members move together. To disconnect a dimension from the alignment group, right-click the dimension and select Break Alignment.

To create an ordinate dimension, follow these steps:

  1. **Choose Tools⇨Dimensions⇨Ordinate.**

     The pointer changes to indicate that the command is active.

  2. **Click the first item (edge or vertex, for example) from which all others will be measured to be the base (the 0.0 dimension).**

  3. **Click again to place the dimension outside the model.**

4. **Click the edges, vertices, or arcs you want to dimension using the same ordinate.**

   As you click each item, the dimension is placed in the view and aligned to the zero ordinate, as shown in Figure 7-11. The Dimension PropertyManager appears.

5. **Set display options in the PropertyManager.**

6. **Press Esc to exit from Ordinate mode.**

   Newly placed ordinate dimensions automatically jog to avoid overlapping text. The size of the jog is determined by the size of the text and the potentially overlapping area of the text.

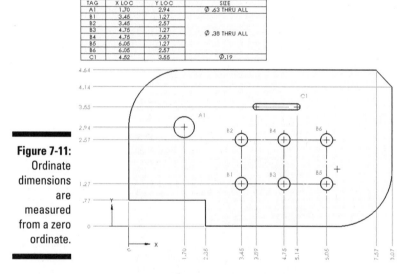

Figure 7-11:
Ordinate
dimensions
are
measured
from a zero
ordinate.

To create a baseline dimension, follow these steps:

1. **Choose Tools➪Dimensions➪Baseline.**

   The pointer changes to let you know that the command is active.

2. **Click the edge or vertex you want to use as a baseline.**

   The edge or vertex turns green when you select it.

3. **Click each of the edges or vertices you want to dimension.**

   Those items also turn green.

4. **Click to place the dimensions.**

   If you select an edge, dimensions are measured parallel to the selected edge. If you select a vertex, dimensions are measured point to point from the selected vertex.

   The Dimension PropertyManager appears.

5. **Set display options in the PropertyManager.**

6. **Click OK.**

Adding Reference Annotations

When you finish adding and inserting dimensions into your drawing views, you want to add *annotations.* These notes, symbols, and text define engineering characteristics and parameters in your model and in your drawings (see Figure 7-12).

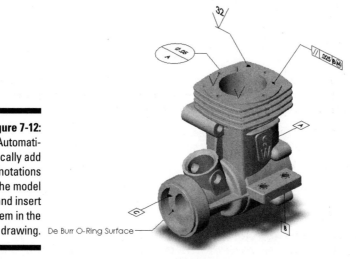

Figure 7-12: Automatically add annotations to the model and insert them in the drawing.

De Burr O-Ring Surface

Annotations behave like dimensions in each type of SolidWorks document. You can add annotations in a part or assembly document and then insert them in the drawing views, or you can create annotations in the drawing. (You insert model annotations into the drawing by using the Insert Model Items command, as covered in Chapter 8.)

In the following sections, I tell you how to add each type of annotation to any SolidWorks document, not just to the drawing.

Note

Notes are virtual sticky notes with a little extra feature. A note can contain text, symbols, a border, parametric text, and hyperlinks. (That's the extra feature). You can include or omit leaders in your notes. *Leaders* point to items in the drawing. Notes can include multiple lines of text and multiple text styles (font type or bold, for example), in case you want to "fancy them up."

To insert a note, follow these steps:

1. **Click Note on the Annotation toolbar, shown in Figure 7-13.**

   The Note PropertyManager appears, and a small rectangle appears near your pointer. If you move the pointer over an object, the object turns red and a leader extends from the note to the object.

Figure 7-13:
The
Annotation
toolbar.

2. **If you want a note with no leader, click in the graphics area to place the note. If you want a note with a leader, click an object and then click again in the graphics area to place the note.**

   The Formatting dialog box appears, with tools that allow you to change the font and style of the text.

3. **Type your text.**

   Text doesn't wrap automatically. To add multiple lines, press Enter.

4. **Adjust text properties.**

   You can change the appearance (font, size, and color) of the text by selecting text and then clicking the format tools in the Formatting dialog box (see Figure 7-14).

Figure 7-14:
Text
formatting
tools.

5. **Click the right corner of the Formatting dialog box to close the box.**

   The dialog box closes so that you can see more of the graphics area.

6. **Add symbols or links to the note by using the buttons in the Text Format section of the Note PropertyManager.**

   For symbols, place the pointer in the note text box where you want the item to appear and then click a symbol. Hyperlinks and custom properties link to the entire note. Your choices include

   - *Insert Hyperlink:* Click to include a hyperlink in the note. The text and characters in the note turn blue.

   - *Link to Property:* Click to link to a custom property. Linking to custom properties ensures that if the model changes, the note is updated.

   - *Add Symbol:* Insert a standard symbol from a symbol library. In the Symbols dialog box, select a library from the Symbol library list, then select a symbol name from the list, and click OK. The symbol's name is displayed in the text box, and the actual symbol appears in the note.

   - *Anchor:* Fixes the note in place to the current location.

   - *Geometric Tolerance:* Insert a Geometric Tolerance symbol into the note. The Geometric Tolerance PropertyManager and the Properties dialog box open so that you can define the symbol.

   - *Surface Finish:* Insert a Surface Finish symbol into the note. The Surface Finish PropertyManager opens so that you can define the symbol.

   - *Datum Feature:* Insert a datum feature symbol into the note. The Datum Feature PropertyManager opens so that you can define the symbol.

7. **Set other options in the PropertyManager.**

   Here are your choices:

   - *Leader:* Change the style and appearance of the leader.

   - *Border:* Click the options in the Border section to change the border around the note.

   - *Layer:* Indicate which drawing layer you want to attach the note to.

8. **Click OK.**

You can edit notes. Click a note to display the Note PropertyManager. Double-click a note to display the Formatting dialog box and the Note PropertyManager.

Balloon

You can create balloons in a drawing document. The balloons label the parts in the assembly and relate them to item numbers on the bill of materials. (You can find out how to insert a bill of materials into a drawing by reading the "Bill of materials" section, later in this chapter.)

However, you don't have to insert a bill of materials table into a drawing in order to add balloons. If the drawing has no bill of materials, the item numbers are the default values that SolidWorks would use if you inserted a bill of materials. If the active drawing sheet has no bill of materials but another sheet does, SolidWorks uses the numbers from the other bill of materials.

You can also add balloons in assembly documents and then import those balloons from an assembly document into a drawing view. (Chapter 8 explains more on how this process works.)

To insert a balloon, follow these steps:

1. **Click Balloon on the Annotation toolbar.**

   The Balloon PropertyManager appears, and a small circle follows your pointer around in the graphics area. If you move your pointer over an edge, the edge turns red. You can also place balloons on the surface of an object; note that the leader changes from an arrow to a dot.

2. **In the PropertyManager, in the Balloon Settings section, set the following:**

   - *Style:* Select from the list a style for the shape and border of the balloon. The style None displays the balloon text with no border.

   - *Size:* Select a size from the list — either a specified number of characters or Tight Fit, which adjusts automatically to the text.

   - *Balloon text:* Select the type of text for the balloon. Custom allows you to type the text. Item Number puts the item number in the bill of materials. Quantity adds the number of this part needed for the entire assembly.

3. **In the PropertyManager, in the Layers section, select a named drawing layer to add the balloon to.**

   The default is None. This option doesn't appear if you're adding balloons to an assembly.

4. **Click a part and then click to place the balloon.**

   A leader extends from the balloon to the part.

5. **To add balloons, repeat Steps 2 through 4.**

6. **Click OK.**

   The Balloon PropertyManager closes.

You can edit any balloon by clicking it to display the Balloon PropertyManager or pressing Delete on the keyboard.

Auto Balloon

You can speed the process of adding balloons to drawing views by using the Auto Balloon command. The Auto Balloon command automatically inserts balloons for all the components in a selected drawing view. SolidWorks inserts the balloons into the appropriate views without duplicates.

To insert balloons into a drawing view, follow these steps:

1. **Click Auto Balloon on the Annotation toolbar.**

   The Auto Balloon PropertyManager appears.

2. **Click the drawing view that you want to add balloons to.**

   You see a preview of the balloons appear around the view.

3. **In the PropertyManager, in the Balloon Layout section, specify how you want the balloons to align around the view.**

   You can choose a square pattern, on the top or to the left, for example. The balloons are placed outside the view border, and the leaders do not intersect. At this point, you can change the placement of all balloons by selecting a balloon and dragging it to a new position. This action changes the distance of the placed balloons from the Model view.

4. **In the Balloon Layout section, select the Ignore Multiple Instances check box.**

   When you select this option, balloons do not appear on multiple instances of a part.

5. **In the PropertyManager, in the Balloon Settings section, set these options:**

   • *Style:* Select from the list a style for the shape and border of the balloon. The style None displays the balloon text with no border.

   • *Size:* Select a size from the list — either a specified number of characters or Tight Fit, which adjusts automatically to the text.

- *Balloon text:* Select the type of text for the balloon. Custom allows you to type the text. Item Number puts the item number in the bill of materials. Quantity adds the number of this part needed for the entire assembly.

6. **In the PropertyManager, in the In Layers section, select a named drawing layer to add the balloon to.**

   The default is None. This option doesn't appear if you're adding balloons to an assembly.

7. **Click OK.**

   After you close the PropertyManager, you cannot open it again to change the orientation of the balloons. You can delete the balloons or undo the Auto Balloon command and then reinsert the balloons. You can drag a group of balloons or a single balloon.

Surface finish

You can specify the surface finish and texture of a part face by using a Surface Finish symbol. You can select the face in a part, an assembly, or a drawing document.

To insert a Surface Finish symbol, follow these steps:

1. **Click Surface Finish on the Annotation toolbar.**

   The Surface Finish PropertyManager appears.

2. **Click a button for a symbol type in the PropertyManager.**

3. **Enter a symbol layout value.**

   Different symbol types require different codes to specify manufacturing method or texture requirements, for example. You can enter these values, and they appear with the symbol in the graphics area.

4. **Set other options in PropertyManager.**

   You have these options:

   - *Format:* Use the document font or choose another font.

   - *Angle:* Set the angle or rotation for the symbol.

   - *Leader:* Select a leader style.

   - *Layer:* Select a named layer (or none) if you're adding symbols to a drawing.

5. **Click the graphics area to add a symbol.**

- *Multi-jog Leader:* A *multi-jog leader* adds bends to the normally straight leader line. Before placing the symbol, right-click and choose Use Multi-jog Leader to add a multi-jog leader. Click in the graphics area to place the arrow end of the leader and then move the pointer and click to add each jog point. To complete the leader and place the symbol, either double-click or right-click and choose End Leader.

- *Multiple instances:* Click as many times as necessary to place multiple copies.

- *Editing each instance:* You can change text and other items in the dialog box for each instance of the symbol.

- *Leaders:* If the symbol has a leader, click once to place the leader and then click a second time to place the symbol.

- *Multiple leaders:* While dragging the symbol and before placing it, press Ctrl. The note stops moving, and a second leader is added. While still holding Ctrl, click to place the leader. Click as many times as necessary to place additional leaders. Release Ctrl and click to place the symbol.

6. **Click OK.**

To edit a Surface Finish symbol, click the symbol, and the PropertyManager appears.

Geometric tolerance

A slight variation always occurs in the manufacturing process. *Tolerancing symbols* indicate how precisely the manufacturer needs to make a part. You can place Geometric Tolerancing symbols, with or without leaders, anywhere in a drawing, a part, an assembly, or a sketch, and you can attach a symbol anywhere on a dimension line. The Properties dialog box for Geometric Tolerance symbols offers selections based on the symbol you choose. Only the attributes that are appropriate for the selected symbol are available.

To add a Geometric Tolerance symbol, follow these steps:

1. **Select the face or edge of a part for the tolerance symbol.**

   Preselecting the location makes placement easier.

2. **Click Geometric Tolerance on the Annotation toolbar.**

   The Geometric Tolerance PropertyManager appears, and the Properties dialog box appears in the graphics area, where you can create a symbol.

3. **In the Properties dialog box, create a symbol.**

   Select any symbol, tolerance, datum references, and material conditions for the geometric tolerance.

4. **Set the display properties in the PropertyManager.**

   Choose the leader type, the font, and a named drawing layer (if you're working on a drawing) to apply the symbol to.

5. **Click OK.**

Datum target

Datum targets are used in conjunction with, and define the location and area for, Geometric Tolerance datum symbols. These annotations indicate how to set up the datums to inspect for accuracy after the part is manufactured. You can attach a datum target and symbol to a model face or an edge of any document.

To create a datum target and symbol, follow these steps:

1. **Click Datum Target on the Annotation toolbar.**

   The Datum Target PropertyManager appears.

2. **Set the following properties in the Settings section of the PropertyManager:**

   - *Styles:* Select a target symbol style.

   - *Target Area:* Select the target area display. You can choose an x, a circular or rectangular target area, or none.

   - *Target Area Size:* Enter the width and height for rectangles or the diameter for Xs and circles.

   - *Leader:* Select a leader style and an arrow style.

   - *Layer:* In drawings with named layers, select a layer.

3. **Click in the graphics area to place the target and then click again to place the symbol. If you selected No Target Symbol in the PropertyManager, click only once to place the annotation.**

   The datum target appears in the drawing. The command stays active, so you can place as many as you like.

4. **Continue inserting as many symbols as needed.**

5. **Click OK.**

   The PropertyManager closes.

You can move a datum target symbol by selecting the symbol and dragging the item. To edit the datum target symbol, select the symbol.

Datum symbol

Datum Feature symbols are used in conjunction with Geometric Tolerance symbols. These annotations indicate how inspection machines should check a part for accuracy after the part is manufactured. You can attach a Datum symbol to the following items:

- ✔ In a part or assembly, you can attach a symbol to a planar model surface or a reference plane.

- ✔ In a drawing view, you can attach a Datum symbol to a surface that appears as an edge (not a silhouette) or to a section view surface.

- ✔ If your model contains a Geometric Tolerance symbol frame, you can attach a Datum symbol to it.

- ✔ You can also put a Datum symbol in a note.

To add a datum feature, follow these steps:

1. **Click Datum Symbol on the Annotation toolbar.**

   The Datum Symbol PropertyManager appears.

2. **Edit the options in the Datum Symbol PropertyManager.**

   - *Label:* Enter the character to appear in the Datum Feature box.

   - *Use Document Style:* Select this check box if you want to use the document style, which follows the standard (ANSI or ISO, for example) specified in the Document Properties section. (Choose Tools➪Options. On the Document Properties tab, select Detailing and set options.) If you deselect this check box, you can select a different style of box and attachment. Each box has a different set of attachment styles.

   - *Layer:* In drawings with named layers, select a layer.

3. **Click in the graphics area to place the leader and then click again to place the symbol.**

4. **Continue inserting as many symbols as needed.**

   SolidWorks automatically increments the label in the datum feature box (A, B, and C, for example).

5. **Click OK.**

Cosmetic thread

A *cosmetic thread* represents the inner diameter of a thread on a boss (a bolt is an example of a boss) or the outer diameter of a thread on a hole and can include a hole callout. If you add a cosmetic thread while working in a drawing view, the part or assembly is updated to include a cosmetic thread feature.

To add a cosmetic thread, follow these steps:

1. **Choose Insert⇨Annotations⇨Cosmetic Thread.**

   The Cosmetic Thread PropertyManager appears.

2. **Select the holes to add cosmetic threads.**

   On a cylindrical feature (a boss, a cut, or a hole), select the circular edge where the thread begins. If the feature is a conical hole, select the major diameter. If the feature is a conical boss, select the minor diameter.

3. **Set the options in the PropertyManager for the end conditions (how deep) and enter the outer thread diameter.**

4. **Click OK.**

Center mark

You can place center marks in circles or arcs in drawings and use them as references for dimensioning. Center marks are available as single marks, in linear patterns, or in circular patterns.

To add a center mark to a drawing, follow these steps:

1. **Click Center Mark on the Annotation toolbar.**

   The Center Mark PropertyManager appears.

2. **Set Options in the PropertyManager.**

   - *Single Center Mark:* Insert a center mark into a single circle or arc. You can change the display attributes and angle of the center mark.

   - *Linear Center Mark:* Insert center marks into a linear pattern of circles or arcs. You can select connection lines and display attributes for linear patterns.

   - *Circular Center Mark:* Insert center marks into a circular pattern of circles or arcs. You can select circular lines, radial lines, a base center mark, and display attributes for circular patterns.

3. **Select a circular edge or an arc for center mark insertion.**

   You have three options, shown in Figure 7-15. Pick the single, linear, or radial centerline. The example shows all three types. A preview of the center mark appears.

4. **Click OK.**

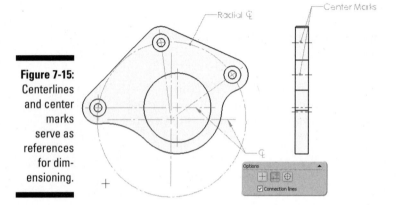

Centerline

Centerline annotations in drawings mark the center of a feature, such as when you see a hole viewed on an edge. The center marks are shown within the right side view in Figure 7-15.

To add a center mark to a drawing, follow these steps:

1. **Click Centerline on the Annotation toolbar.**

   The Centerline PropertyManager appears.

2. **Select one of the following:**

   - Two edges (parallel or nonparallel)
   - Two sketch segments (except splines)
   - A face (cylindrical, conical, toroidal, or swept)
   - A drawing view in the graphics area (except isometric orientation)
   - A feature, component, or drawing view in the FeatureManager design tree
   - The Insert Component Centerline option on the component short-cut menu or in the graphics area (assembly drawings only)

3. Click OK.

Centerlines appear in all appropriate segments of the selected entities.

To repeat any command, just press the Enter key, which restarts the last used command.

The display of annotations is controlled through the FeatureManager Annotations folder:

- ✔ **To turn the display of annotations on or off:** Select the Annotations folder in the FeatureManager. Then right-click the folder and select or deselect Display Annotations.

- ✔ **To display only certain types of annotations:** Select the Annotations folder. Then right-click it and choose Details. From there, you can choose the annotations types to display.

You can define standard annotations once and then reuse them by storing them in the Design Library. For example, you can create a standard note that you use often and save the annotation to the Design Library. To save the note (or any annotation) to the Design Library, right-click the item and choose Add to Design Library. When the Save As dialog box opens, type a name for the annotation, navigate to the proper folder, and click Save.

You can automatically insert centerlines and center marks when you create views by choosing Tools⇨Options. Then click the Document Properties tab. In the Detailing section, in the Auto Insert on View Creation field, select the Centerlines and Center Marks-Holes and Center Marks-Fillets check box.

Checking Spelling

A helpful feature that works on drawings is the Spelling Check tool. It's one of my favorite tools. (Just ask my editors.) This tool checks the spelling of notes, dimensions that include text, and drawing title blocks (when you're in Edit Sheet Format mode). Spelling Check operates similarly to the spell checker in Microsoft Office applications. SolidWorks identifies words that may be misspelled and provides suggested corrections based on a built-in dictionary. You can specify to correct the word, ignore the word, or add it to the dictionary. In fact, this function uses the Microsoft Word dictionary, so you need to have Microsoft Word 2000 or higher loaded on your computer to use it. The tool also has a special user dictionary (swengineering.dic) that picks up on SolidWorks terminology, and you can add custom dictionaries.

To check the spelling on a drawing, follow these steps:

1. **Choose Tools⇨Spelling.**

   The Spelling Check PropertyManager appears, and Spelling Check begins to scan your drawing. If it finds a misspelled word, the word appears in the PropertyManager. In the Suggestions section, a list of possible alternative spellings appears.

2. **If you want to change the spelling, select an alternative and click Change. Otherwise, click Ignore or Add to Dictionary.**

   Spelling Check continues to scan your document, picking up on any curiously spelled words.

3. **Continue until all misspellings are corrected.**

4. **Click OK.**

Defining Drawing Tables

Tables are a wonderful way to keep track of information, and they prove useful in SolidWorks drawings for a number of purposes. This section covers the bill of materials, revisions, and hole tables.

When you insert a table, a section in the PropertyManager for that table asks you to select a template. You can find standard templates for these items in `<install_dir>\lang\<language>`.

You can define many of the properties for tables described herein in the Tables sections of the Document Properties tab. Choose Tools⇨Options. On the Document Properties tab, select Detailing and then Tables.

Bill of materials

A *bill of materials,* generally referred to as simply BOM, lists all the parts and subassemblies in an assembly. The BOM is an important piece of literature. Suppliers use the bill of materials to quote jobs and to order parts.

All companies have their own BOM formats that they like to use. In this section, I focus on creating a simple bill of materials table. The section "Changing and customizing tables," at the end of this chapter, explains how to change and customize the different types of tables.

SolidWorks maintains a list of items that go into an assembly and tracks the part numbers, quantity, and other attributes. A drawing can contain a

Anchors away!

Anchors make tables easier to place in the drawing. You can define anchors in the drawing format by editing the sheet format. Right-click a sheet in the FeatureManager design tree and choose Edit Sheet Format. Right-click the corner of the existing geometry within the sheet format to use as an anchor in the graphics area and choose the table type from the Set As Anchor menu.

When you insert a table, set the Table Anchor corner to use for the table. If you have a predefined anchor, select the Attach to Anchor check box to attach the table to the anchor within the table's PropertyManager.

table-based BOM or a Microsoft Excel–based bill of materials, but not both. In this chapter, I cover the table-based BOM.

You can use custom properties defined in the individual part and assembly documents to fill in the BOM table so that you don't have to enter values in the BOM table manually. You can make formatting changes to the table after you save it to a template. By doing this little bit of extra work up front, you make inserting a BOM, as shown in Figure 7-16, into a drawing simple and straightforward.

To insert a BOM table, follow these steps:

1. **Choose Insert⇨Table⇨Bill of Materials.**

   The Bill of Materials Table PropertyManager appears, and a message prompts you to select a view.

2. **Click a drawing view to identify the assembly from which to extract the BOM.**

   The PropertyManager expands to show several other options.

3. **In the Table Template section, click the Open Table Template for Bill of Materials button.**

   The Select BOM Template dialog box appears.

4. **Select a table template and click Open.**

   The name of the template appears in the Table Template field.

5. **In the Table Anchor section, select the Attach to Anchor check box and click an option for the anchored corner.**

   This option determines which corner of the table is fixed to the drawing.

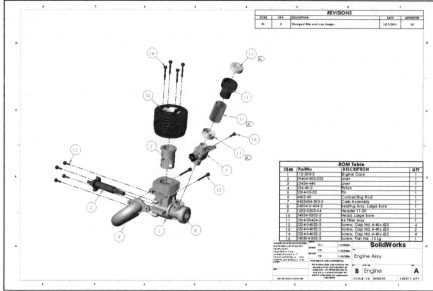

Figure 7-16:
A bill of materials lists all parts in an assembly, along with part numbers and quantity.

6. **In BOM type, select a check box next to one of these options:**

   • *Top-Level Only:* Lists parts and subassemblies but not subassembly components.

   • *Parts Only:* Doesn't list subassemblies; lists subassembly components as individual items.

   • *Indented Assemblies:* Lists subassemblies; indents subassembly components below their subassemblies without item numbers.

7. **In the Configurations section, manually select the configurations to include quantities in the bill of materials or click Select All Configurations or Unselect All Configurations.**

8. **Click OK and, if you did not select Attach to Anchor in Step 5, click the graphics area to place the table.**

   The table appears in the drawing and in the FeatureManager design tree.

Revision table

Drawings can go through a lot of changes, and it's important to track the who, what, when, and why of every revision the document goes through and to track approvals, too.

With this in mind, SolidWorks allows you to insert a revision table into a drawing. Figure 7-16 (refer to the preceding section) denotes the revisions with five-sided flags (my personal preference). The revision table gives you a place to track changes and revision numbers by date. You can type a description of the change, and the table has a column for approvals.

In Figure 7-16, you can take advantage of drawing layers for your revision symbols. Before you insert the revision table, define the layer for revision marks with a different color, which does two things:

✔ Highlights the revision marks in another color

✔ Lets you turn off the revision marks by turning off the layer

When creating the Revision symbol, select the layer used for Revision symbols.

If the layer doesn't exist, open the Layer dialog box by selecting the Layer toolbar. Click New, enter the layer name in the Name field, and click OK within the Layer dialog box. If the Layer toolbar isn't active, turn it on by choosing View➪Toolbars➪Layer. (See Chapter 8 for more details on layers.)

To insert a revision table into your open drawing, follow these steps:

1. **Choose Insert➪Tables➪Revision Table.**

   The Revision Table PropertyManager appears.

2. **Set the following properties in the PropertyManager:**

   • *Table Template:* Browse for a template to choose a standard or custom revision template.

   • *Table Anchor:* Set the anchored corner.

   • *Attach to Anchor:* Attach the specified corner to the table anchor.

   • *Revision Symbol Shapes:* Select a border shape for a revision symbol.

   • *Options:* Select a check box for the Enable symbol when adding a new revision. You can click in the graphics area to place Revision symbols when you add a revision table. If you clear this option or add a symbol later, right-click in a row of the revision table, choose Revisions➪Add Symbol, and then click in the graphics are to place symbols. If you edit revision text, the symbols are updated.

3. **Click OK and, if you did not select the Attach to Anchor option, click the graphics area to place the table.**

   The table appears in the drawing and in the FeatureManager design tree.

To add a revision to the table, follow these steps:

1. **Right-click in the revision table and choose Revisions⇨Add Revision.**

   If the Revision Symbol option is turned on, the symbol appears next to the cursor after the table is placed. If you don't want to place a symbol now, press Esc before continuing to Step 2.

2. **Double-click inside a revision field.**

   The field is highlighted, and the text inside the box is selected. The Note PropertyManager appears in the left pane.

3. **Type the new text.**

4. **To change the style or justification of the text, highlight the text and enter the new style in the Note PropertyManager.**

   The text is updated in the revision table.

5. **To add a Revision symbol, click where you want to add the symbol and click Add Symbol in the Note PropertyManager.**

   The Symbols dialog box opens.

6. **In the dialog box, select a symbol library by using the pull-down arrow.**

   A list of available symbols appears in the box below the Library field. If you select a symbol, a preview appears in the dialog box.

7. **Choose a symbol and click OK.**

   The symbol appears in the revision table.

8. **Click OK in the Note PropertyManager.**

The DrawCompare command compares all entities between two documents. The differences between the drawings are displayed in color codes. When you use this command to compare two versions of a drawing, you can check for any design changes that were left unmarked in the revision table. Choose Tools⇨DrawCompare. In the DrawCompare dialog box, browse to select a drawing for Drawing 1 and Drawing 2. In each of the fields, select a color. The two drawings appear side by side. In the Differences field, you can see what was removed and what was added.

Hole tables

Hole tables in drawings measure the positions of selected holes from a specified origin. SolidWorks labels each hole with a tag that corresponds to a row in the hole table (see Figure 7-17).

The Hole Table command creates a table that shows the XY coordinates and hole size for each hole you select. If you make a change to the model, the change is reflected in the hole table.

To insert a hole table in an open drawing, follow these steps:

1. **Choose Insert⇨Tables⇨Hole Table.**

   The Hole Table PropertyManager appears with the Origin field active.

2. **In the graphics area, select a vertex to specify the origin datum.**

   You can select an X axis and a Y axis to define a vertex for the datum. You can also drag the origin into position after you place the table. The Edges/Faces field becomes active.

3. **Select hole edges or select a model face.**

   The holes are added to the Edges/Faces field. If you select a face, all the holes are added to the table.

4. **In the PropertyManager, select a template or anchor.**

5. **Click OK and, if you did not select the Attach to Anchor option, click the graphics area to place the table.**

   The hole table appears in the drawing and in the FeatureManager design tree.

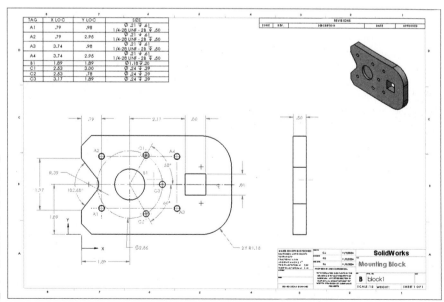

Figure 7-17:
Hole tables in drawings track holes and are updated with the model.

Changing and customizing tables

You're not stuck with the standard table templates. You can customize them to fit your requirements. The table types have similar formats but also some differences — for example, BOM format for bill of materials or Revisions for revision tables).

To edit table values, click once inside the table to summon the Table Formatting dialog box, as shown in Figure 7-18. You can change the values in the selected cell or select another area to change. When you're editing a table, an additional grid appears around the table and shows row and column labels.

When you select a single table cell, the Table Formatting dialog box appears and displays buttons for text formatting options, such as font, alignment, and fit or rotate text. If you select an entire column, the Column PropertyManager also appears for setting column property options. If you click the upper-left corner of the table, the Table PropertyManager appears with options of its own. Some of the most important items are described in this list:

- **Cell Properties:** *When you're selecting a single cell,* specify the justification and orientation of text in the cells and the font style. You can select the table font (as specified in the Table Format PropertyManager) or specify a new font. In the bill of materials table, you can use Cell Properties to total the rows or columns.

- **Column Properties:** *When you're selecting a column,* click to access table column properties. In the Column PropertyManager, you can select a column type — for example, Revision or Approved — and change its header in the table.

✔ **Table Properties:** *When you're selecting the upper-left corner,* display the Revision Table PropertyManager, where you can choose a corner for anchoring the table. For the revision table, you can also select Revision symbol shapes, change the border around the table, and specify a named layer to associate the table to.

You can move an entire table to a new position on your drawing sheet. Put your pointer around the upper-right or -left corner of a table. When the pointer changes to a set of four arrows pointing in each direction, click and drag the table. Releasing the mouse sets the final position of the table.

You can customize your favorite table formats and save them as templates. Right-click a table and choose Save As Template. In the Save As dialog box, type a name for the template and browse to its saved location. Make sure that you store these templates in a common location for all users to access. To set the location for storing templates, choose Tool⇨Options. On the Systems Options tab, select File Locations. Show folders for the template you want to save, click Add, and browse for the folder location.

Chapter 8

Speeding It Up: Automating the Drawing

In This Chapter

▶ Marking dimensions in the model for importing into the drawing

▶ Organizing drawing information with layers

▶ Picking favorites to speed drawing creation

▶ Linking the sheet format to custom properties

*I*n this chapter, I give you hints, tips, and shortcuts that you can use to speed up the drawing creation process. You discover how to import dimensions, annotations, and reference geometry directly from the model. You also find out how to make the most of custom properties and how to create templates to jump-start your drawings. (For information on creating a drawing, see Chapter 7.)

Planning for the Drawing

The devil's in the details, and this saying is especially true when you're creating manufacturing drawings. The person who designs a product is the one who knows the most about it. As the designer, you need to communicate that wealth of information in your head to the person making the product, by including the right amount of detail (not too much, and not too little) in your drawings.

SolidWorks lets you incorporate manufacturing details into your model. You can mark dimensions and add finishing symbols, geometric tolerances, and other annotations to the model that you want to import into the drawing. Your model should contain all the information you need to create the drawings.

Here are the basic steps to follow as you design:

1. When you design the model, create the sketches the way you want them to show up in the drawing. Add annotations to the model and mark in the Modify dialog box the dimensions you want to import into the drawing. (The next section explains how to do so.)

2. Set up your sheet formats and drawing templates in advance and put them where they're readily available to the design team. Include links to custom properties and the drawing symbols you use most often.

3. After you place the drawing views, use the Model Items command to insert dimensions, annotations, and reference geometry automatically. (See the next section for more on this command.)

Inserting Model Items

In Chapter 7, I tell you ways to insert dimensions and annotations manually in both the model and the drawing. In this chapter, I introduce you to Model Items, a powerful command in SolidWorks that allows you to insert dimensions, annotations, and reference geometry into the drawing views automatically.

Here's how it works: When you create a dimension in a model, you can mark it for import into the drawing. This option is usually turned on by default, but if not, in the Modify dialog box, which appears when you add a dimension to a model, click the Mark Dimension to Be Imported into Drawing icon. (To deselect a dimension for import, click the icon again.) Be sure to add any annotations and symbols in the model that are important to the manufacturing process.

After you place all the drawing views, you can use the Model Items command to automatically insert the dimensions, annotations, and reference geometry from the model. Model Items gives you the option to import all dimensions or only those marked for import. You can also select the specific types of annotations and reference geometry you want to import.

Model Items imports model dimensions, also known as *driving dimensions* because they drive changes in the model geometry. SolidWorks shows model dimensions in black. You can read more about dimension types in Chapter 7.

There are several advantages to using Model Items:

✔ **You save time inserting items automatically.** If you couldn't insert dimensions automatically, you would first have to dimension the sketches to create the part features and then re-create those dimensions again in the drawing, creating twice the amount of work.

✔ **You can capture design intent in the part, not as an afterthought when creating a drawing.** When you create the part features, why not spend a little extra time adding the information you need in your drawings?

✔ **If tolerance or dimension values change in the drawing, your part is updated automatically.** Conversely, any change to the model is updated in the drawing. You don't need to redo work on either side.

The example shown in Figure 8-1 shows how I used Insert Model for the profile feature and the holes. Model Items requires no extra cleanup. Simply define the placement and other dimension attributes in the sketch and mark the dimension for import. I also used Model Items to import surface-finish annotations.

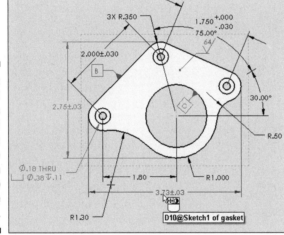

Figure 8-1:
The Model Items command lets you select the dimension types to import to the drawing.

Before using the Model Items command, you should place all your drawing views. To insert Model Items into an open drawing, follow these steps:

1. **Choose Insert⇨Model Items.**

   The Model Items PropertyManager appears, as shown in Figure 8-2. You should carefully set all options in the PropertyManager.

2. **In the Source/Destination area, select one of these options:**

   • *Entire Model:* Model Items inserts entities (dimensions, annotations, and reference geometry) from the entire model.

   • *Selected Feature:* Model Items inserts entities from only the features or components you select in the graphics area.

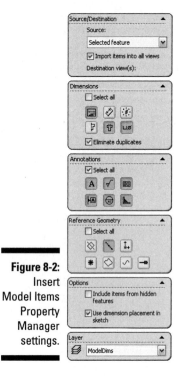

Figure 8-2:
Insert
Model Items
Property
Manager
settings.

If you want to import items into all views, select the Import Items into All Views check box. Otherwise, deselect the option and select a single model view.

If you select a model view, the items appear in that view.

3. In the Dimensions area, click the dimension type you want to insert:

- *Marked for Drawing:* Inserts only the dimensions marked for drawing in the Modify dialog box.

- *Instance/Revolution Counts:* Inserts only the number of instances for linear or circular patterns.

- *Hole Wizard Profiles:* Inserts only dimensions for Hole Wizard profiles.

- *Hole Wizard Locations:* Inserts only dimensions for Hole Wizard locations.

- *Hole Callout:* Inserts only dimensions for hole callouts.

- *Eliminate Duplicates:* Prevents duplicate dimensions from appearing in different drawing views.

4. **In the Annotations area, click Select All if you want to import all annotations in the model. Otherwise, click to select the specific types.**

   You can import notes, surface finishes, geometric tolerances, datums, datum targets, or welds. Cosmetic threads can be imported into assembly drawings only.

5. **In the Reference Geometry area, select the Select All check box if you want to import all reference geometry in the model. Otherwise, click to select the specific types.**

   Selection options include planes, axis, points, origins, surfaces, curves, and routing points.

6. **In the Options area, select the check box for the following options:**

   - *Include Items from Hidden Features:* Imports items that are in features or parts that are hidden.

   - *Use Dimension Placement in Sketch:* Inserts model dimensions from the part in the same locations in the drawing.

7. **In the Layer area, if the drawing has named layers, select one to add the items to it.**

8. **Click OK.**

   The Model Items PropertyManager closes, and the dimensions and annotations appear in the drawing view or views.

If your drawing view is cluttered with dimensions after using model items, you can hide some dimensions so that they're no longer visible. Right-click a dimension and choose Hide. You can click and drag to move a selected dimension.

Managing Drawing Clutter with Layers

Layers are a clever way to organize information in your drawings. *Layers* are "transparent" sheets that stack up to form the final drawing. You can create as many layers as you want, depending on how complex the drawing is, and group information on the various layers. One layer may contain all the holes in an assembly, and another may contain only dimensions and annotations.

You can turn layers on and off, depending on what you want to display or print, and you can move entities from one layer to another. And, so that you can find your way around, SolidWorks lets you assign a line color, thickness, and style for the entities on the different layers.

TIP

To make sure that you apply layers consistently in all your drawings, define layers within the document templates for drawings. Create the standard layer names and then assign the 2D sketch entities to the appropriate layer. To move a selected entity to a new layer, click the Move button within the Layer dialog box.

Creating layers

To create a new drawing layer in a drawing, follow these steps:

1. **Click Layer Properties on the Line Format toolbar.**

   You may have to add the Line Format toolbar to the CommandManager. (Chapter 2 explains how to customize the CommandManager.)

   The Layers dialog box, shown in Figure 8-3, has Name, Description, On/Off, Color, Style, and Thickness column headings. If you can't read a column heading, you can expand it by clicking the vertical line between the headings and dragging it one way or the other.

Figure 8-3:
In the
Layers
dialog box,
you define
line color
and style for
layers.

2. **Click New.**

   Layer1 appears in the Name column for the first new layer. The text is highlighted so that you can type a new name over it.

3. **Enter a name for your new layer.**

   The new layer name appears in the Name column. A yellow arrow in front of the name indicates that this layer is active. (The layer named FORMAT is included within a drawing and is not selected.)

TIP

   To create the most benefit from using layer organization, give your layer a name that clearly indicates what the layer will contain.

4. **To add a description for the new layer, double-click the Description column and enter the text.**

   The description appears in the Description column.

5. **To specify the line color for the parts on this layer, click the Color box, select a color in the Color dialog box, and then click OK.**

   The box is set to the new color. The Color dialog box also has a Define Custom Colors option. You can use it to define and add custom color options.

6. **To specify a line style, click in the Style column and select the desired line style from the list.**

   Style types include Solid, Dashed, and Phantom, for example.

7. **To specify a line thickness, click in the Thickness column and select a line thickness from the list.**

8. **Repeat Steps 2 through 7 to add any other layers you need.**

9. **Click OK.**

   The Layers dialog box closes, and your new layers are created. When you add new entities to a drawing, they appear on the active layer.

Working with layers

You can activate a layer, move layers, and maneuver between layers from inside the Layers dialog box. To activate or edit layers, click Layer Properties on the Line Format toolbar. You can choose one of these options:

✔ **Active:** An arrow indicates which layer is active. To activate a layer, click next to the layer name, and an arrow appears.

✔ **On/Off:** A yellow light bulb appears when a layer is visible. To hide a layer, click its light bulb. The light bulb turns gray, and all entities on the layer are hidden. To turn on the layer again, click the light bulb.

✔ **Move:** To move entities to the active layer, select the entities in the drawing and click Move. You can select multiple items by holding down the Ctrl key when you click them.

✔ **Delete:** To delete a layer, select the layer name and press Delete on your keyboard.

Automating Drawing Creation

Unless you like repetition, you can work smarter when you're creating drawings. This section covers various SolidWorks features that allow you to reuse information and churn out drawings faster.

Using custom properties

Custom properties are metadata about a part or assembly document. *Metadata* is data about data. Think of a book: The book has pages full of information and also contains information about the book itself, such as the author, publisher, and copyright. This detailed information is metadata.

Information that SolidWorks stores about the model includes the who, what, why, and when of file creation as well as material, vendor information, and approvals, for example. You can create custom properties in a model that carry over to drawings. The title block, notes, and bill of materials include links to custom properties. Other downstream applications (such as analysis and product data management software) also use custom properties from the model. COSMOSWorks, for example, reads the material type and weight of a model to perform its calculations for finite element analysis.

You can add custom properties to any active drawing, part, or assembly document. To access custom properties, open a SolidWorks document and choose File⇨Properties. The Summary Information dialog box, shown in Figure 8-4, appears.

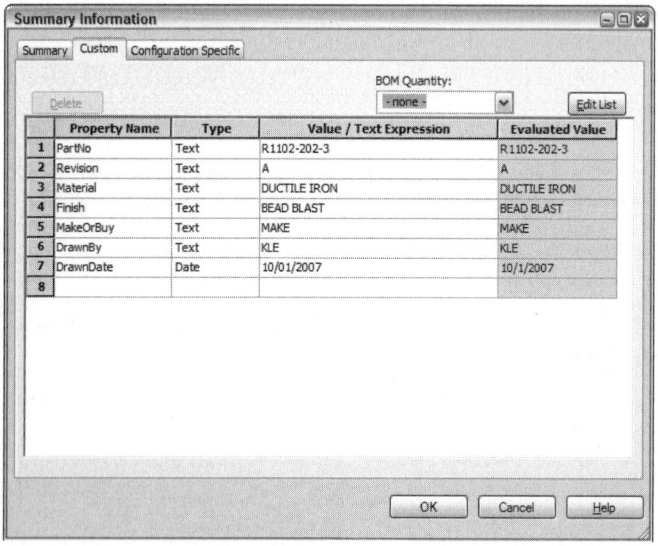

Figure 8-4:
On the Custom tab in the Summary Information dialog box, you can set custom properties for the entire document.

Summary Information
Summary	Custom	Configuration Specific

BOM Quantity:
- none - ▾   Edit List

Delete

	Property Name	Type	Value / Text Expression	Evaluated Value
1	PartNo	Text	R1102-202-3	R1102-202-3
2	Revision	Text	A	A
3	Material	Text	DUCTILE IRON	DUCTILE IRON
4	Finish	Text	BEAD BLAST	BEAD BLAST
5	MakeOrBuy	Text	MAKE	MAKE
6	DrawnBy	Text	KLE	KLE
7	DrawnDate	Date	10/01/2007	10/1/2007
8				

OK   Cancel   Help

The dialog box contains three tabs for parts and assemblies; for drawings, you see only two tabs (drawings don't include the Configuration Specific tab):

✔ **Summary:** See a basic summary of the document, such as author, key-words, comments, title, and subject. This tab also has a Statistics box that tells you when the document was created and last saved and who saved it last.

✔ **Custom:** Enter custom properties that apply to the entire document. These properties are document specific, which means they're controlled by the SolidWorks document (part, assembly, and drawing) templates and apply to all part and assembly configurations.

✔ **Configuration Specific:** Define custom properties that vary from one configuration to another. *Configurations* are variations of a model stored in the same document. The table on the Configurations Specific tab has the same heading as the one on the Custom tab, but you can specify which configuration in the document it applies to.

To add custom or configuration properties to an open part or assembly document, follow these steps:

1. **Choose File⇨Properties.**

   The Summary Information dialog box appears. The dialog box has three tabs: Summary, Custom, and Configuration Specific.

2. **Select the Custom or Configuration Specific tab.**

   A table appears with the following headings: Property Name, Type, Value/Text Expression, and Evaluated Value. The Configuration Specific tab has a field in which you can select the configuration to which you want to apply the property.

3. **If you are defining a property on the Configuration Specific tab, in the Applies To field, select a configuration from the drop-down list.**

   Now any custom properties you set in the table apply to only the configuration that appears in the Applies To field.

4. **Click the first blank cell in the Property Name column and then type a name or choose one from the list.**

   To move between cells in the table, press Tab or Enter, or click in the cell you want to move to.

   To add custom properties to the drop-down list, click Edit List in the Summary Information dialog box, type a new name in the Edit Custom Property List dialog box, and click Add. Select a property and click Delete, Move Up, or Move Down to delete or move a custom property in the list.

5. **Select a type from the drop-down list.**

   Type describes the value you can enter in the Value/Text Expression cell. Type options include text, date, number, and yes or no. For example, if you want someone to be able to indicate whether a part is a fastener by using the IsFastener custom property, select the Yes or No type option.

6. **In the Value/Text Expression column, enter a custom-property value that's compatible with the selection in the Type cell.**

    You can type a value, or you can select a value from a drop-down list if it's available. For example, if you select Yes or No for type, Yes or No appears in the drop-down list in the Value/Text Expression cell. You must enter a valid type.

7. **Press Tab or Enter.**

    The value of the property appears in the Evaluated Value column.

8. **Repeat Steps 2 through 7 to add any other custom properties.**

9. **Click OK.**

    The Summary Information dialog box closes, and custom properties are added to the model.

If you enter a date in the custom properties, it must be a valid date. Don't enter a date that's valid but inaccurate. For example, the created date is unlikely to be 10/12/1947.

To ensure that custom properties are available on each document, you should define the custom properties in the drawing, part, and assembly document templates. (Chapter 2 explains how to create templates.)

Setting up a drawing sheet format

A *drawing sheet* is a page in a drawing document. A *sheet format* is the background for your drawing and typically includes elements such as page size, orientation, standard text, borders, and title block. Sheets in a drawing can use different formats. You select a sheet format when you open a new drawing.

Standard sheet formats in SolidWorks include links to custom properties. You can edit a title block in a sheet format by using the steps I outline in Chapter 7. You can use the Note PropertyManager, which appears when you edit text in the title block, to edit or add links to custom properties in the drawing document or in the model. For example, you can include links to the model that include the author, comments, and filename. The links are populated if the information exists in the custom properties of the model.

One advantage to using custom properties to define the information in the title block is that after you set up the title block, you can use custom properties to edit all the values, and you don't have to use the Edit Sheet function. Figure 8-5 shows the custom properties used to automatically annotate the drawing format.

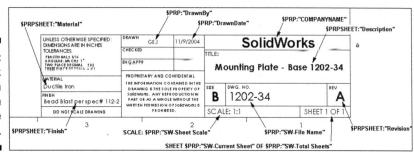

Figure 8-5: You can link to custom properties in the title block.

The text notes link to the custom properties. The notes shown (with labels) link to custom properties defined in the drawing. These notes link to values by using the following formats:

- ✔ **($PRP:<value>):** Links to the custom properties in the model used to create the drawing views
- ✔ **($PRPSHEET:<value>):** Links to custom properties from the current drawing document
- ✔ **($PRP: "SW-Total Sheets"):** Lists special SolidWorks system values (for example, total sheets, sheet number, and filename)

The Link to Property feature links the contents of the text note to a custom property, as shown in Figure 8-6.

SolidWorks lets you customize sheet formats and save them for future use as files with an .slddrt extension. You can store these files in the Design Library. You can also create drawing templates that use custom sheet formats.

Chapter 7 explains how to edit a drawing sheet format. The following steps tell you how to save a drawing sheet format for use in other drawings.

To save a new format as the standard A-Landscape format, follow these steps:

1. **Choose File⇨Save Sheet Format.**

   The Save Sheet Format dialog box opens. The Save As Type option defaults to Sheet format (*.slddrt).

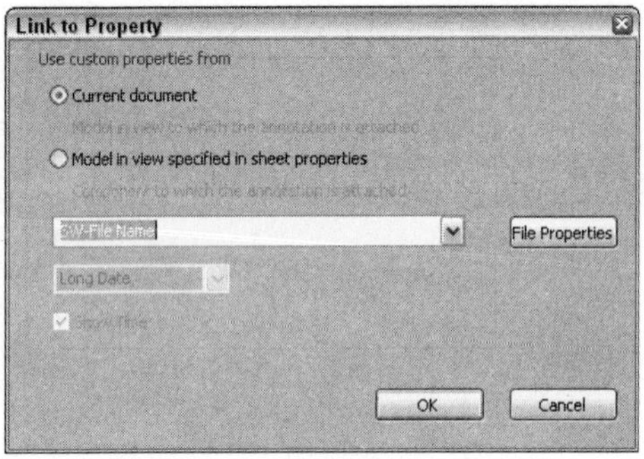

Figure 8-6:
You can
create and
edit links to
custom
properties.

2. **In the Save In box, use the drop-down menu to navigate to the folder *<install_dir>*\data\.**

   You see the saved format for various sheet sizes.

3. **Click a-landscape.**

   The text *a-landscape* appears on the File name drop-down list.

4. **Click Save.**

   SolidWorks notifies you that the file already exists and asks whether you want to replace it.

5. **Click Yes to confirm that you want to overwrite the existing sheet format.**

   The new format is saved. Now, when you open a new drawing, those changes appear anytime you select that drawing sheet size.

Using predefined views to start drawings

After you start a drawing, you need to insert and position the drawing views. You also may need to adjust the scale of the drawing views. (SolidWorks formats are a 1:1 size ratio; no scaling required.)

Wait — there's a simpler way. When you start a drawing, use a drawing template with predefined views. After you set up the predefined views once, you just need to apply the template each time you apply a new document, and the template takes care of the rest for you.

You can create templates with the drawing sheet size and types of views that are commonly used (top, front, right, and isometric). Figure 8-7 shows an example of four predefined views saved within a drawing template. Predefined drawing views are similar to the Multiple View option.

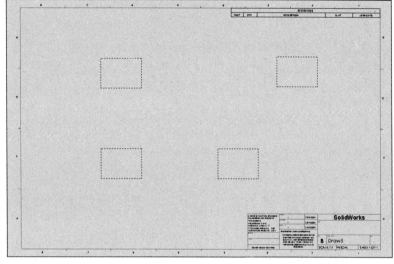

Figure 8-7:
You can
speed
drawing
creation
with
predefined
views.

To insert a predefined view into a drawing, follow these steps:

1. **Click Insert➪Drawing View➪Predefined.**

   A box appears near the pointer.

2. **Click in the graphics area to place the view.**

   The Drawing View PropertyManager appears in the left pane.

3. **In the PropertyManager, leave the Insert Model option blank.**

   By leaving it blank, the views automatically propagate when you make a drawing from a part or model and choose this template.

4. **Set remaining options in the PropertyManager:**

   • *Orientation:* Select a standard view.

   • *Scale:* Select Use Sheet Scale, or Use Custom Scale and select or enter a scale ratio.

   • *Dimension Type:* Select Projected or True.

5. **Click Project View from the Views toolbar to add more views to the drawing.**

6. **Click in the graphics area to place the view.**

   The Drawing View PropertyManager appears in the left pane.

   7. Repeat Steps 5 and 6 to create any other views.

   8. Click OK.

   The PropertyManager closes.

   9. Click Save As and save the drawing as a template.

   Chapter 2 offers more detail on how to save templates.

You can populate predefined views in a few ways. For example, you can drag a model from the FeatureManager design tree of an open part or assembly document into the drawing document. All available predefined views are populated.

Working with Dimension Favorites

Dimension favorites is another feature that saves you time in drawing creation and makes the styles more consistent. It lets you define standard dimension styles (decimal precision and line style, for example) that you can use throughout a drawing, and using it is similar to using styles in Microsoft Word.

You define dimension favorites in the Dimension PropertyManager, which appears when you insert or select a dimension to edit in a drawing view. The Favorites section (see Figure 8-8) is at the top of the PropertyManager. Any properties you can define within the dimension PropertyManager can also be saved as dimension favorites.

Figure 8-8:
The dimension favorite Property Manager field.

Here are the options in the Dimension PropertyManager that you can use to add, edit, or delete a favorite:

   ✔ **Apply the Default Attribute to Selected Dimensions:** Resets selected dimensions to the document defaults.

✔ **Add or Update a Favorite:** Opens the Favorite dialog box, where you can type a name to add a new favorite to the current document. Or, choose a Favorite from the list to do either of the following:

- *Update All Annotations Linked to This Favorite:* All annotations using the selected favorite style are updated with the changes to the selected annotation.

- *Break All Links to This Favorite:* All links between the selected favorite and annotations are broken. The annotations retain the attributes previously applied by the favorite unless the annotations are subsequently reset to the document default.

✔ **Delete a Favorite:** Deletes the selected favorite in the document.

✔ **Save a Favorite:** Opens the Save As dialog box with Favorite (.sldfvt) as the default file type to save an existing favorite.

✔ **Load Favorites:** Opens the Open dialog box with Favorite (.sldfvt) as the active file type. You can use Ctrl or Shift to select multiple files.

✔ **Set a Current Favorite:** Choose a favorite style from the list to apply to selected dimensions or to delete or save the favorite.

To ensure that dimension favorites are available in all document types, you should define them within the document templates. You can define them by setting them up from scratch or loading them from another drawing and then saving the new drawing as a template file.

Creating the Drawing Template

Templates are important tools in creating drawings. You can use templates to capture all your design standards and open one each time you start a new drawing. Here are the basic steps for creating a drawing template. (See Chapters 7 and the earlier sections in this chapter for all the details.) You may want to think of these steps as a sort of checklist:

1. **Open a new drawing document.**

   This new document will become your custom template. After you make changes to it, you should save this document in the template format so that it appears in the Advanced mode of the New SolidWorks Document dialog box. Chapter 2 provides details on how to create a template.

2. **Define the custom properties.**

   Custom properties link to the sheet format. Read the section "Using custom properties," earlier in this chapter, for details.

3. **Edit the sheet format.**

   The sheet format is the background of your drawing and contains the title block. You can link text in the title block to custom properties in the model, such as the author's name and the revision date. (See Chapter 7 for steps on how to edit a title block.)

4. **Put the drawing format on its own layer.**

   This step allows you to easily turn on or off the drawing format so that you can see it.

5. **Set options in Document Properties.**

   With a document active in SolidWorks, choose Tools⇨Options and select the Document Properties tab. You can set all the standards for how you want things in the document to look, from the font style for dimensions to the units of measurement to use throughout the document. (You can read more about document properties in Chapter 2.)

6. **Save the drawing as a document template.**

   In the Save As dialog box, select Save As Type `.drwdot`.

Chapter 9

Changes, Changes, Changes

*I*n the wonderful world of design, nothing stays the same. New information rolls in, people change their minds, and the CAD model continually evolves.

The good news is that SolidWorks makes it easy to update designs. Because SolidWorks is a *parametric* software, changes you make in one area ripple through all other areas of your design automatically. You don't have to manually update all the related geometry, assemblies, or drawings. If you did, you would probably consider a new line of work.

An added benefit to all this is that you can use SolidWorks to tinker with numerous what-if design scenarios, such as "What if I add five inches to this fan blade?" or "What if I make a bicycle with three wheels?"

In this chapter, I show you how to update SolidWorks documents so that you're always working with the current document. I also show you how to query a design for information, such as measurements, mass properties, and rebuild statistics.

Changing the Design

No matter how hard you try to be clairvoyant and figure out what a design will ultimately look like, it just doesn't happen. In the design world, change is the name of the game. The three areas you can change in a design include part features, visual properties, and document references. In the following sections, you find out how to tinker with each area.

Changing dimensions and features

You change features in SolidWorks by modifying dimensions. *Dimensions* define the size and the shape of a part.

Typically, you create dimensions as you create each part feature and then insert those dimensions into drawing views. In SolidWorks, when you change a dimension in the model, the drawing is updated. By the same token, when you change a dimension in a drawing, the model is updated.

The way to change a part feature (a cut or an extrusion, for example) is to change the model dimensions associated with that feature. You can change model dimensions in the part, the sketch, or the drawing.

Driving dimensions are sometimes called model dimensions. *Driven dimensions* are another type of dimension used only for reference. In SolidWorks, driving dimensions are black, and driven dimensions are gray. (You can find out more about dimensions in Chapter 3.)

When you double-click a dimension to change it, the Modify dialog box appears (see Figure 9-1).

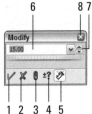

Figure 9-1:
The Modify
dialog box.

The following list describes the Modify dialog box functions.

> **1 OK:** Saves the current value and closes the dialog box.
>
> **2 Cancel:** Restores the original value and closes the dialog box.
>
> **3 Rebuild:** Regenerates the model (shows the changes) with the current value. You can use Rebuild to evaluate different values before closing the Modify dialog box.
>
> **4 Spin box value:** Sets the value for the spin increment (up and down arrows). To define the spin default value, choose Tools➪Options. On the System Options tab, select Spin Box Increments. Set the values in the Spin Box Increments dialog box.

5 Mark dimension to be imported into a drawing: Marks the dimensions in part or assembly documents that you want to import into a drawing when you use the Model Insert command. (Read more about this command in Chapter 8.)

6 Dimension value: Displays the current value, which you can change by typing a new one or by sliding the nifty thumb wheels back and forth to increase or decrease the values. The default units (inches) are shown after the value.

7 Spin box: Increases or decreases the dimension value by a specified increment when you click the up or down arrows.

8 Close: Closes the dialog box without saving changes.

When you change the value of a dimension within the Modify dialog box, the size or shape of a part isn't automatically updated. You need to rebuild the model with any changes you made. To do so, simply click the Rebuild button in the Modify dialog box. Rebuilding a change while you're still in the Modify dialog box allows you to play with a number of what-if scenarios and make additional adjustments, if necessary.

When you add a brand-new dimension, you typically go back and double-click it to display the Modify dialog box, where you enter an exact value. If you want to save a bit of time, choose Tools⇨Options. In the General section of the Systems Options tab, select the check box for Input Dimension Value. When you check this option, the Modify dialog box appears automatically each time you insert a new dimension.

You can change a driving dimension in a part, a sketch, an assembly, or a drawing by completing the following steps:

1. **Open a drawing, part, or assembly document.**

2. **Double-click the part feature you want to change in the FeatureManager design tree or within the graphics area.**

   The dimensions appear as lines with the values next to them. You can edit only driving dimensions, which appear in black. You can't edit reference dimensions, which appear in gray.

3. **Double-click the dimension you want to change.**

   The Modify dialog box appears.

4. **Enter a new value in the dialog box.**

5. **Click Rebuild in the Modify dialog box.**

   The model is updated to reflect any changes.

6. **Click OK.**

   The changes are saved, and the Modify dialog box closes.

You can also change the way you define a feature (extrusion or fillet, for example). When you modify a feature, the original PropertyManager that you used to define the feature appears. You can change the values in the PropertyManager to change or redefine the feature.

To change the way an existing feature was defined, follow these steps:

1. **Open a drawing, a part, or an assembly document.**

2. **In the FeatureManager design tree, right-click the feature you want to change and choose the Edit Feature icon.**

   The feature's PropertyManager appears.

3. **Change the values and definition of the feature in the PropertyManager.**

   Each feature has a different PropertyManager. (Chapter 5 explains the different types of features and how they're defined.)

4. **Click OK.**

   The value and property changes appear within the part.

Changing visual properties

SolidWorks lets you create models that look and act like the real thing. You can assign materials, such as aluminum or cast iron, to parts. Each material has its own associated characteristics, such as density, color, and texture. In parts and assemblies, you can adjust the direction, intensity, and color of light in the shaded view of the model to create more realistic lighting effects.

Material properties stay with the model. Downstream applications, such as the SolidWorks add-ins COSMOSWorks for analysis and PhotoWorks photo-rendering software, use these material properties to calculate their results. At times, however, you may need to edit the material properties.

You can create custom document templates with predefined materials and lighting and store these templates on a shared server for others to use. To find out more about how to create and save templates, see Chapter 2.

Setting materials properties

SolidWorks lets you assign material properties to parts. This process isn't automatic; a part gets a material property only if you assign it one or if you preset the material property in the document template. What's more, only individual parts can have material properties. You cannot assign a single material property to an entire assembly, for example.

To find what material (if any) is assigned to a part, open the document and look in the FeatureManager design tree. You see the material name and type that are listed. If the part has no material, you see Materials <not selected>.

To assign or change the material of a part, follow these steps:

1. **Right-click the part in the FeatureManager design tree and choose Appearance⇨Edit Material.**

   The Materials PropertyManager, shown in Figure 9-2, appears.

2. **Select a materials library in the Materials section.**

   SolidWorks Materials is the main library. Any custom libraries may appear here as well. After you select a library, the library contents are displayed. You see a list of material classes (Steel and Alloy Steel, for example).

Figure 9-2:
You can assign a material property to a part by using the Materials Property Manager.

3. **Select a material from the library contents.**

   Click the plus sign next to a material class to find the material type you want.

4. **Click OK.**

   The Materials Editor PropertyManager closes. The material is assigned to your part and shows up in the FeatureManager design tree. The visual appearance of the model is updated to reflect its material properties.

Let there be light

Another way to change the visual appearance of a SolidWorks model is with lighting. Lighting applies to both part and assembly documents. Think of lighting like this: When a professional photographer prepares to take a portrait of your child, he tinkers with the lighting. He adds, directs, and adjusts the light to create an overall good picture. You can make similar lighting adjustments in SolidWorks.

SolidWorks offers different lighting types that you can choose for your model. The properties of the light sources work together with the material properties of the model. If you change material properties of the model, you can enhance or reduce the effect of the light properties.

You can choose several light sources in the same document. Here's what SolidWorks gives you to work with:

- **Ambient light:** Illuminates the model evenly from all directions. In a room with white walls, the level of ambient light is high because the light reflects off the walls and other objects.

- **Directional light:** Comes from a source that's infinitely far away from the model. It's a columned light source consisting of parallel rays from a single direction, like the sun.

- **Point light:** Comes from a very small light source located at a specific coordinate in the model space. This type of light source emits light in all directions. The effect is like a tiny light bulb floating in space.

- **Spot light:** Comes from a restricted, focused light with a cone-shaped beam that is brightest at its center. You can aim a spot light at a specific area of the model. You can adjust the position and distance of the light source relative to the model, and you can adjust the angle through which the beam spreads.

You can define the following properties for a light source inside its PropertyManager:

- **On/Off:** Turns the light source on or off.

- **Color:** You can also choose the color of light. The default is a white light, but you can use a different color to give the model more warmth.

✔ **Ambient:** Controls the intensity of the light source by using a value between 0 and 1.

✔ **Brightness:** Controls the brightness of the light by using a value between 0 and 1.

✔ **Specularity:** Controls the extent to which shiny surfaces exhibit bright highlights where the light strikes them by using a value between 0 and 1.

✔ **Light position:** Controls the position of the light relative to the model.

To see the types of light in your model, open a part or assembly document in SolidWorks and double-click the Lighting folder in the FeatureManager design tree. The default lights are ambient and directional, but you can adjust them or add other lights. A few rules apply:

✔ You can turn the ambient light on or off, but you can't delete it or add other ambient lights.

✔ You can turn the directional light on or off or delete it.

✔ You can add additional directional light sources.

✔ You can add point light and spot light sources.

✔ In any document, you can have up to nine light sources (the ambient light and eight others in any combination).

To add a light source, follow these steps:

1. **Right-click the Lighting folder in the FeatureManager design tree.**

   A menu appears with these choices:

   - Add Directional Light

   - Add Point Light

   - Add Spot Light

2. **Choose the type of light you want to add.**

   After you make a selection, the lighting type appears in the Lighting folder immediately, as shown in Figure 9-3. You can add up to nine light sources to the model.

You can also modify a light source. To modify the lighting properties, follow these steps:

1. **Expand the Lighting folder in the FeatureManager design tree by clicking the plus sign next to the folder.**

   The contents of the Lighting folder appear.

Figure 9-3:
You can add
as many as
nine light
sources for
any model.

2. **Right-click a light source and choose Properties.**

   The PropertyManager for that light source appears.

3. **Edit the properties to change light qualities.**

   The available light properties depend on the type of light source. You can move the slider on the bar to change the ambient, brightness, and specularity properties from a value of 0 to 1.

   As you edit, a graphical representation of the light source appears in the graphics area to show the color and direction of the light.

4. **Click OK.**

To quickly edit the properties of a light source, in the FeatureManager design tree, double-click the icon of the light source you want to modify.

To delete a light source, follow these steps:

1. **Click the plus sign to expand the Lighting folder in the FeatureManager design tree.**

2. **Select the light source to delete and press the Delete key.**

To turn off a light without deleting it, follow these steps:

1. **Click + to expand the Lighting folder in the FeatureManager design tree.**

2. **Right-click the light source and choose Off.**

   This option toggles. If the light source is on, you turn it off, and vice versa.

Changing document references

An assembly may go through many revisions in its design life. Changes are especially common in a multiuser environment where several users are working on individual parts and subassemblies. You can change assembly components by using three methods:

- ✔ **Add:** You can add a new component to an assembly using the methods I cover in Chapter 6 of this book. You can drag a component from File Explorer or use the Insert Component PropertyManager (choose Insert⇨Component).
- ✔ **Delete:** Deleting a component is as easy as 1-2-3. Open the assembly, select the component you want to delete in the FeatureManager design tree, and press the Delete key. SolidWorks asks you for confirmation before deleting the component.
- ✔ **Replace:** A safe, efficient way to update an assembly is to replace the components or subassemblies when you need to.

To replace parts or components in an assembly, follow these steps:

1. **Choose File⇨Replace.**

   The Replace PropertyManager, shown in Figure 9-4, appears.

2. **In the graphics area, click the component or components to replace.**

   The components you select appear in the Replace These Component(s) section of the Replace dialog box.

3. **If you want to replace all copies of the part, select the All Instances check box.**

   This feature allows you to automatically replace all occurrences of a part within an assembly, without having to manually select every one.

4. **Click Browse to locate the replacement component for the With This One section.**

   The Open dialog box appears.

5. **Locate the replacement part on your computer and click Open.**

   The Open dialog box closes, and a link to the replacement part appears in the With This One section of the Replace dialog box.

Figure 9-4:
You can
replace an
assembly
component
with the
Replace
PropertyMa
nager.

6. **In the Configuration area, select Match Name to allow the software to try to match the configuration name of the old component with a configuration in the replacement component.**

If you're the do-it-yourself type, select Manually Select so that you can choose the matching configuration in the replacement component.

7. **Select Re-attach Mates to allow the software to try to reattach existing mates to the existing components.**

8. **Click OK.**

The selected component instances are replaced. If you chose Manually Select, choose the configuration to open in the Configurations dialog box. If you selected the Re-attach Mates check box, the Mated Entities PropertyManager appears. (You can read about mates in Chapter 6.)

Mates position a component in an assembly precisely with respect to each other. Mates defines how the components move and rotate together.

The Replace feature works well when you're replacing a component with a similar component. But if the assembly components aren't similar to one another, you're better off deleting the existing component and adding the new one manually.

Getting Information from Your Design

Another advantage to having a 3D design is the wealth of information in the design after it's complete. And that's a good thing because someone always wants to know how big a model is, how much it weighs, or what it's made of.

You can query the SolidWorks model in three ways:

- ✔ Measure your design.
- ✔ Calculate mass properties.
- ✔ Review your document's statistics.

The following sections explain how it's done.

Measuring your design

You can choose from a few ways to measure entities in a SolidWorks design. One way is to extract the dimensions. You can make dimensions of a part visible in the default view. With your part document open, in the FeatureManager design tree, right-click Annotations and choose Show Feature Dimensions. (A check mark next to Show Feature Dimensions indicates that the feature is already selected.) Your dimensions should already appear in your drawing, so you don't need to do anything to see drawing dimensions.

Dimensions are easier to see when you view the part as shaded. (Click Shaded on the View toolbar.) Some dimensions become more readable when you rotate the part. If you want to display dimensions for a feature, double-click the feature in the FeatureManager design tree.

An easy way to measure entities is with the SolidWorks Measure tool. To open the Measure tool, choose Tools⇨Measure. The Measure dialog box, which is really more like a toolbar (see Figure 9-5), appears.

Figure 9-5:
The
Measure
tool.

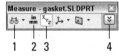

You have the following options:

1 Arc/Circle Measurements: Select to specify the distance to display when arcs or circles are selected to measure.

- *Center to Center:* Measures the distance between the centers of the circles (the default).

- *Minimum Distance:* Measures the distance between the closest points on the circles.

- *Maximum Distance:* Measures the distance between the farthest points on the circles.

2 Units/Precision: Select to display the Measure Units/Precision dialog box, where you can display the custom measurement units and precision.

3 Show XYZ Measurements: Select to display *dX, dY,* and *dZ* measurements between selected entities in the graphics area. Clear to display only the minimum distance between selected entities.

4 Expand or contract the information window: Use when you want to copy the information to a clipboard.

In most cases, the Measurement tool is straightforward to use. Simply select an entity to measure. To select more than one entity, just keep clicking. To unselect an item, click it again.

As long as you select a valid measurement, SolidWorks displays the values in the Measure dialog box and in the graphics area. If SolidWorks can't take a measurement, a message in the Measure dialog box says "Invalid combination of selected entities."

If you select too many items at one time, the Measure tool displays nothing, and you need to restart the Measure tool. You can clear the selections by clicking in an area of the graphics area where no geometry appears.

Figure 9-6 shows three examples of entities that I selected in a gasket part and used the Measure tool to measure:

- ✔ **Arc selected:** Displays the radius and center *(X, Y, Z)* values.

- ✔ **Line selected:** Displays the length of a line.

- ✔ **Two circles selected:** Displays the center distance, or the distance between the holes, and the *dX* and *dY* values. The *dX, dY,* and *dZ* values are the change (delta) in the distance along the *X, Y,* and *Z* axes.

Displaying mass properties

SolidWorks calculates mass properties and section properties for parts and assemblies. These properties include density, mass, volume, and surface area, for example.

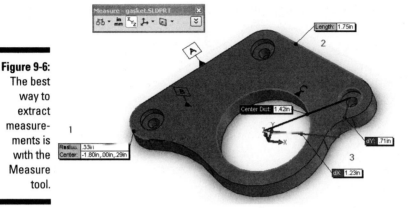

Figure 9-6:
The best
way to
extract
measure-
ments is
with the
Measure
tool.

Mass properties look at the entire part or assembly, and *section properties* look at multiple faces that are in parallel planes. You can assign values for mass and center of gravity to override the calculated values. The ability to assign values is useful when you want, for example, to assign the correct mass and center of gravity to a simplified representation of a component.

When either mass or section property is calculated, a tricolored reference 3D triad is displayed at the origin of the part or assembly along with the mass properties or section properties.

To display mass properties, follow these steps:

1. **Choose Tools⇨Mass Properties.**

   The Mass Properties dialog box appears, as shown in Figure 9-7.

2. **Click a part or an assembly in the FeatureManager design tree.**

   The part or assembly name appears in the Selected Items area. If you choose more than one entity, you see the calculated mass properties for the combination of those entities.

3. **Select from these options:**

   • *Include Hidden Bodies/Components:* Select to include hidden bodies and components in the calculations.

   • *Show output Coordinate System in Corner of Window:* Select to display the tricolored reference 3D triad in the corner of the graphics area, or clear to show the triad at its origin.

   • *Assigned Mass Properties:* Select to assign values for mass and center of gravity to override the calculated values. You can assign properties to only a single entity, not to a combination.

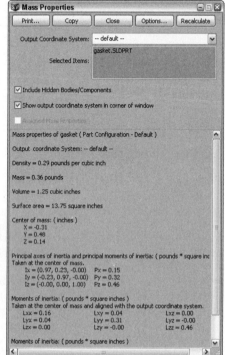

Figure 9-7:
The Mass
Properties
dialog box
gives the
density of
this gasket.

4. **Choose Recalculate in the Mass Properties dialog box.**

   The mass properties are displayed in the dialog box. If you chose an assembly file, you see the mass properties for the assembly as a whole.

5. **To clear an entity, select the entity and press Delete on the keyboard.**

   The items are cleared from the Selected Items area. You can then select another item for a new mass properties calculation.

6. **Click Close to close the dialog box.**

If you want mass properties to be displayed in different units (feet rather than meters, for instance), select Options in the Mass Properties dialog box. In the Mass Property Options dialog box that appears, select a different unit of measure, and click OK.

Mass property calculations are based on the physical properties of a part. To change a part's physical properties (aluminum to iron ore, for instance), right-click the material name or Material <not selected> in the FeatureManager design tree, and select Edit Material. In the Materials Editor PropertyManager, select a new material, and click OK.

The default unit of measure for the mass property calculation is set in the document template. You can change the default unit of measure by choosing Tools⇨Options⇨Document Properties⇨Units in an open document. You can also define default material properties in the template.

You can use the Section Property feature to display the area, centroid (sketch and part origin), and other information for a 2D sketch.

To display section properties for multiple entities, follow these steps:

1. **Edit or create a sketch.**

   To edit an existing sketch, select the feature, right-click, and choose Edit Sketch.

2. **Choose Tools⇨Section Properties.**

   The results appear in the Section Properties dialog box.

3. **Click Close to close the dialog box.**

Getting the stats on your documents

Understanding what makes up a document from a feature, size, and complexity standpoint is useful information when you're reviewing a design or working on a new design. Each SolidWorks document type has statistics. No, the document statistics are not a description of how your drawing likes to take long walks on the beach and is looking for a caring, sensitive partner to spend free time with. I'm talking about rebuild statistics.

When you make changes to a SolidWorks document, you need to rebuild the model to check for geometry errors. In a large assembly, rebuilds can take a lot of time. The Feature Statistics tool tells you how much time it takes to rebuild each feature in a part or each part in an assembly.

Depending on the document type you have open, the Feature Statistics dialog box displays different information and a different user interface. The following information appears:

- ✔ **Drawing statistics:** The number of drawing sheets, number and types of drawing views, and number and types of drawing annotations (such as notes, dimensions, and symbols).

- ✔ **Feature statistics:** In a part file, the Feature Statistics dialog box lists all features in the part with their rebuild times in descending order (see Figure 9-8). In the case of an unusually long rebuild time, you may consider reworking the geometry (so that the feature takes less time to rebuild) or suppressing the feature in a rebuild. A feature that takes up 60 percent of the rebuild time for a part isn't always a bad thing. It's just good to know in case you're heading to happy hour in 15 minutes.

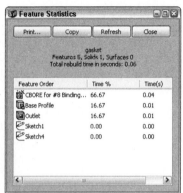

Figure 9-8:
Find out in the Feature Statistics dialog box which features take the most time to rebuild.

In Figure 9-8, the counterbored hole is the key contributor to the rebuild time in the gasket model. In this case, that's okay. The idea is to use the information as a reference and not to get too worked up on how to remodel the feature to save time. Some features have longer build times than others. Get an idea for what they are, and if something doesn't pass the smell test (it smells fishy), further investigation may be warranted.

✔ **Assembly statistics (AssemblyXpert):** Displays the total number of components, number of unique parts and subassemblies, number of mates that exist, and number of top-level mates and components. When you're taking assembly performance into consideration, a large number of top-level components and mates can be a performance drag. The AssemblyXpert also analyzes the performance of your assembly, and may suggest ways to help improve the overall performance of very large assembly files.

To get feature statistics (or drawing or assembly statistics), follow these steps:

1. **Open a part document (or a drawing or assembly document).**

2. **Choose Tools⇨Feature Statistics.**

    If you're working on an assembly document, the command is labeled AssemblyXpert; on a drawing, it's Drawing Statistics.

    The Feature Statistics dialog box appears with a list of all the features and their rebuild times in descending order.

3. **Click Feature Order to sort the features to match the FeatureManager design tree.**

4. **Click one of the following:**

   - *Print:* Prints the statistics.

   - *Copy:* Copies the statistics so that you can paste them into another file.

   - *Refresh:* Refreshes the feature statistics.

5. **Click Close.**

When displaying Feature Statistics for a part, the features (by default) appear in order of their rebuild times. You can reorder the list by clicking one of the category headings; for example, if you click Feature Order, the features appear in the same order as they do in the FeatureManager design tree.

Chapter 10

Leveraging Your Existing Designs

SolidWorks offers several tools that let you get extra mileage out of existing designs. For example, many engineers have a stockpile of product designs that exist as old *(legacy)* drawing files. With SolidWorks, you don't have to throw that 2D data in the trash and start from scratch. You can maintain those files in their native formats or import them into SolidWorks and use them as a basis for 3D models.

Multiple configurations are another way to get more play out of designs. *Configurations* are variations of an existing design. Think of a screw that comes in different lengths. Rather than have to create 50 different files, you can create those variations in SolidWorks in a single document. This way, you can manage files more easily and edit all configurations consistently.

You also can use SolidWorks to create exploded views of an assembly that you can use in technical documentation. The views show the assembly with the components separated so that you can see how items fit together.

Maintaining Old Drawing Files

Few new products are totally new. More often, they're built on existing designs. Many of these existing designs are in DWG or DXF drawing formats. These formats generally mean that someone created the drawings in AutoCAD, a 2D design program that was popular before 3D modeling programs, such as SolidWorks, existed. Engineers often refer to DWG and DXF files as *legacy* programs, even if the documents were created in recent versions of AutoCAD. Many SolidWorks users come from an AutoCAD background, and they still have a lot of AutoCAD files that they want to maintain.

SolidWorks offers tools that allow you to work with these drawing files. You can import a DWG or DXF file into SolidWorks using an import wizard so that you can use the file as the basis of a 3D design. If you need to make only a minor change, the SolidWorks tool DWGEditor allows you to work with an AutoCAD DWG or DXF file in its native format. DWGEditor lets you open and save any file created in AutoCAD version 2.5 through 2007 without file conversions. DWGEditor has an AutoCAD-like interface (see Figure 10-1), so it's familiar to use if you have an AutoCAD background.

DWGEditor also allows you to save a file back to an earlier version of AutoCAD. If you work with a vendor that has AutoCAD 2000, you can save drawing files in that version's format to work on the vendor's system.

You can use DWGEditor independently of SolidWorks. To access DWGEditor in Windows, choose Start⇨All Programs⇨SolidWorks 2008⇨DWGEditor. If you import a DWG or DXF file into SolidWorks, the DXF/DWG Import dialog box appears, as shown in Figure 10-2.

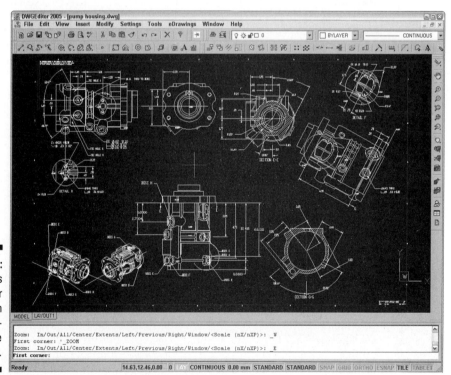

Figure 10-1:
SolidWorks DWGEditor offers an AutoCAD-like interface.

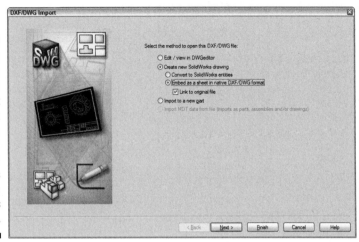

Figure 10-2:
The
DXF/DWG
Import
dialog box
lets you use
an AutoCAD
drawing file
as the basis
of a
SolidWorks
drawing.

You can use DWGEditor in several ways:

✔ **Perform a quick change to a DWG or DXF file in its native format, without going through any file conversions.** When you're finished making the change, you can save the file in its native format so that AutoCAD can open it again.

✔ **Import a DWG or DXF file and use it as the basis of a SolidWorks part.** You can do this in a few ways; my preference is to open a DWG or DXF file in DWGEditor and use Windows copy (Ctrl+C) and paste (Ctrl+V) functions to paste directly into the SolidWorks sketcher the DWG geometry you want to use.

✔ **Import a DWG or DXF file and use it as the basis of a SolidWorks drawing.** In SolidWorks, choose File➪Open. When the Open dialog box appears, change the Files of Type to DWG or DXF and browse to the file you want to open. Click the file to select and then click Open. When the DXF/DWG Import dialog box appears, select the Create New SolidWorks Drawing option and the Embed As a Sheet in Native DXF/DWG Format option (refer to Figure 10-2). The file is imported into a new SolidWorks drawing sheet.

During installation, SolidWorks gives you the option to associate DWG and DXF files with the SolidWorks DWGEditor. If you select this option, the DWGEditor DXF/DWG Import dialog box opens automatically when you double-click a DWG or a DXF file in SolidWorks Explorer or the Design Library or when you check a DWG or a DXF file out of the PDMWorks Workgroup vault.

To edit a DWG or DXF file in its native format using DWGEditor, follow these steps:

1. **In SolidWorks, choose File⇨Open (or you can run the program independently).**

   The Open dialog box appears.

2. **Select DWG or DXF for Files of Type. Browse to the location of the file you want to open, click it, and select Open.**

   The DXF/DWG Import dialog box appears.

3. **Check the option Edit/View in the DWGEditor and click Finish.**

4. **In the DWGEditor, make whatever changes to the drawing that you need to make.**

5. **Choose File⇨Save As.**

   The Save As dialog box appears. In the Save As Type box, you can specify whether to save the file in the current version of AutoCAD or in an earlier version.

6. **Click Save to close the dialog box and save the file.**

Managing Configurations

At times, you need to create several variations of a design. For example, you may want to create a family of screws, or you may want to create multiple configurations of a carburetor. After all, a single carburetor won't fit all vehicle types. If you have to create a different file for each design scenario, it will take a lot of time — and patience. Even a simple geometry change may make for a long day at the office.

Fortunately, there's a better way. The ConfigurationManager in SolidWorks manages multiple configurations of a part or an assembly in the same document to save you time and reduce errors. And you don't have to re-create the wheel each time you create a smaller one. ConfigurationManager lets you create various design scenarios by simply suppressing part or assembly components and features, or in the case of that screw family, by varying dimensions and parameters.

You can create design variants in two ways: manually or with Design Tables. You can use a *Design Table* to build multiple configurations of parts or assemblies by applying the values in the table to the dimensions in the part. Design Tables are the best way to create a family of screws that vary in width, length, and number of threads. If you want to show a door in open and closed positions, it's easier to create those variations manually.

Some of the purposes of configurations are described in this list:

- ✔ **Produce multiple versions of a model or to display optional features in a part or optional components in an assembly.**

- ✔ **Create a simplified part configuration to use in a large assembly so that the assembly loads into memory faster.** Smaller parts and assemblies rebuild more quickly when you use simplified configurations. Also, editing a document is easier when you have less visual clutter.

- ✔ **Create additional drawing views.** A single drawing can display multiple configurations of a part or assembly in the different views.

- ✔ **Create exploded views of assemblies.** You can use different design configurations to document a multistep installation process.

- ✔ **Define multiple positions of a part for motion studies.** For example, you can show how a car door looks open and closed by creating one configuration of the door at 0 degrees and another at 90 degrees.

- ✔ **Define custom properties per configuration.** A *custom property* is a file attribute (such as the revision date or part number or a description of the document) defined within the original document template. You can define these properties by choosing File⇨Properties. In the Summary Information dialog box, click the Custom tab for properties that apply to the entire document, or the Configuration Specific tab for properties that vary from one configuration to another.

To view the different configurations in your document, click the ConfigurationManager tab at the top of the FeatureManager design tree and double-click the configuration names.

Varying the design

When you create variations of a design, the idea is to simply make your changes to the model and save those changes as a different configuration, rather than as a different document. The next two sections explain how to do that. For the moment, here's a list of ways that you can vary a part or an assembly design to create new configurations.

You can vary a part configuration by

- ✔ Modifying feature dimensions
- ✔ Suppressing features, equations, and end conditions
- ✔ Defining configuration-specific properties

You can vary an assembly configuration in several ways:

- ✔ Change the suppression state (Suppressed or Unsuppressed) or visibility (Hide or Show) to highlight different components.
- ✔ Change the referenced configuration of components.
- ✔ Change the dimensions of distance or angle mates or the suppression state of mates.
- ✔ Modify dimensions or other parameters of features that belong to the assembly (not to other components), including cuts and holes, component patterns, reference geometry, and sketches.
- ✔ Define configuration-specific properties, such as end conditions and sketch relations.

You can *hide* features or components to highlight other items in a document. When you hide an item, you make it "invisible." (The item is still there — you just can't see it.)

You can use the *suppressed* state to temporarily remove a feature from a part or a component from an assembly, without deleting it. The item is no longer a functional member of the part or assembly, so you can't select, reference, or edit its children. And because SolidWorks removes the suppressed item from memory, the document is loaded, rebuilt, and displayed faster.

To access the Hide/Show and Suppress/Resolved commands, in the Feature Manager design tree, right-click a feature in a part or component in an assembly and choose the command. If a component is hidden, the word *Show* appears on the menu. If a component is suppressed, the word *Unsuppressed* appears.

Creating a configuration manually

You have two ways to create a configuration in SolidWorks: manually and with Design Tables. If you want to make a few variations on a complex assembly, you should do it manually.

Here's how to manually make a new configuration of a part or an assembly:

1. **Open a part or assembly file in SolidWorks.**
2. **Click the ConfigurationManager tab at the top of the FeatureManager design tree.**

   In place of the FeatureManager, you see the ConfigurationManager.

3. In the ConfigurationManager, right-click the part or assembly name and choose Add Configuration.

The Add Configuration PropertyManager appears (see Figure 10-3).

4. In the Add Configuration PropertyManager, type a configuration name and specify properties for the new configuration.

Always give your configurations meaningful names so that you can recognize them easily.

You have room In the PropertyManager to add a descriptive name and a comment. These fields make it easier for someone who later reviews or modifies your design to understand what you were trying to do.

Advanced Options properties control what happens when you add new features and components to other configurations and then activate this configuration again. By default, SolidWorks suppresses in this configuration any new components or features that you add to another.

5. Click OK.

Figure 10-3: You can name your configuration and add a description and comments in the Configuration Property-Manager.

After you create the new configuration, you can make overall changes to the design. The reason to create the configuration first and make changes later is so that you know which configuration you're making changes to.

To change an existing configuration, in the ConfigurationManager, double-click the configuration you want to change to make it active. Any changes you make apply to only that configuration.

When you double-click a driving dimension to change it, a Modify dialog box appears, as shown in Figure 10-4. In the Modify dialog box, you can specify which configuration you want to apply your change to by selecting All Configurations, This Configuration, or Specify Configuration(s).

Figure 10-4:
Applying a
change
inside the
Modify
dialog box.

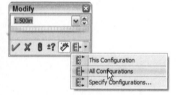

A *driving dimension* is one that changes the size of a model when you update it. *Driven dimensions* are for information only. You can modify only driving dimensions.

Creating configurations with Design Tables

Design Tables allow you to create an infinite number of variations on a single design. SolidWorks uses Microsoft Excel to create the design table, so you need to have a copy of the program on your computer to use this feature.

To create a Design Table, you insert a new, empty Design Table in the model and enter the Design Table information directly in the worksheet. You enter the names of the configurations you want to create, specify the parameters you want to control, and assign values for each parameter. Parameters can be dimensions, features, or parts. When you finish entering information, SolidWorks creates the new configurations for you. And, if your configuration data already exists, you can add it to the table automatically.

The first column of the worksheet lists the different configuration names. Parameters are in the first row of cells, and dimensions and suppression values are beneath each parameter. When you change a dimension value in a Design Table, the configuration is updated with the specified value. In addition to changing dimension values, you can change the suppression state of a feature in Design Tables. You can suppress or unsuppress a feature.

Figure 10-5 displays row values (4–40 x .500, for example) and column headings (Head Dia@Profile, for example) that define the configuration name (row name) and the driving value (column name).

Figure 10-5: Row column format for a design table.

	Head Dia@Profile	Head Thickness@Profile	Length@Profile
4-40 x .500	0.125	0.055	0.5
6-32 x .125	0.14	0.066	0.125
6-32 x .250	0.14	0.066	0.25
6-32 x .375	0.14	0.066	0.375
6-32 x .500	0.14	0.066	0.5
6-32 x .625	0.14	0.066	0.625
6-32 x .750	0.14	0.066	0.75

The SolidWorks 2008 Help file contains a list of valid design table parameters. For example, proper parameter syntax for a feature dimension is *dimension @feature_name.* Legal values under this parameter heading include any decimal number. To find the SolidWorks 2008 Help file, choose Help from the main menu in SolidWorks.

A Design Table that uses named features and comments is easy to understand and to modify. It's a waste of time to have to continually close the spreadsheet to review features and dimension names in the model. The example just shown in Figure 10-5 uses decipherable names for the dimension values.

To create a Design Table, follow these steps:

1. **Open a part or assembly document in SolidWorks.**

2. **Choose Insert⇨Design Table.**

   The Design Table PropertyManager appears, as shown in Figure 10-6.

3. **In the PropertyManager, in the Source section, select Auto-create.**

   Auto-create extracts from the model some data that is valid in the Design Table, such as a list of dimensions.

4. **In the PropertyManager, select options for Edit Control and Options.**

   Select one of these options in the Edit Control section:

   • *Allow Model Edits to Update the Design Table:* Any changes you make to the model are updated in the design table.

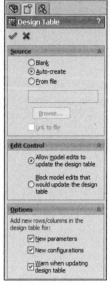

- *Block Model Edits That Would Update the Design Table:* Any changes you make to the models aren't updated in the design table. You cannot make changes in the model that affect the design table's parameters.

Select from the following options in the Options section:

- *New Parameters:* Adds a new column to the design table if you add a new parameter in the model.

- *New Configurations:* Adds a new row to the design table if you manually add a new configuration to the model.

- *Warn When Updating Design Table:* Warns you that the design table will change based on the parameters you updated in the model.

5. Click OK.

The PropertyManager disappears, an embedded worksheet appears in the window, and Excel toolbars replace the SolidWorks toolbars.

6. Enter configuration names in the first column.

Cell A1 contains the design table name, and cell A2 is blank. So the first column includes cells A3, A4, and so on. If configurations already exist in the document, they appear in these columns. Any new configurations you add here are updated in the model according to your selections in the PropertyManager (see Step 4).

Working with configurations

Here are some more useful notes and tips on configurations:

✔ You can't delete an active configuration. To delete a configuration, make another configuration active and then delete the configuration.

✔ The comment field is a good place to include a description of the reasons for, and the function of, the configuration.

Comments help document the intent and the purpose of the configuration.

✔ To activate a configuration, double-click the configuration name within the ConfigurationManager.

✔ The FeatureManager displays the active configuration to the right of the part name in the ConfigurationManager.

To add a new configuration, enter a new name in column A under the last configuration.

7. Enter parameter names in the first-row columns.

Enter your parameter names in cells B2, C2, and so on. (The design table name is in the first row.) Parameter names should reflect the feature or dimension in the model you want to vary. To add a parameter name to the design table, place your pointer in a cell and then double-click the feature or dimension you want to add in the FeatureManager design tree.

8. Enter dimension and suppression values in the appropriate cells.

You can enter dimension and suppression values beneath the parameter name in the row of the corresponding configuration. Dimension values are decimal numbers. Suppression values are S (Suppressed) or U (Unsuppressed).

9. Click outside the Design Table window to close the design table.

Here are a few tips to keep in mind when working with a design table:

✔ To edit a design table, in the ConfigurationManager, right-click the Design Table icon and choose Edit Table.

✔ Microsoft Excel lets you add comments. To add a comment in Excel, right-click the cell you want to comment on and choose Insert Comment. In the box, type the comment text.

✔ If you make an entry in a cell within the design table that doesn't have a corresponding row (leftmost cell in the row) and column (topmost cell in column) heading, Design Table treats the cell contents as a comment.

Using configurations to create exploded views

After you design a product, the manufacturing department needs to know how to assemble it, and the maintenance department needs to know how to take it apart. Another way to get more mileage from your SolidWorks assembly design is to create exploded views. *Exploded views* show the assembly components separated so that the viewer can visualize how parts fit together. You can use configurations to show a series of exploded views to create product documentation.

An exploded view consists of one or more explode steps. You create these steps by selecting and dragging parts in the graphics area. When you're done, SolidWorks stores the exploded view with the assembly configuration you created it with. Each configuration can have only one exploded view.

Figure 10-7 shows an exploded view of a personal water propeller. SolidWorks lets you toggle between the exploded and collapsed views.

Figure 10-7: This exploded view of a personal water propeller shows how parts fit together.

To create an exploded view of an assembly, follow these steps:

1. **Open an assembly file.**

2. **Click the ConfigurationManager tab at the top of the FeatureManager design tree.**

   In place of the FeatureManager, you now see the ConfigurationManager, which lists the configurations in the design.

3. **Double-click the configuration you want to explode.**

   This step makes the configuration active.

4. **Click the Explode View icon on the Assembly toolbar.**

   The Explode PropertyManager appears.

5. **In the graphics area, select one or more components to include in the first explode step.**

   A manipulator with three handles (red, green, and blue) appears in the graphics area. In the PropertyManager, the components appear in the Settings section.

6. **Move the pointer over the manipulator handle pointing in the direction that you want to explode the part.**

   The pointer changes to a blue drag handle.

7. **Drag a manipulator handle to explode the components, as shown in Figure 10-8.**

   The explode step appears in the Explode Steps area.

8. **Create more explode steps until you're done.**

9. **Click OK.**

   The assembly appears in the exploded state and is saved with the active configuration.

Figure 10-8:
Drag a
component
to create an
explode
step.

Drag to explode in this direction

To change an exploded view, open the ConfigurationManager and click the explode step that you want to edit. For example, to change the location of the nose cone in the personal watercraft assembly, click the Exploded View icon, below the configuration name and, in the graphics area, move the blue arrow handle to reposition the component.

Animating the explode or collapse sequence

You can do more than just explode or collapse the assembly. You can animate the explode or collapse sequence to show the assembly components move apart and then move back together again. Figure 10-9 shows the Animation Controller toolbar. The Save As AVI button on the toolbar lets you save the explode sequence as an AVI file that you can send or include in an eDrawings file. (Chapter 14 offers more information on viewers.)

Figure 10-9:
The
Animation
Controller
toolbar.

To animate the explode or collapse of an exploded view of an assembly, follow these steps:

1. **Open an assembly file.**

2. **Click the ConfigurationManager tab on top of the FeatureManager design tree.**

   In place of the FeatureManager, you now see the ConfigurationManager, which lists the configurations in the design.

3. **Click the plus sign (+) beside the configuration that contains the exploded view you want to animate.**

   You see the Exp│View feature, which contains each step in the explode process.

4. **Right-click the Exp│View feature and choose Animate Collapse or Animate Explode.**

   The assembly explodes or collapses, and the Animation Controller toolbar appears.

You can use the playback controls to animate the explode or collapse. The two controls on the rightmost side of Figure 10-9 allow you to slow it down (x1/2) or speed it up (x2).

Adding exploded views to a drawing sheet

You can add exploded views to a drawing sheet. To change a drawing view to the exploded state, open a drawing file, right-click a view, and choose Properties. The Drawing View Properties dialog box appears. In the Configuration Information section of the dialog box, select the Show in Exploded State check box, shown in Figure 10-10, and click OK.

Figure 10-10:
You can select the Show in Exploded State check box.

Chapter 11

Printing and Plotting

In This Chapter

▶ Adding a printer to the network

▶ Defining the SolidWorks document settings

▶ Printing SolidWorks parts, assemblies, and drawings

▶ Understanding the different printing methods

*N*o matter what people say about a paperless workplace, sometimes nothing can replace a physical copy of a SolidWorks document. Hard copies of large engineering drawings are easier to read than electronic copies on tiny computer screens. Some companies require printed copies for reviews and recordkeeping. Other folks might not have the means to view electronic copies. And, whereas CAD files contain proprietary information, hard copies protect your interests.

In this chapter, I take you through the steps of setting up your printer in Windows and show you the best ways to print SolidWorks documents.

Delving into Printing and Plotting

You can print flat images of parts and assembly models by using a regular office printer, but for high-quality, large-scale engineering drawings, a *plotter* is best. A printer simulates lines by printing a closely spaced series of dots, whereas a plotter uses a pen to draw continuous lines. A *multicolored plotter* uses different colored pens to draw different colored lines. Plotters are considerably more expensive than printers, but they're called for when precision is mandatory.

You can access any printer or plotter, local or remote, by using the standard Windows operating system. Printing from SolidWorks is similar to printing from any Microsoft Office application, so if you know how to do that, you're halfway there.

You can print SolidWorks documents directly from SolidWorks or from the eDrawings Viewer or the SolidWorks Viewer, two free programs that let you view SolidWorks documents without the SolidWorks software. (Chapter 14 offers more information on viewers.) You can download both viewers at www.solidworks.com/pages/products/designtools.html.

Installing a Printer in Windows

In a larger organization, the job of adding a printer to a network is one that generally belongs to the IT group. In the case of a small business or home office, that IT person may be you.

The good news is that most new printers and plotters support Plug and Play in Windows. If you have a plug-and-play printer (look for Plug and Play on the printer's list of features), just plug the printer into your computer, and Windows takes care of the setup.

If you have an older printer or you're connecting your printer to a network, you need to take a few extra steps. First, make sure that you have handy the CDs that came with your printer. The Add Printer Wizard installs the printer drivers from the CDs. If you don't have the CDs, you can get the driver from the Web site of the printer manufacturer.

To install an older printer without plug-and-play technology on Windows XP or Windows Vista (the Windows operating systems now supported by SolidWorks), follow these steps:

1. **Choose Start⇨Settings⇨Printers and Faxes or choose Start⇨Printers and Faxes, depending on how your Start menu is configured.**

   A list of currently defined printers and fax devices appears.

2. **Choose File⇨Add Printer.**

   The Add Printer Wizard appears, to walk you through installing a printer or making a printer connection.

3. **Click Next.**

   The next frame of the wizard asks whether you have a local or network printer.

4. **Determine whether you have a local printer or a network printer.**

   Click the local printer option if the printer is attached to your computer or if it's a network printer not attached to a print server.

   If the printer is on a network, click the network printer option.

5. **Click Next.**

   The Specify a Printer dialog box appears.

6. **Specify a printer by checking one of these three options:**

   - *Find a Printer in the Directory:* Click this option to locate the printer on your computer.

   - *Connect to This Printer:* Click this option and type the name of the printer below it.

   - *Connect to a Printer on the Internet or on a Home or Office Network:* Click this option if the computer is on a network, and type the URL for the printer.

7. **Click Next.**

   The Browse for Printer dialog box appears.

8. **Set the printer as the Windows default.**

   Select either the Yes or No check box to indicate whether the printer should be the system default.

   The *default* printer is the one your documents print to automatically unless you select another output device. To set a printer as a default printer at any time, from the Windows Start menu, choose Settings➪ Printers and Faxes. Right-click a printer and select Set As Default. A check mark appears next to the default printer icon in the Printers and Faxes section.

9. **Click Next.**

10. **Click Finish.**

   The new printer is added to the system and is available for printing.

Setting Printer and Document Preferences in Windows

After you add a printer to your network (see the preceding section), Windows allows you to change print preferences. Keep in mind that the preferences you set for a printer could become the default settings for any user who connects to the printer. Some of the commands described in this section may not be available on every printer. If an option you want isn't available (it appears in gray), see your system administrator.

To access the following commands in Windows, choose Start⇨ Settings⇨ Printers and Faxes. Then right-click your printer name and choose a command:

- ✔ **Open** opens the print queue for the printer, which shows active print jobs. Use this option to cancel, reprint, or pause a print job.

- ✔ **Set As Default Printer** sets the printer as the default printer for all applications.

- ✔ **Printing Preferences** defines the default print quality, number of pages per sheet, input and output paper trays, paper orientation.

- ✔ **Pause Printing** pauses any current print job. To resume, right-click the printer icon again and choose Resume Printing.

- ✔ **Sharing** allows other users on the network to use the printer. When this option isn't enabled, only you can use the printer.

- ✔ **Rename, Delete, or create a Shortcut** allows you to rename the printer, to delete it, or to create a shortcut on the desktop.

- ✔ **Properties** include the printer's name, port, sharing, and security.

Choosing Print Options in SolidWorks

You can also set many print properties within the SolidWorks document, as I explain in the sections that follow. And, if you have a consistent way of printing — for example, you always print part documents in a landscape orientation scaled to 90 percent — you can set these preferences directly in the SolidWorks document template.

 To save time, you can save a SolidWorks document (for example, a part, an assembly, or a drawing) as a template document for reuse. A *template* forms the basis of a new SolidWorks document. SolidWorks saves these files by using a different file extension, much like Microsoft Word templates do. SolidWorks assigns the extension .prtdot to a part template, .asmdot to an assembly template, and .drwdot to a drawing template.

You can make a new template by saving any SolidWorks document as a template. To do so, select the appropriate file format in the Files As Type section of the Save As dialog box. (See Chapter 2 for more details on document templates in SolidWorks.)

Defining printer page setup properties

In the Page Setup dialog box, you can change printer settings, such as resolution, scale, and paper size. The preferences are set automatically to those of the default printer. In SolidWorks, you can keep those preferences or override them. Either way, these preferences are saved with the document.

To define the printer page-setup properties in an open document, follow these steps:

1. **In SolidWorks, choose File➪Page Setup.**

   The Page Setup dialog box, shown in Figure 11-1, appears. This dialog box contains the default printer settings.

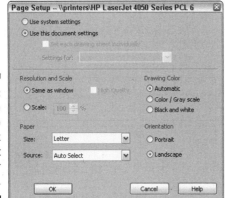

Figure 11-1:
Use the
Page Setup
dialog box
to adjust
printer
settings.

2. **Select the setting defaults and other options.**

   Specify whether to use the system printer settings or the document settings. You can also define resolution and scale, paper size and source, drawing color, and orientation by using this option.

3. **Click OK to accept the changes.**

   SolidWorks saves page setup changes with the document so that the document prints the same way next time. If you don't want the changes to the page setup to be permanent, close the document without saving after you finish printing.

Setting options within the Print dialog box

You can set a number of options within the SolidWorks document by using the Print dialog box, as shown in Figure 11-2. Similar to the page setup options (see the preceding section), SolidWorks saves with the document any changes you make to these printer setup values.

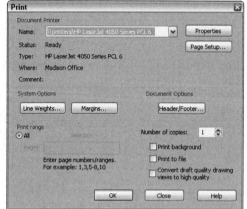

Figure 11-2:
You select
options in
the Print
dialog box.

To access the Print dialog box in an open SolidWorks document, choose
File⇨Print. The dialog box contains these areas:

✔ **Document Printer** specifies these printer options:

  • *Name:* Specifies the printer: The system provides read-only status
    about the printer's status, type, and location.

  • *Properties:* Specifies options specific to the selected printer.

  • *Page Setup:* Specifies page setup options and advanced printer
    options, such as scale, orientation, and resolution.

✔ **System Options** defines the line weights (see Figure 11-3) and printer
  margins.

Figure 11-3:
Set printer
line weights
in the
System
Options
section of
the Print
dialog box.

Line Weights		
Thin: 0.00208661in	Thick(3):	0.02755906in
Normal: 0.00984252in	Thick(4):	0.03937008in
Thick: 0.01377953in	Thick(5):	0.05511811in
Thick(2): 0.01968504in	Thick(6):	0.07874016in

By default, the margin default values are set to the printer margin and
rarely need to change. The line weights correspond to the thickness value
that you set for line fonts. (To access line fonts in the open document,
choose Tools⇨Options. Look for the Line Font section on the Document
Properties tab.)

These two buttons appear in the System Options field:

- *Line Weights:* Specifies the line weights that work best with your printer or plotter

- *Margins:* Specifies values for the top, bottom, left, and right margins of the document

✔ **Document Options** defines header and footer values (see Figure 11-4). Click the Header/Footer button to specify headers and footers for only the active document. You can select a predefined header or footer or create new ones. Headers and footers can include information, such as page number, total pages, date, and filename.

Figure 11-4:
Create a header and footer with a page number, the date, and the filename in the Page Setup section of the Document Options dialog box.

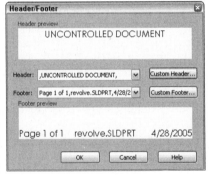

✔ **Print Range** allows you to select the sheets you want to print in a drawing. Here are your options:

- *All:* Prints all pages in the document.

- *Pages:* Prints the sheets you specify (drawings only).

- *Selection:* Prints a selected area of a drawing sheet at a scale you specify (drawings only).

Other options in the dialog box are described in this list:

✔ **Number of Copies:** Sets the number of copies to print.

✔ **Print Background:** Prints the window background in addition to the model or drawing.

✔ **Print to File:** Prints to a file rather than to the printer. If you select this check box, you're prompted to type a name for the file in the Print to File dialog box.

✔ **Convert Draft Quality Drawing Views to High Quality (Drawings Only):** Converts the current draft quality view into high quality for printing purposes only.

After setting the options, click OK to close the dialog box. The next time you print the document, it uses the new settings.

Printing a Document

After you configure the printing, you're ready to print a document. The first thing you should know is that not all SolidWorks documents print the same way, and the way a document prints is based on its type:

✔ **Parts:** SolidWorks prints the active document on the screen, using the current setting for zoom, view orientation (front, back, and isometric, for example), and display mode (wire frame, hidden lines visible, or hidden line removed).

✔ **Assemblies:** SolidWorks prints assemblies as it does parts, in the active display setting and using the current zoom, orientation, and display mode.

✔ **Drawings:** SolidWorks print a full-size copy of the active sheet, regardless of the current zoom scale. You can print all the sheets in a multiple sheet drawing or specify selected sheets to be printed.

You can print a document in SolidWorks in one of three ways: from the Print Preview screen, from the Print dialog box, or by using the Print icon at the top of the menu bar.

Printing from the Print Preview screen is my favorite method. The Print Preview feature shows you how a document will look when it prints. You can use this preview to judge any necessary adjustments to the header, footer, and margins. A quick look at the print preview saves paper and time.

To preview the printed image of an active document, follow these steps:

1. Click the Print Preview icon.

A preview of the document appears. Use the command buttons at the top of the window to scan different pages of a multipage document, zoom in and out, and print the document. If you want to make changes to what you see, click Cancel to close the window. Otherwise, continue to Step 2.

2. **Click Print.**

   The Print dialog box appears.

3. **Review and set the printing options, if necessary.**

   If you're not sure what these options are, see the earlier section "Setting options within the Print dialog box." If you're satisfied with the default settings, continue to Step 4. Otherwise, make changes to the print properties and page setup.

4. **Click OK to print.**

To print quickly within SolidWorks, open a document in View-Only mode and print. To do so, choose File➪Open and check View-Only in the Open dialog box, as shown in Figure 11-5. In View-Only mode, the document loads faster for viewing and printing, but you can't edit the document or see features in the FeatureManager design tree.

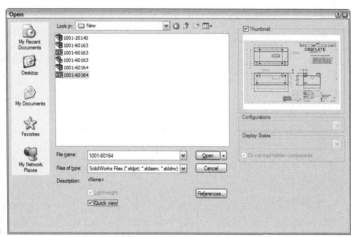

Figure 11-5:
If you want to print quickly, open a document by using the View-Only option in the Open dialog box.

Part IV

Playing Nicely with Others (And Picking Up Your Toys)

The 5th Wave
By Rich Tennant

"I don't care what your friends at school say.
You are not redrawing plans for the house with
SolidWorks so that you can have a bigger room."

In this part . . .

Working well with others in the design process is a key to success. Your job of collaborating with team members, vendors, and customers is easier and more effective when you know which data they need and how they need it formatted. In this part, I tell you everything you need to know about working with others and introduce eDrawings.

Chapter 12

Managing the Clutter

In This Chapter

▶ Exploring different data management options

▶ Setting up a file structure for data management

Data is one of your company's most valuable assets. In an engineering -company, that data includes not just CAD files but also project specifications, design review information, finite element analysis results, and engineering change orders. This data constitutes the basis of your products, so managing it properly is important.

You can manage design data in two ways: automatically, by using product data management (PDM) software, or manually, by setting up a system of file structures. This chapter tells you what to look for when you set up a PDM system and how to set up file directory structures to manage data manually in SolidWorks.

Managing Data with or without a Net

One of the most important decisions to make when you implement SolidWorks is how to manage the data. The safest bet (I call it "managing with a net") is to implement product data management (PDM) software, which manages and tracks product data automatically. PDMWorks is the PDM software made to work with SolidWorks, but others on the market also work with SolidWorks.

However, if your design team is small, you can opt to organize your data manually with a system of directories and file folders that you organize on a shared network server. You can also take advantage of SolidWorks collaboration settings, which allow you to control who has access to which data so that you can be sure that one person doesn't overwrite another's changes. (See Chapter 13 for more details on collaborating with others.)

Checking your list

Whether you choose to implement a PDM system or you decide to manage your data manually, consider this important checklist:

- ✔ **Ease of use:** I'm a firm believer that any system you want others to use should follow this rule of automation: It needs to be easy, offer value, and save time. Otherwise, no one will use it, or if they do, they'll use it so inconsistently that the value of the investment is lost.

- ✔ **Data security:** As anyone who has experienced a computer hard drive crash knows, data is never as valuable as when it's gone. In a multiuser environment, you want to put all your design data on a network server, develop a good backup plan, and stick to it.

- ✔ **Performance:** Working with large files over a network server can be slow. PDMWorks copies data to a local workspace (on the user's computer) and updates the information to the server periodically. Do you have a similar plan for your manual system?

- ✔ **Search capabilities:** The ability to quickly find data is one of the most important features in a data management system. PDMWorks has search tools built in. With a manual approach, the best way to find data is to use Windows Search to search by custom properties and filename.

- ✔ **Product life cycle:** Designs go through several revisions and changes throughout their life cycles (sort of like software does). You need a system for tracking various versions and for storing documents that are in different development phases, such as in progress, released, or obsolete.

- ✔ **Document access:** When working with other users on the same design project, you need to know who's working on what and when a new revision of a document is available. You also need a way to communicate that information back to other team members.

- ✔ **Metadata:** These custom properties, used in drawing title blocks, are stored in the document. Choose File➪Properties and then click the Custom tab in the Summary Information dialog box to see which values are defined within each type of document. A good PDM system can generate reports based on metadata stored in SolidWorks documents.

- ✔ **File manipulation:** How does the system copy, rename, archive, and delete documents and projects?

- ✔ **Tracking versions:** How does the system handle legacy (old) versions of documents? Does the system allow others to access old versions of drawings after a new change?

Deciding which way to go

The ways that you can manage your CAD data can be divided into three categories:

- ✔ **Manual,** such as a system of file folders that contain project data. You should keep these types of folders on a shared network server.
- ✔ **Workgroup-level PDM,** such as PDMWorks Workgroup, is a simple, inexpensive, easy-to-deploy data management system.
- ✔ **Enterprise-level PDM,** such as PDMWorks Enterprise, provides advanced data management tools, such as work flow and integration into other corporate computer systems.

Each of these categories has pros and cons, which I list in Table 12-1.

Table 12-1	Comparison of Data Management Tools	
Category	*Pros*	*Cons*
Manual	Simple; no additional software required.	A manual, error-prone process; lacks search capabilities. It's difficult to track versions (Rev A, Rev B, and so on) and keep old design history.
Workgroup-level PDM	A less expensive application that's easy to install. It has a vault, or central database.	Limited advanced capabilities, API, and integration support.
Enterprise-level PDM	Scalable (size of installation and scope of application). It has more advanced features.	More expensive and difficult to implement.

The rest of this chapter covers manual data management. Although you don't need a PDM system to create great designs in SolidWorks, the process is easier and more straightforward when you have one.

Managing your data manually is time consuming and can resemble running around with sharp sticks — you take the risk of falling and jabbing yourself. Similarly, at some point, trying to manage multiple documents manually is a problem.

For more information about PDMWorks, visit www.solidworks.com/pages/products/solutions/datamanagement.html.

Managing Your Data Manually

Whether you work alone or with a team of designers, if you don't have a PDM system, you need to manage files manually. For a manual system to be even remotely workable, you need to define a meaningful directory structure for storing projects and their related documents. You also need a strategy for creating and storing backups.

Setting up a good directory structure

Here's an example of a directory structure setup in Windows:

- **Main-level directories:** Use these top-level directories to organize your data. You could have two top-level directories, one named Released (for documents that have been checked and approved) and one named WIP (for works in progress or copies of files being changed). When you're looking for released files, you know to look in the Released directory. Likewise, files being worked on are in the WIP directory.

- **Standard part directories:** If a lot of your work entails the use of standard parts, put the standard part models in a shared network drive so that others can access the files and use them in designs. You may want to make the directory read-only so that only the CAD administrator can make changes or additions.

- **Project-level directories:** Below the main directories might be several levels of folders, used to further organize the data. Examples of second-level directory folders are Standard (for standard parts), Projects (named project number), Part Numbers (setup directories based on part numbers), and Part Type (motors and brackets, for example).

Having too many levels of directories and folders can make documents hard to find. Try to keep it simple so that everyone can quickly find what they're looking for.

When you name SolidWorks documents, don't include the revision number in the filename. For example, don't name a plate model plate-RevA, because any changes in plate-RevB aren't reflected in any drawing or assembly file which references that part. You have broken the reference. Instead, create a separate directory where you keep original copies for later reference. By using a directory structure like this one to store different versions, you more easily ensure that you don't edit the production copy. It's a bad day when your boss asks for Revision B and all you have to show her is Revision E.

Making backups

In the area of manual data management, you have to remember to back up your data regularly. At the office, you may work on a server for which the IT department manages backups. If you're part of a smaller operation, invest in large, external hard drives that connect to your computer via USB or look into an online backup service for storing data. You need enough space to store your large SolidWorks documents. In addition, you may want to back up data to another building location, in case your office disappears in a flood, a fire, or an earthquake and you need to go to work the next day.

Keep non-SolidWorks copies (such as eDrawings or PDF files) of all your released drawings. This way, you have a simple backup and additional references for all released drawings.

Copying Files with SolidWorks Explorer

When you start a new project or revise an existing project, you need to copy files. You're better off making copies using SolidWorks Explorer, not Windows Explorer. Windows Explorer isn't SolidWorks-*aware,* which means that it can't identify document references. If you use Windows Explorer to copy a SolidWorks drawing, the next time you open the drawing, you see a message telling you that the file cannot locate its references.

SolidWorks Explorer has the following advantages over Windows Explorer:

- ✔ **You can copy, replace, and rename SolidWorks documents without breaking links to external reference documents.** When you copy a drawing, for example, SolidWorks Explorer gives you the option to copy any part or assembly files that the drawing references.

- ✔ **You can view and change the custom properties of a document.**

- ✔ **You can find out which other SolidWorks documents reference or use the file.** If the file is a model of a standard component, you can find out which assembly designs are using the component. The limitation is that you can search only one directory at a time. You may need to change the directory and run the search again several times.

✔ **You can operate the aforementioned functions without opening a SolidWorks document.** This feature offers a performance advantage, especially when dealing with massive assembly files that take a long time to load.

You can run SolidWorks Explorer independently of SolidWorks. To copy a file in SolidWorks Explorer, follow these steps:

1. **Choose Start➪All Programs➪SolidWorks <version and service pack>➪SolidWorks Explorer 2008.**

   The SolidWorks Explorer window appears, as shown in Figure 12-1.

2. **In the File Explorer pane, browse to and choose the document you want to copy.**

3. **Right-click the document name and select the SolidWorks Pack and Go option from the pop-up menu.**

   The Pack and Go dialog box appears, as shown in Figure 12-2, where the file appears. If you're copying a drawing or assembly file, all related (or *child*) documents also appear.

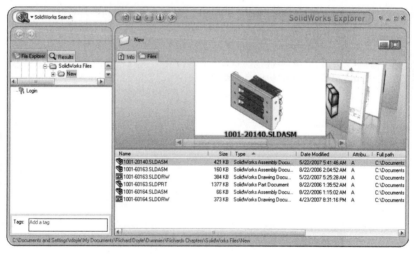

Figure 12-1:
The best way to copy files is with SolidWorks Explorer.

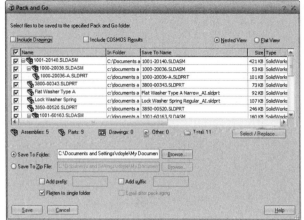

Figure 12-2:
The Pack
and Go
dialog box.

4. **Select the Save to Folder radio button.**

   Click the Browse button to select a location for the files to be copied. If you don't want to copy certain files, clear the check boxes next to their filenames. To change the name of any document, double-click in the Save to Name column and type a new filename.

5. **Click Save.**

By default, the Save to Folder defaults to the current directory. To copy to a new location, use the Browse button in the Save to Folder field.

Chapter 13

Collaborating with Team Members

· ·

· ·

As a designer, rarely do you work on a design alone. More likely, you're part of an extended design team, with members spread out across the country or around the world. In a multiuser environment, keeping projects on a network server allows everyone to access the files. At the same time, you need to control who is working on what so that one person doesn't overwrite another's changes. You also want to store common design elements in a design library to save time and rework.

This chapter introduces SolidWorks tools that allow you to collaborate and work with other designers in a multiuser environment.

Keeping Everyone on the Same Page When Collaborating

In a *multiuser environment,* multiple designers are accessing and revising assembly files at the same time. One of the biggest issues in this type of situation is figuring out how to manage the data. A SolidWorks assembly can include hundreds of part and subassembly documents, manufacturing drawings, and other engineering material. To complicate things even more, many documents reference other documents, so one change can ripple through thousands of other documents. For this reason, you need to keep a close watch on who modifies what and when, or else an entire project can go down the gurgler.

Many people use *project data management* (PDM) software to manage data in a multiuser environment. PDMWorks, a PDM software program that runs inside the SolidWorks environment, stores documents in project directories in a vault (usually on a server). PDMWorks controls projects with procedures for checkout, check-in, revision control, and other administrative tasks.

Not everyone feels the pull to go the PDM route. If your design team has only a few members and you're not yet ready for the additional software investment, you can opt to manage your data manually by placing the data on a server (or otherwise making it available on a network) and setting up Windows folders for different projects.

SolidWorks offers tools to manage access to data in a multiuser environment where there's no PDM system. One of those tools is the Collaboration Mode option.

When Collaboration mode is enabled, it offers several advantages. You can

- ✔ **Mark parts and subassemblies for read and write access.** *Read-only* means that users can review the parts and subassemblies but cannot make changes to them. If someone tries to make a change, a message warns that the document is read-only. Users can modify only documents marked write-access.

- ✔ **Identify who is working on what.** When the assembly is open, a ToolTip in the FeatureManager design tree informs you, by using visual clues on the component icons, whether a part or subassembly is write-access or read-only. If another user with write access has a document open, a ToolTip names the user.

- ✔ **See the status and properties of items at a glance.** In File Explorer, modified files appear in bold, read-only files appear in orange, and write-access documents appear in black. Icons for files open in SolidWorks are solid. Icons for referenced components that are in memory but not open are transparent. The File Explorer tab (see Figure 13-1) is in the SolidWorks Resource task pane, to the right of the graphics area.

Figure 13-1:
In File Explorer, icons for files that are open in SolidWorks appear solid.

Setting the Collaboration mode options

Okay, so you decided to manage your data manually. You'll be fine as long as your design team is relatively small and you set up a system that others can follow. First, be sure to put project data in a central location, such as a networked server, so that others can access it. Next, organize your projects in Windows folders. (Read more about organizing projects in file directories in Chapter 12.) Finally, have each design team member turn on Collaboration mode in SolidWorks, to ensure that one person doesn't inadvertently overwrite another's changes when you're working on the same assembly. Collaboration mode allows you to set documents as read-only or write-access.

Here's how to set up Collaboration mode:

1. **Choose Tools⇨Options.**

   A dialog box appears. If you have a document open, it contains two tabs. If no document is open, only the System Options tab appears.

2. **On the System Options tab, click Collaboration.**

   The Collaboration Mode options appear in the right panel.

3. **Select the Enable Multi-User Environment check box, as shown in Figure 13-2.**

   After you select this option, other options become available.

4. **Select the check boxes for these two other options:**

   • *Add Shortcut Menu Items for Multi-User Environment:* Selecting this option adds menu items for Make Read-Only and Get Write Access, which are accessible when you right-click an assembly component in the FeatureManager design tree. You can now switch the read and write access of any document with a single right-click.

   • *Check If Files Opened Read-Only Have Been Modified By Other Users:* When this option is enabled, at a time interval you specify (the default is every 20 minutes), SolidWorks checks files that you've opened as read-only to see whether they've been modified in one of the following ways: Another user saves a file that you have open in SolidWorks, making your file out of date, or another user relinquishes write access to the file that you have open in SolidWorks by making the file read-only, allowing you to take write access. If the system detects a change, a ToolTip in the lower-right corner of the graphics area points to an icon on the status bar. Click the icon to access the Reload dialog box.

5. **Click OK.**

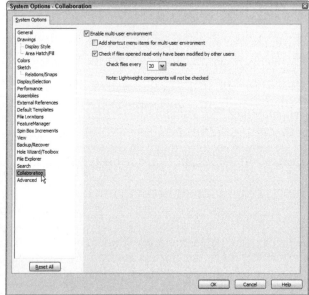

Figure 13-2:
Collabor-
ation
mode
allows you
to manage
access to
documents.

Giving users read/write access

Collaboration mode allows you to make any assembly component read-only or write-access. Here's how to wield your power:

1. **Open the assembly document.**

   A list of components appears in the FeatureManager design tree.

2. **Right-click a component in the FeatureManager design tree.**

   A pull-down menu appears.

3. **Choose Get Write Access or Make Read-Only.**

   The part changes to write-access or read-only.

If you want to check whether anyone has updated one of the documents in your current assembly, click Check Read-Only Files on the Standard toolbar, as shown in Figure 13-3. (You may have to add the Check Read-Only Files button to your standard toolbar; see Chapter 2.) If the files haven't changed, a message appears. If any files have changed, the Reload dialog box appears. This dialog box gives you the choice of reloading modified items into your current session or reloading the original version of a document without closing SolidWorks.

Figure 13-3:
Read-only
files appear
on the
Standard
toolbar.

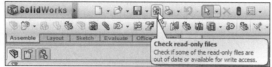

Figure 13-3:
Read-only
files appear
on the
Standard
toolbar.

Covering the bases: External references

In SolidWorks, many documents reference others. For example, an assembly
may reference dozens of part and subassembly documents. Any change to one
of those external references may affect the assembly. The External Reference
option in SolidWorks automatically marks as read-only any documents that
an assembly references while you have that assembly open. Here's how you
activate this feature in SolidWorks:

1. **Choose Tools➪Options.**

   A dialog box appears with one or two tabs, depending on whether you
   have a document open.

2. **In the dialog box that appears, select the System Options tab, as
   shown in Figure 13-4.**

   The System Options options appear.

3. **Select External References.**

   The External References options appear in the right pane.

4. **Select the check boxes for the following options:**

   - *Open Referenced Documents with Read-Only Access:* SolidWorks
     makes all referenced documents read-only by default.

   - *Don't Prompt to Save Read-Only Referenced Documents (Discard
     Changes):* When you save or close a parent document, SolidWorks
     doesn't prompt you to save its read-only reference documents.
     (Otherwise, the multitude of prompts can get annoying.)

5. **Click OK.**

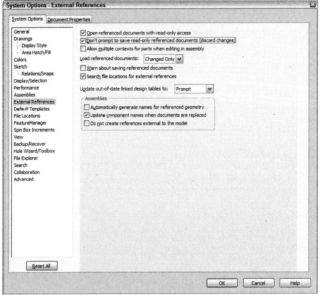

Figure 13-4:
You can set
External
References
options
so that
SolidWorks
doesn't
prompt you
to save any
read-only
references
of an
assembly.

Exploring Standard Design Elements

Whenever possible, reuse information. Redesigning standard components is a waste of time, especially if the supplier makes component models available through online supplier catalogs. Likewise, you don't want your design team to create the same features repeatedly. Find or build the components once, and then put them somewhere that everyone can grab a copy. On the SolidWorks Design Library tab of the SolidWorks task pane (see Figure 13-5) are four folders where you can store standard components and design elements for use by your entire design team.

Here's a brief description of each folder:

- **SolidWorks Design Library:** Located in a separate folder (of the same name) on the Design Library tab, the Design Library is where you can store company-standard features, annotations, and components.

- **SolidWorks Toolbox:** Contains a library of standard hardware (bolts, nuts, washers, and standoffs, for example) that is integrated with the SolidWorks software.

- **3D ContentCentral:** Has links to component supplier Web sites and a library where SolidWorks users can share CAD models that they design.

Figure 13-5:
The
SolidWorks
Design
Library
stores
standard
design
elements.

✔ **SolidWorks Content:** Has links to additional SolidWorks content, including predefined blocks and structural members used for creating weldments. You can download the content to your local folders by holding down the Ctrl key and clicking the items you want to download.

Inside the Design Library

The Design Library (which you should put on a shared network server if you work in a multiuser environment) is a place for you to store the design components and elements you use most often. The library contains separate folders for parts, assemblies, and features, for example. SolidWorks supplies content for these folders, but you can add new folders and customize existing ones by adding your own content over time.

One criterion I use to decide whether a part belongs in the Design Library or in the PDM vault (if you use PDM software) is whether your organization has design control over the part. If you designed the part and need to maintain a design history of it, put the part in the PDM vault. If the component is a purchased part, it's a good candidate for the Design Library.

Finding your way around in the Design Library is straightforward. The following command buttons are available on the Design Library tab:

✔ **Add to Library:** Adds content to the Design Library.

✔ **Add File Location:** Adds an existing folder to the Design Library.

✔ **Create New Folder:** Creates a new folder in the Design Library.

✔ **Refresh:** Refreshes the view of the Design Library tab.

If you want to use an item in the Design Library, simply select the item and drag it onto your design. Similarly, you can also drag items from your design into folders in the Design Library. When you drag an item into a folder, the Save As dialog box appears and lists the item's default file type. You need to type only an optional part description and click Save.

Design Library folders accept all document types. You can save a part file in a folder marked Assemblies just as you can put socks in your underwear drawer. The folder names are there only to keep you organized.

Here are a few other ways to copy design elements into the Design Library:

✔ **To copy an assembly or part into the Design Library:** Select the item in the FeatureManager design tree and drag it to an appropriate folder in the lower pane of the Design Library tab.

✔ **To copy annotations or blocks into the Design Library:** Hold down the Shift key on your keyboard and drag the annotation or block from the graphics area to the lower pane of the Design Library.

✔ **To copy a feature into the Design Library:** Drag the feature from the FeatureManager design tree or the graphics area. Features are saved as library feature parts with the extension .sldlfp.

By default, SolidWorks installs the Design Library in C:\Program Files\ SolidWorks\data\design library. If you plan to use SolidWorks in a multiuser environment, copy the Design Library to a network directory and make it read-only so that only the system administrator can make changes.

Using SolidWorks Toolbox

If you're like me, you keep a box of nails, screws, and other parts that you can reach into whenever you need to fix or build something at home. You don't want to run to the hardware store each time you need a nut or a bolt. SolidWorks has something similar: a virtual toolbox.

SolidWorks Toolbox includes a library of standard fasteners (bolts, nuts, chain sprockets, and timing belts, for example) that you can add to your SolidWorks assembly. Here's how Toolbox works: Say that you want to attach a hinge to a door or fasten a waste pipe to a sink. Simply select the standard screws and washers included in SolidWorks Toolbox and drag them into your design. This way, you don't have to make additional parts to complete your assembly.

Searching for a bolt or a nut in Toolbox is like thumbing through the pages of a part catalog. Similar to a catalog, SolidWorks Toolbox folders are divided by standard (ANSI, BSI, or CISC, for example), category (washers, pins, screws), or type (lag screws, machine screws, miniature screws).

SolidWorks fills Toolbox folders with some standard items, but you can customize Toolbox to include those parts that you refer to most frequently. You can also make a copy of any Toolbox part and edit it as needed.

Because SolidWorks Toolbox is an add-in, it isn't available with the standard SolidWorks program. You have to buy it separately or as part of the SolidWorks Office Professional or SolidWorks Office Premium bundles. After you install Toolbox, open SolidWorks and choose Tools➪Add Ins. In the Add-Ins dialog box, select the SolidWorks Toolbox and the SolidWorks Toolbox Browser options. Click OK.

Inserting the hardware

You can easily add fasteners to your assembly by dragging them out of Toolbox and dropping them into your model. You can also configure fasteners to your exact needs. Here's how to edit a Toolbox fastener and insert it into your open assembly:

1. **Click the Design Library icon on the SolidWorks task pane.**

   The task pane displays the contents of the Design Library.

2. **Click the Toolbox folder.**

   The Toolbox folder expands to reveal several folders that represent standard part catalogs.

3. **Click the plus sign (+) to the right of a standard folder.**

   The folder expands to reveal more folders.

4. **Drill down through the folders (standards, categories, types, fasteners) to find the fastener you need.**

5. **Drag the part into your assembly.**

   A PropertyManager dialog box appears for the part you selected (see Figure 13-6). You can use this dialog box to set the property values for the part or to change the part number or to add a description before adding the part to the assembly.

6. **Find the property you want to update and then select a value from the pull-down list next to it.**

   For parts included with SolidWorks Toolbox, the values in the list are valid standards-based values for the selected part.

7. **Continue to update the remaining properties and values until the size is correct.**

8. **Click the green check mark icon.**

   The part appears in the assembly.

Figure 13-6:
You can use Toolbox to insert standard fasteners into an assembly.

SolidWorks marks a Toolbox file with an attribute (IsFastener) that identifies the file as a fastener. If you add new components to Toolbox, you can run a utility to mark the new files as Toolbox content. You can find this utility at `<SolidWorks install directory>\Toolbox\data utilities\ sldsetdocprop.exe`. Open the utility and select the Toolbox directory that you want to update by using the Add Files or Add Directories button. Browse to the directory and click OK. Select Update Status to update the document property.

Adding fasteners the smart way

Toolbox allows for the use of Smart Fasteners, a SolidWorks feature that automatically inserts bolts and screws into your assembly where there's a hole, hole series, or pattern of holes (see Figure 13-7) sized to accept the standard hardware. Smart Fasteners use fasteners that come from the Toolbox library, but you can also add your own, custom designs to the Toolbox database and use them within Smart Fasteners.

Figure 13-7: Smart Fasteners add fasteners to an assembly automatically.

Smart Fasteners can also add nuts and washers to your fasteners. Bolts and screws can have an associated Top Stack (washers under the head of the fastener) and Bottom Stack (washers and nuts added to the end of the fastener). You can use Smart Fasteners to insert bolts, screws, nuts, and washers to your assembly in a few simple steps (refer to Figure 13-7).

To add Smart Fasteners to an open assembly, follow these steps:

1. **Choose Insert⇨Smart Fasteners.**

   The Smart Fastener PropertyManager appears.

2. **If you want to add fasteners to all holes in the assembly, in the Selection area, click Populate All.**

   Smart Fasteners fills the holes in your assembly with fasteners.

   If you're working on a very large assembly, SolidWorks may prompt you with the message "This operation may take a long time. Do you want to continue?" If you have time on your hands, click Yes and skip to Step 5. Otherwise, click No and proceed to Step 3.

3. **If you want to add fasteners to only certain areas of your assembly, select a hole (or holes), a face, or a component.**

   The selected items appear in the Selection area. If you want to remove an item, select the item and press the Delete key.

4. **To add fasteners to the items, select Add in the Selection area.**

   Fasteners are added to the items you selected. If you selected a component, Smart Fasteners finds all available holes in that component. If you selected a face, Smart Fasteners finds all available holes that pass through the surface. Fastener types appear in the Fastener field.

5. **If you want to change a fastener type or the top or bottom stacks, in the Fastener field, right-click the item and choose Change Fastener Type.**

   The Smart Fasteners dialog box for the fastener type is displayed.

6. **Select a replacement fastener by using the pull-down menus in the Standard, Category, Type, and Fastener boxes.**

7. **Click OK.**

   The Smart Fasteners dialog box closes, and the model is updated with the new fastener types.

8. **Click OK (the green check mark).**

   The Smart Fastener PropertyManager closes.

A place for sharing: 3D ContentCentral

Designing standard parts when you can find ready-made CAD models online is a waste of time. 3D ContentCentral helps you find the part models you need in a format you can use. This online resource offers direct access to timesaving CAD models from leading suppliers and from individual SolidWorks users worldwide. You find two main areas in 3D ContentCentral:

- ✔ **Supplier content:** The Supplier Content folder provides links to the Web sites of suppliers who use SolidWorks 3D PartStream.NET to create their online part catalogs. Some of the part models in the catalogs are configurable so that you can tailor them to suit your needs.

- ✔ **User library:** In this section, you can share parts with other designers. You can download a ready-made part model to use in your design or post one of your own for others to access. When you post a component, your name appears on the download page of that part.

Anyone can access 3D ContentCentral at `www.3dcontentcentral.com`. The benefit of getting there directly from the SolidWorks software is that you don't have to register to use the site. (Some individual supplier sites, however, require a separate registration to download the models.)

The following sections explain how to use the most popular features on the site.

Finding a part for your model

To use a component from 3D ContentCentral, follow these steps:

1. **In the SolidWorks task pane, click the Design Library tab, as shown in Figure 13-8.**

Figure 13-8: You can access 3D Content Central from the Design Library.

2. **Click the plus sign (+) to expand the 3D Content Central folder.**

   Folders named Supplier Content and User Library appear.

3. **Select Supplier Content or User Library.**

   In the lower pane, folders appear for All Categories and All Suppliers if you chose Supplier Content, or Home Page if you chose User Library.

4. **Double-click a folder — All Categories, for example.**

   An icon appears that serves as a link to the 3D Content Central Web site.

5. **Click the 3D Content Central icon to open the home page, where you can begin your search for models.**

6. **Click to select a supplier name from the alphabetized list, or use the Search bar to locate a specific part type.**

   If you click a supplier name, a Web browser opens in SolidWorks and takes you to the supplier's online part catalog, where you see a selection of parts to peruse. Supplier sites vary slightly, and some allow you to configure components to your specifications (see Figure 13-9).

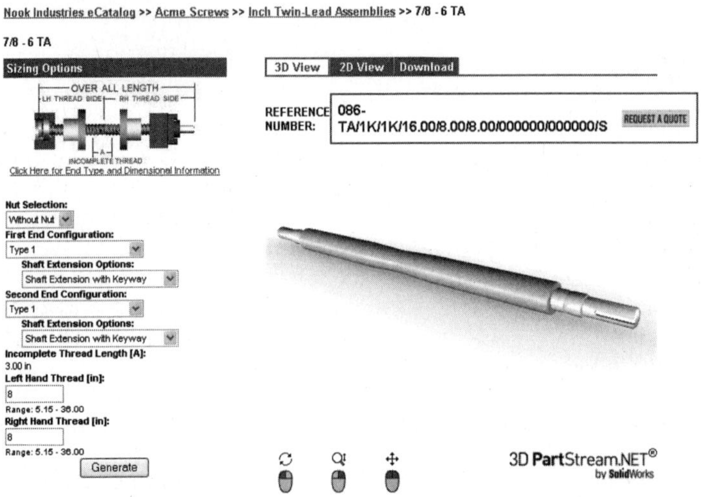

Figure 13-9: Some supplier sites allow you to configure components before you download them.

If you select User Library, you see a Web page that contains a gallery of parts. Clicking a category opens another page that shows all part types in that category. When you click the icon of the part type you're looking for, a list of models appears. You also see a detailed description of the part, an image of the model, and the name of the user who designed the part. Some users include their e-mail addresses. Click a model to download it.

7. **Locate a part and click its icon.**

   After you click the part icon , you can configure and download the model. Some models let you choose the file format, although in the User Library, the models are generally offered in only the SolidWorks format.

8. **When the part is ready, click and drag the file into your assembly.**

9. **Close the Internet browser window.**

Adding a model you want to share

If you want to submit a model to the 3D ContentCentral User Library, right-click 3D ContentCentral and choose Share a Model. Follow the directions on-screen to enter your profile information and upload your model. SolidWorks Corporation reviews your model and informs you whether the model has been accepted for sharing.

The SolidWorks Resources section of the Task Pane also has an engineering search engine that you can use to locate engineering-related topics you want to read about. The search is conducted by the GLOBALSPEC search engine.

Working with Different File Formats

At times, you may need to exchange files with people who use other CAD systems — or no CAD system. For example, you may need to communicate with a vendor who doesn't accept native SolidWorks files or to show a design to a customer (or someone in your own, internal marketing department) who doesn't have access to a CAD system.

Become familiar with the different translation formats so that you can send and receive information easily, without the extra work of having to verify and clean up imported documents.

In general, you need to be familiar with these four important topics:

- **Types of formats:** Knowing the different types of CAD and image formats you can use makes life easier when transferring SolidWorks documents.

- **Exporting files:** You need to know a few things about how to send documents to other systems.

- **Importing files:** The importing features enable you to you work with documents sent from other systems.

- **Fixing import and export issues:** When you have issues with imported data, sometimes there's an easy fix.

In the sections that follow, you find details about each of these topics.

Looking at types and uses of data formats

During your career as a designer, whether you work on a team or as a lone contractor from your home, you may often have to swap files with other people. Here are a few examples I've encountered:

- A supplier wants to send you a CAD model of a standard component so that you can check it for fit and clearance within your assembly.

- You need to export a file to a customer for review and approval.

- Your internal marketing department wants a graphical image of the model to create advertising materials for print products and the Web site.

- A supplier needs 3D data of the product to program his computer-aided manufacturing (CAM) software with.

- The shop floor wants a manufacturing drawing of the product so that it can see how to assemble it.

- A customer sends you an existing DWG or DXF sketch of the product, and you need to import the sketch file into SolidWorks as the basis for a model.

Luckily for you, SolidWorks can import and export in several different file formats so that you can share files with other users. Table 13-1 describes the data format categories.

Table 13-1	Data File Format Categories
Name	**Description**
SolidWorks	Native SolidWorks documents (parts, assemblies, drawings, library features, and templates, for example).
eDrawings	A lightweight 2D and 3D viewing format. You can publish an eDrawings file from inside SolidWorks or any major CAD system.
Neutral	Neutral 2D and 3D file formats, which are non-system-specific and include DXF, DWG, IGES, STEP, ACIS, and Parasolid.
Vendor specific	Formats native to other systems (AutoDesk Inventor, Unigraphics, and Solid Edge, for example).
Graphical	Image formats (JPEG and TIFF, for example).

How you save your SolidWorks document depends on the recipient's plans for the document and his type of system. If the recipient uses SolidWorks, you can send him a native SolidWorks file. But, if you want him to get only a general idea of the model, you might send an eDrawings file. Although SolidWorks supports many different file formats, keep these points in mind:

- ✔ Use SolidWorks native files whenever possible.

- ✔ If the other system is Parasolid-based (Unigraphics NX and Solid Edge), use the Parasolid format. Because SolidWorks is also built on the Parasolid kernel, it makes sense to send files in the neutral Parasolid format.

- ✔ Consider sending more than one neutral format (IGES and STEP) when working with a new supplier, to allow for troubleshooting in case one file doesn't convert properly.

Exporting SolidWorks files

When you export a SolidWorks document, all you're really doing is saving it in a different format using the Save As dialog box. To export a file for use in another program, follow these steps:

1. **Open the file to export, and choose File⇨Save As.**

   The Save As Document dialog box appears.

2. **From the Save As Type drop-down list, choose the format in which you want to save the file.**

   If you're not sure of the best format to use, refer to Table 13-1.

3. **Click Save.**

   Your document is saved in the new format. The "exporting" part is up to you. Depending on the size of the file and your time constraints, you can send the file by e-mail or snail mail, post the file on an FTP site, or hand the job over to an overnight courier service.

Importing non-SolidWorks files

When you're working with other members of your design team, importing files is no problem because they all use SolidWorks. Trouble arises when you receive *non-native files,* which are created in another system (such as Mechanical Desktop, Pro/Engineer, or Solid Edge) or when you receive inter-mediary 3D file types, such as IGES or STEP.

CAD files can be large and complicated. It isn't uncommon for a CAD program to have difficulty interpreting information that arrives in a different format. Most problems occur because a CAD system has trouble re-creating faces or edges on the model when importing the file. (The next section, on problem-solving, covers how to correct this type of issue.)

To import a file from another application, follow these steps:

1. **Choose File⇨Open.**

   The Open Document dialog box appears.

2. **In the dialog box, select a file type (for example, DWG, IGES, or STL) in the Files of Type field.**

   Be sure that the file extension of the file you're importing is correct. If the filename is `Newpart.dwg`, use the DWG file format.

3. **Browse to select the file that you want to open, and click Open.**

   Your file opens inside SolidWorks.

   If you're importing a DXF or DWG file, the DXF/DWG Import Wizard appears. You can choose to edit the file in the DWGEditor or to import it to a sheet in a native format (view only) in addition to importing it to a part or drawing document.

   If you import an IGES, STEP, or other 3D file that contains surfaces, SolidWorks reads the surfaces this way:

   - *If the file has surfaces that are hidden,* SolidWorks imports the surfaces and adds them to the FeatureManager design tree as surface features.

   - *If SolidWorks can knit the surfaces into a solid,* the solid appears as the base feature (named Imported 1) in a new part file. You can add features (bosses and cuts, for example) to this base feature, but you cannot edit the base feature itself.

   - *If the surfaces represent multiple closed volumes (or bodies),* one part is made for each closed volume. An assembly file also is made that includes the imported parts positioned relative to the assembly origin, according to how the surfaces are defined in the imported file.

     For ACIS files, if the imported ACIS file has only surfaces, SolidWorks creates only surfaces even though the surfaces represent multiple closed volumes, no matter which import options you choose. If the ACIS file contains data about multiple solid bodies (or bodies), SolidWorks creates parts or surfaces, depending on the import option you choose.

   - *If SolidWorks can't knit together the surfaces,* the surfaces are grouped into one or more surface features (named Surface-Imported 1, Surface-Imported 2, and so on) in a new part file.

Solving common import problems

The process of importing documents doesn't always go smoothly. Errors can occur for a number of reasons. The problem may have to do with the method that the other system used to write the document, the way SolidWorks reads the file, or an incompatible feature type in the neutral file. When you import from another system and you get a surface body rather than a solid body, it's an indication that SolidWorks had trouble reading the file and turning the surfaces into a solid body. Bad surface geometry, gaps in surfaces, and surfaces that overlap can all cause these problems. Fortunately, SolidWorks has an Import Diagnostics tool, which can help you identify and fix problems.

Here's how you can tell that a file hasn't been imported properly:

- ✔ After importing the file, SolidWorks displays a warning and a prompt to open the diagnostics function, as shown in Figure 13-10.

- ✔ After SolidWorks opens the part, a warning or an error message appears next to an imported feature in the FeatureManager design tree.

Figure 13-10:
SolidWorks warns you when a file doesn't import properly.

The Diagnosis tool diagnoses and repairs gaps and faces on imported features. To diagnose and fix or simplify faces, follow these steps:

1. **Right-click the imported feature in the FeatureManager design tree and choose Import Diagnostics.**

   SolidWorks automatically runs a diagnostics test of the imported geometry.

2. **If Import Diagnostics finds face errors, you can hover the pointer over the faces listed in the Faulty Faces box to see a ToolTip that reports the problem.**

3. **Click Attempt to Heal All.**

   Alternatively, you can select either Attempt to Heal Faces or Attempt to Heal Gaps. A third option is to right-click each listed face or gap and choose Heal Face or Heal Gap.

To simplify entities with a tolerance greater than 1.0e-8 meters and less than 1.0e-5 meters, you must manually select the relevant faces and then click Attempt to Heal All Faces.

1. **Select the two faces in the graphics area.**

2. **Click Attempt to Heal All Faces.**

   If the two faces are meant to be one (for example, the two halves of a cylindrical face), the two faces merge. The diagnosis performs an in-depth check on all entities in a model.

3. **Click OK.**

   If the imported body still shows rebuild error markers even though a body check and the Import Diagnosis PropertyManager report no surface problems, the body is probably valid.

4. **Click Rebuild to clear the rebuild error markers.**

   You can merge multiple edges into a single edge by using Heal Edges on the Features toolbar. To view and fix gaps, follow these steps:

   a. *Right-click the Imported feature in the FeatureManager design tree and choose Import Diagnostics.* The PropertyManager reports the number of gaps found.

   b. *View and fix the gaps by using the Attempt to Heal All Gaps tool.*

   c. *Click OK.*

If you run into a dead end and, no matter how hard you try, the methods in this section don't seem to fix the problem, here are some ideas:

✔ Call the sender and ask him to send you a native format, if possible.

✔ Ask for another file type or another version of the file format.

✔ Use a direct translator (available through SolidWorks partners).

✔ Manually identify and clean up the problem areas by using the Import Diagnostics tool described in this section. Then remove and re-create the faces in question.

Chapter 14

Viewing and Reviewing Documents

Sharing your design with others doesn't mean that you have to continually send huge CAD (computer-aided design) files via overnight courier services. Instead, you can take advantage of CAD viewers to save time and be more efficient. CAD viewers allow people without CAD licenses to view, mark up, and measure your CAD design without having to own or operate expensive or complex software.

Imagine that you want to send a model of your stovetop espresso maker to a vendor to see whether the vendor can manufacture it. You can e-mail a lightweight version of the model so that the vendor can take measurements and add comments and then return it by e-mail to you the next day.

In this chapter, I introduce you to two CAD viewers that let you look at SolidWorks drawings, parts, and assembly documents: eDrawings and the SolidWorks Viewer.

I also briefly touch on graphics files and embedded and linked documents so that you know how to include SolidWorks documents in your presentations.

Viewing with CAD Viewers

When you work with other design team members, vendors, or customers, the ability to communicate design ideas quickly is vital. But sometimes you don't want to or need to, or simply cannot, send someone an entire SolidWorks file.

CAD files, for example, tend to be very large — a SolidWorks assembly can easily reach 150MB — which makes them cumbersome and tricky to send. And they contain propriety information, so you don't want to send your CAD files to just anybody. You may want to send someone only enough information to take accurate measurements or to see how an assembly fits together.

CAD viewers help in this process. A *CAD viewer* lets you look at 2D and 3D design data in its non-native format, without having to own or operate complicated or expensive CAD software. (Not that SolidWorks is either of those things, but a less technical person may consider it so.)

Two CAD viewers — eDrawings and the SolidWorks Viewer — allow you to review and print SolidWorks documents in a non-native format. Both viewers are free and available at the SolidWorks Web site (`www.solidworks.com/pages/products/designtools.html`).

Here are a few scenarios where a CAD viewer may come in handy:

- ✔ **Request quotes from vendors:** You can send a compressed eDrawing file (see the later section "Communicating with eDrawings") to a vendor who can then use the markup tools in eDrawings to request changes or additions.

- ✔ **Perform virtual design reviews:** What better way to distribute design data than in an e-mail? CAD viewers give you that advantage. Your design team can view a document and mark it up and then send back comments.

- ✔ **Make customer presentations:** Your customers don't want to invest in SolidWorks just to see your works of art. A CAD viewer lets a customer view a CAD file without having any special knowledge of CAD. If you send your customer an eDrawings file, a special animation feature plays the design so that it rotates automatically through different orientations.

- ✔ **Send engineering change notices:** Design engineers spend their entire careers making changes to designs. A CAD viewer can make it easier to check and approve designs and send back comments.

Keep in mind that CAD viewers aren't the only way to present your design brilliance to people. Graphical formats (such as TIF, BMP, and JPEG) are great for sharing, too. The only problem is that they're flat images that contain no real CAD data, so you can't measure them or check for mass properties.

Sharing Models and Data with eDrawings

eDrawings is a free e-mail–enabled program included with SolidWorks that lets you share designs with the people who need to see them, no matter which CAD program they have — or don't have. eDrawings is easy to use and comes in two parts: Viewer and Publisher. A Professional version includes additional capabilities to mark up and measure a model. The standard Viewer and Publisher are free, but you have to pay for the Professional version.

You can download the standard eDrawings Viewer and Publisher or the Professional version of eDrawings at `www.eDrawingsViewer.com`. If you download Publisher or the Professional version, the viewer downloads automatically, so you don't have to download it again. You need the viewer to save any eDrawings files you publish in your CAD system.

eDrawings Publishers are available for SolidWorks and most major CAD systems. Anyone with the eDrawing Viewer can read an eDrawing file.

Using eDrawings offers you many advantages:

- eDrawings Viewer reads and prints any eDrawings file; native SolidWorks drawing, part, and assembly file; and also any DWG and DXF drawing files.

- eDrawings Publisher produces a lightweight, compressed format, making your CAD design small enough to send in an e-mail.

- Although an eDrawings file hides proprietary data, it retains external graphical details as well as the dimensions and mass properties of your model. This feature makes eDrawings accurate enough for proper measurements.

- You can send an eDrawings file with a built-in viewer in a self-extracting e-mail. The recipient just double-clicks the attachment, and the CAD model or drawing appears.

- With the extra collaboration features included in eDrawings Professional, you can measure and mark up files, add comments, and manage markups from other design team members.

- eDrawings also offers several tools that give you a better understanding of the design. A Play button moves the model or drawing through different views automatically. You can interrogate the model and examine it up close with zoom, rotate, and pan functions.

Creating an eDrawings file

With eDrawings Publisher, you can publish native SolidWorks documents as eDrawings files, which anyone can view with the free eDrawings Viewer. Because eDrawing Publisher is a SolidWorks add-in, a Publish eDrawings 2008 File command icon appears on the SolidWorks main toolbar.

eDrawings 2008 comes standard with SolidWorks, but just like with other add-ins, you need to select it in the Add-Ins dialog box so that it appears on the SolidWorks Standard toolbar. In SolidWorks, choose Tools➪Add-Ins. When the Add-Ins dialog box appears, select eDrawings and click OK.

To publish an eDrawings file from within SolidWorks, follow these steps:

1. **Open the drawing, part, or assembly file that you want to publish.**

2. **Choose File➪Publish eDrawings 2008 File.**

   The eDrawings Viewer appears, displaying the new eDrawings file you just created.

   Your file isn't saved automatically. You must save it using eDrawings Viewer.

3. **Within eDrawings Viewer, choose File➪Save As.**

   The Save As dialog box appears.

4. **In the Save In drop-down list, browse to the location where you want to save the document.**

5. **Enter the name for the file in the File Name field.** The default name is based on the original SolidWorks document. To change the name, type a new name for the file.

6. **In the Save As Type field, select the file format in which you want to save the file.**

   In addition to using the standard EDRW, EPRT, or EASM format, you can also save your file as a 2D image file, such as a JPG, TIF, or PNG file.

7. **Click Save.**

Creating an eDrawings file from SolidWorks

Creating an eDrawings file directly from SolidWorks allows some additional control over the model data. Using the Save As eDrawings option, you can allow the receiver to measure (or not measure), to output (or not output) a solid model or assembly to the STL format, view (or not view) the drawing in shaded mode, or view (or not view) any animations included in the file.

To create an eDrawings file, follow these steps:

1. **Open the drawing, part, or assembly file that you want to publish.**

2. **Choose File⯈Save As.**

   The Save As dialog box appears.

3. **In the Save In drop-down list, browse to the location where you want to save the document.**

4. **Enter the name for the file in the File Name field. The default name is based on the original SolidWorks document. To change the name, type a new name for the file.**

5. **In the Save As Type field, select eDrawings.**

6. **Click the Options button, and select any other options you want to apply.**

   Depending on the file type you're saving, other options include

   - *Okay to Measure This eDrawings File:* By checking this option, if you have eDrawings Professional, you enable the recipient to measure your design.

   - *Save Shaded Data in Drawings(Drawings Only):* This option saves the shaded data from a drawing in the eDrawings file.

   - *Allow Export to STL for Parts and Assemblies (Parts and Assemblies Only):* This option allows the recipient to save the eDrawings file as an STL (stereolithography) file for output on a rapid prototype machine.

   - *Save Animator Animations to eDrawings File:* This option saves any animations from the SolidWorks model and allows the receiver to play them using eDrawings.

Sending an eDrawings file

A benefit that sets apart eDrawings is the ability to send a file with eDrawings Viewer encapsulated in an e-mail. This way, the receiver has nothing to download. He simply clicks the attachment, and the eDrawings drawing or model appears. Firewalls don't like executable files because they look like virus attachments; however, eDrawings offers several sending options to ensure that your file gets through.

To send an eDrawings file, follow these steps:

1. **Open the eDrawings file in eDrawings Viewer.**

2. **Choose File⇨Send.**

   The Send As dialog box appears.

3. **Choose how you want to save your file.**

   Your options include

   - *eDrawings File (.edrw, .eprt. or .easm):* Allows you to send a file as an eDrawings file. The recipient needs to install eDrawings Viewer, but this option is best for the smallest file size.

   - *Zip File (.zip):* Creates a firewall-friendly zip file that contains the self-extracting eDrawings Viewer; the recipient needs to have the software to unzip the viewer.

   - *HTML File (.htm):* Displays the eDrawings file within a firewall-safe HTML Web page that the recipient can view with Internet Explorer. Installs Viewer automatically.

   - *Executable File (.exe):* Creates a self-executable file with Viewer attached. The least firewall-friendly option, it's also the most likely to have the recipient's antivirus program strip it from the e-mail. The file is larger (1.4MB) because of the embedded viewer.

4. **Click Save.**

   eDrawings generates an outgoing e-mail with the file attached.

5. **Type the recipient's e-mail address and click Send.**

Measuring and marking up

The standard version of the eDrawings Viewer includes interrogation tools (Spin, Pan, and Zoom) that allow you to get a closer look at a design. If you want the collaboration tools, including the ability to mark up and measure, get your hands on the Professional version.

A unique feature of eDrawings Professional is that it automatically publishes eDrawings files as *review-enabled.* Anyone who receives a review-enabled file — whether that person has the Professional version or not — can use the Markup and Measure functions in eDrawings Viewer. This feature lets other designers, customers, or vendors use these advanced tools without having to purchase the Professional version.

If you want the receiver to see only certain measurements and not others, you can disable the eDrawings Measure tool (in the SolidWorks Save As dialog box options, deselect the Enable Measure option) and use basic dimensions to indicate, for example, the length, width, and diameter of your model.

Measuring a model

The Measure tool is a handy eDrawings feature. Vendors often need accurate measurements of your product. For example, a vendor who makes packaging may need to measure your television design to make sure that it fits inside the Styrofoam packaging he's designing.

To measure a model, the eDrawings file you're viewing must be Measure-enabled. Look for a measuring tape icon in the lower-right corner of the user interface. A red line through it means that measurement is disabled.

To measure an eDrawings file in the eDrawings Viewer, follow these steps:

1. **Choose File⇨Open to open the eDrawings file you want to measure.**

2. **Choose Tools⇨Measure.**

   The Measure tab appears in the eDrawings Manager.

3. **Move the pointer to the graphics area.**

   The pointer changes to a measuring tool. When the pointer detects a potential measurement starting point, that starting point is highlighted. Points are highlighted with a dot; edges and the borders of faces are highlighted with thick solid lines.

4. **Click to set the measurement starting point.**

   Your starting point appears in the Selected Items box on the Measure tab.

5. **Move the pointer over the second point, edge, or face.**

   A measure line appears as you drag the pointer.

6. **Click again.**

   The measurement appears in the graphics area and in the Distance section in the Results box on the Measure tab. The second item appears in the Selected Items box. In the Units box, the unit of measurement defaults to the file setting or to Millimeters if no file setting exists.

Marking up your eDrawings file

If you want to communicate and collaborate with other members of your design team, you can use markup tools in eDrawings Professional (see Table 14-1). Using the markup tools, you can add notes, dimensions, text, and graphical elements to the model (see Figure 14-1). On the Markup tab, you have room to include more lengthy descriptions and comments on the model.

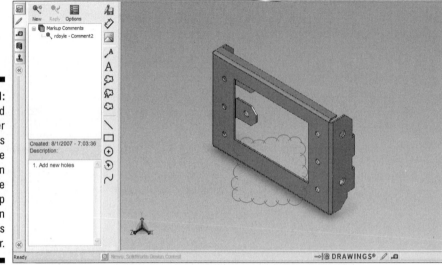

Figure 14-1:
You can add longer comments in the Description box on the Markup tab in eDrawings Viewer.

Table 14-1	Markup Tools
Button	**What It Does**
Save Markup	Saves the markup as a separate file
Dimension	Creates a markup dimension between two points on a drawing

Button		What It Does
	Text with leader	Creates a text note with a leader
	Text	Creates a text note
	Cloud with leader	Creates a cloud with text with a leader
	Cloud with text	Creates a cloud with text inside
	Cloud	Creates a cloud
	Line	Sketches a line by picking the beginning and end points of the line
	Rectangle	Sketches a rectangle by picking the opposite corners of the rectangle
	Circle	Sketches a circle by picking the center and radius locations
	Arc	Sketches an arc by picking the center and radius locations and the start and end points of the arc
	Spline	Sketches a curve by selecting multiple points to create the spline

The markup tools also contain a Comments section, shown in Figure 14-2, where you can reply to, accept, or reject the comments of others, as shown in Table 14-2. eDrawings automatically saves markup files as threaded comments with the eDrawings file. You can also save markup data separately without the models. Reviewers can add their comments and send only the markup file (*.markup). You can open your version of the model and each individual markup file separately to see the comments. Comments appear in the graphics area and on the Markup tab in eDrawings Manager.

Figure 14-2:
eDrawings
saves
markup files
as threaded
comments.

Table 14-2	Markup Comments Tools
Button	*What It Does*
New Comment	Creates a new comment
Reply	Replies to the selected, existing comment
Options	Sets preferences for username, markup color, and other eDrawing configuration values

To mark up your eDrawings, follow these steps:

1. **In eDrawings Viewer, open a document to mark up.**

   When you open a document, several tools appear in the eDrawings interface. eDrawings Manager, on the left side of the interface, displays tabs that let you manage eDrawings information. A complete set of markup tools (refer to Table 14-1) appears to the right of the interface.

2. **Click the Markup tab in eDrawings Manager.**

   You see the following icons appear in the tab window: New Comment, Reply, and Options (refer to Figure 14-2).

3. **On the Markup tab, click Options.**

   The Options dialog box appears.

4. **Select the Markup tab in the Options dialog box.**

5. **In the Comment Preferences section, type your name, phone number, and e-mail address and select a color and font for your comments.**

   This information identifies your comments to other reviewers. eDrawings now saves under your name any future comments you make.

6. **Click OK to save the changes.**

   With your user preferences set, you're ready to mark up your document.

7. **To add a text element, skip to Step 8. To add a geometric element, click one of the following icons and use it as described:**

   - *Line:* To draw multiple lines connected with a vertex, click the graphical image to start the line, move the mouse to draw a line, click to create a vertex, and then continue adding lines and vertices. Double-click in the graphics area to close this tool.

   - *Rectangle:* Click the graphical image to set a corner of the rectangle, and then drag the mouse to create the rectangle size you want. Release the mouse to finish.

   - *Circle:* Click to place the center point, drag the mouse outward, and then click again to draw a circle.

   - *Arc:* Click to place the arc center point. Move the mouse and click again to set the radius. Move the mouse and click again to draw the arc.

   - *Spline:* Click, move the mouse, and then click multiple times to draw a spline. Double-click to exit this tool.

8. **To add a text element, click the icon you want.**

   Your choices are Text, Text with Leader, Cloud, or Cloud with Leader.

9. **Type your comment in the box that appears and click the green check mark to accept your comment.**

   Clicking the red *x* cancels the comment.

10. **Click in the graphical image where you want to insert the text element.**

11. **Add markups, if you want, by repeating Steps 7 through 10.**

12. **Choose File⇨Save.**

    eDrawings saves your comments automatically with the eDrawings file.

Using the SolidWorks Viewer

Similar to eDrawings, SolidWorks Viewer opens native SolidWorks documents and is available for free. And, like eDrawings Viewer, SolidWorks Viewer opens native SolidWorks documents in *read-only mode,* which means that you cannot modify the document but you can look at it. A benefit of read-only mode is that it enables the file to open faster because only a subset of information is opened. You can download SolidWorks Viewer from the SolidWorks download Web page at www.solidworks.com/pages/services/downloads.html.

To view a SolidWorks document by using SolidWorks Viewer, simply open the document as you would in most Microsoft programs.

Including SolidWorks Documents in Your Presentations

You can show off your SolidWorks designs in a few other ways. You can display your model inside a Microsoft application — such as Word, Excel, or PowerPoint — using a clever Microsoft technology known as object linking and embedding (OLE). Or, you can make a 2D graphical image (JPG, TIF, BMP, or PDF) of your design and paste it in a document, presentation, or Web page.

Here are the advantages to using OLE:

✔ You can edit the object directly from within another application. Double-click the object or link, and the menus change to SolidWorks (as long as you have SolidWorks installed on your computer).

✔ A linked object is updated when you make changes to the original document.

✔ You can combine different document types and programs into one document. For example, you can embed a SolidWorks document into a Microsoft PowerPoint report.

✔ You can include and show the object without having the actual application for the OLE object for viewing. The application that created the object launches only if you double-click the OLE object.

The advantages to using images are listed here:

✔ They're simple, typically small, file sizes.

✔ They're easy to create as screen captures to edit and annotate.

✔ You don't need to worry about the location of the actual file.

Linking or embedding models in Microsoft Office programs

You can either link or embed an OLE object into a Microsoft document. A *linked* object contains a link to the original file, so any updates to the original appear when you double-click the link. In contrast, an *embedded* object is just like a copy, with no link to the original. The default in most Microsoft applications is to embed the OLE object into the file.

If you choose to link the object to the original file, you must always have direct access to that file. Otherwise, you receive a warning that some linked files were unavailable and cannot be updated.

When you insert an OLE object, you can either create a new OLE object or add an existing file.

To embed an existing SolidWorks document into a Microsoft document, follow these steps:

1. **Open the document in which you want to embed the SolidWorks file.**

2. **Click in the document where you want the embedded object to appear.**

3. **Choose Insert⇨Object.**

   The Object dialog box, shown in Figure 14-3, appears.

Figure 14-3: Use the Object dialog box to embed an OLE object into your Microsoft document.

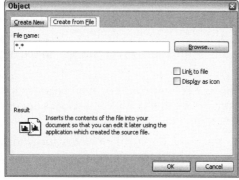

4. **Click the Create from File tab.**

   To create a new file, click Create New, click the application you want, and then create the file.

5. **In the Create from File dialog box, click the Browse button and browse to and select the file you want to embed.**

6. **Click one of these options to indicate how you want the file to be displayed in your document:**

   - *Link to File:* Links the embedded file to the original. Any changes in the original are reflected in the link.

   - *Display as Icon:* Inserts an icon that represents the contents of your file.

7. **Click OK.**

You can make edits to OLE objects. To edit an OLE object, double-click the object and make your changes. To return to the original Microsoft document, click outside the embedded document inside the original document.

Creating an image file of a model

You can create a graphical image of your SolidWorks model in several ways. You can save an eDrawings file as a JPEG, TIFF, or BMP file by selecting one of those formats in the Save As Type field in the Save As dialog box. The SolidWorks Save As dialog box offers similar options, including PDF.

You can take a snapshot of your SolidWorks model by using the Screen Capture tool. Choose View➪Screen Capture➪Image Capture to copy the active SolidWorks window to the Windows Clipboard. The image can then be pasted (press Ctrl+V) into another application.

Part V
The Part of Tens

The 5th Wave — By Rich Tennant

GUS & LILY'S DOG GROOMING — NOW USING SolidWorks SOFTWARE

In this part . . .

No *For Dummies* book is complete without The Part of Tens. In this fun part, I provide information, tips, resources, and links that make your SolidWorks experience more productive and enjoyable. Each of the three chapters in this section lists ten ways (imagine that!) to become more proficient with SolidWorks, extend and reuse your design, and introduce you to the SolidWorks community.

Chapter 15

Ten Tips for Becoming More Proficient with SolidWorks

A craftsman is only as good as his tools, they say. But a tool is only as good as its craftsman, I say. This saying is true of SolidWorks, a brilliant but extensive design tool. To get the most from SolidWorks, you need to become familiar with the nooks and crannies of the program — and there are a lot of them, not to mention the dozens of add-on programs (such as PhotoWorks, COSMOS, and Toolbox) that work inside SolidWorks. The more adept you are at SolidWorks, the more productive and efficient you'll be at design. And the way to hone your SolidWorks skills is through practice and training.

You can follow plenty of other routes in mastering SolidWorks, such as reading books, checking out online sources, and joining SolidWorks user groups. The best way to stay on top of it all is to mix and match several training routines and to stay current. SolidWorks issues a new release of its software every year, and there are always new features and functionality that you'll want to keep up with.

Your efficiency in using SolidWorks translates into the bottom line for you and your company. In this chapter, I cover ten ways that you can make sure that you get the most out of SolidWorks.

Go to Class (Formal Training)

Through an extensive reseller network, SolidWorks offers a variety of training courses in everything from the basics of part and assembly modeling to advanced processes, such as sheet metal design and custom routines.

A word of advice: When you sign up for a class, do some prep work before the class begins. Don't depend on your instructor to download knowledge into your brain. Read some articles about SolidWorks, tinker with the program, and try out the online tutorials located on the SolidWorks Help menu. If you walk into a classroom never having looked at SolidWorks, you'll have a long week, and so will the instructor and the rest of the class. Be prepared. A few warm-up exercises ensure that you get the most out of a course.

You can find an up-to-date list of training courses on the SolidWorks Web site: www.solidworks.com/pages/services/Training/ TrainingCourses.html.

Courses vary by reseller, but here's an list of essential courses for new users:

- **SolidWorks Essentials:** This class takes you through the basics of creating parts, assemblies, and drawings in SolidWorks.

- **SolidWorks Drawings:** After you have part and assembly design under your belt, this class teaches you how to create manufacturing drawings based on your 3D design.

- **Advanced Part Modeling:** In this class, you discover how to use SolidWorks surfacing tools to create swoops, curves, cores, cavities, and other wacky freeform shapes that are now popular in designs.

- **Advanced Assembly Modeling:** This class teaches you advanced techniques for building complex assemblies.

- **Sheet Metal:** Discover how to build stand-alone sheet metal parts, convert parts to sheet metal, and model sheet metal parts in the context of an assembly.

- **Weldments:** Find out how to use the Weldment tools used to create welded structures.

Be Creative (Nontraditional Training)

You don't have to go to class to become a SolidWorks whiz (see the preceding section). In fact, you can stay in your pajamas if you prefer. You can find a plethora of SolidWorks books and online training materials to satisfy all your home-schooling needs. One caveat: These methods of learning are self paced, so depending on the sort of person you are, you may want to apply glue to your chair or put a lock on the fridge. (My personal weakness is the espresso machine.)

Several third-party vendors, including Solid Professor (www. solidprofessor.com), can provide computer-based training. At the SolidWorks Web site, you can subscribe to the online newsletter *SolidWorks Express* to have tips and tricks sent every two weeks to your e-mail address.

One of the best places for getting up to speed in SolidWorks is the SolidWorks program itself. Open SolidWorks and choose Help to find these categories:

✔ **SolidWorks Help:** It contains the SolidWorks *Online User's Guide* and the *What's New Manual.* A Search tool allows you to look up information in these two online sources on just about any SolidWorks feature (see Figure 15-1).

Figure 15-1:
You can use the SolidWorks Help menu to find information on almost any topic.

> ✔ **Moving from AutoCAD:** Many new SolidWorks users are switching over from the 2D AutoCAD program. This guide shows you the differences between SolidWorks and AutoCAD and helps make the transition easier.
>
> ✔ **SolidWorks Tutorials:** SolidWorks includes more than 30 tutorials that are a good launching point for learning how to use the program. These tutorials cover part creation, assembly operations, drawings, and several of the SolidWorks add-in programs.

In SolidWorks, when a command is active, a question mark appears in the PropertyManager. Click the question mark to jump to the Help topic for that command.

Check Local Reseller Events

In addition to formal SolidWorks training courses, SolidWorks value-added resellers (VARs) also hold special events to introduce new users to the SolidWorks program. These events include Night School, Lunch and Learn, and other special programs. At these events, you can find out more about SolidWorks and share your questions and experiences with other users.

Many VARs also hold the SolidWorks Personal Edition Hands-on Test Drive class. After completing this free two- to three-hour seminar, which offers basic instruction in SolidWorks, attendees receive a free copy of the Personal Edition software, which is a noncommercial version of Solid Works. Personal Edition offers all the core features of SolidWorks, but any designs you create don't transfer into SolidWorks.

The availability and scheduling of events varies from VAR to VAR. The best way to find out more about these events is to contact your local VAR.

Join a User Group

Meeting and networking with other SolidWorks users is another great way to discover more about SolidWorks and stay current with happenings in the CAD world. Located around the country and internationally, these user groups are independent groups organized by SolidWorks users. You can find user groups for both SolidWorks and the COSMOS line of analysis software that works inside SolidWorks. Visit www.swugn.org.

Groups vary slightly in structure, but usually it costs nothing to join one. Anyone with an interest in SolidWorks is welcome. Groups meet periodically to discuss and share what they know about SolidWorks. Meetings often offer technical presentations, visits from local resellers, and case studies presented by other users. Users also discuss the newest version of SolidWorks and technical tips. In addition to local meetings, user groups also sponsor regional events. The biggest annual user event is SolidWorks World, usually held in January in a warm locale with a golf course nearby. At this annual conference, you can attend seminars; meet other SolidWorks users, partners, and personnel; and share ideas and find out more about SolidWorks.

Aspire to Be a Superuser

Within every SolidWorks-using company lurks the superuser, the program guru (or geek, whichever you prefer) to whom everyone goes with their questions on the inner workings of SolidWorks. This person saves you from calling technical support or digging through user manuals to learn about a SolidWorks add-in. Some superusers get formal recognition. Others are quietly acknowledged for the services they provide to coworkers.

You too can aspire to be a SolidWorks superuser, or — if you don't have the time to be one — you can cultivate one in your company. To become one, simply do whatever is needed to learn more than anyone else about SolidWorks. To cultivate a SolidWorks superuser, make every effort to recognize, encourage, and grow the SolidWorks geniuses in your organization. Encourage them to take the Certified SolidWorks Professional exam. (See the section "Take the CSWP Test," later in this chapter.) Give them a business title that acknowledges their know-it-all status. Issue a certificate, plaque, or medal that they can proudly display in their cubicles. Send them to the mother of all SolidWorks user group meetings: SolidWorks World. Whatever it is, find some imaginative way to reward them, and they will take root and blossom.

Network Virtually: The Discussion Forum

SolidWorks user groups are a great way to shake hands with other users. If you're not fond of shaking hands or rubbing elbows, though — or your schedule won't permit it — maybe discussion forums are the answer.

SolidWorks discussion forums are another way to exchange ideas with other users. The SolidWorks *discussion forum* is a threaded message board where you can submit questions (which can include document or image attachments that illustrate your confusion) and wait for others to respond.

Of course, you don't always have to be the one asking questions. You can also submit advice based on your own experiences. SolidWorks forums are moderated. Primarily, they consist of users talking to each another, but occasionally someone from SolidWorks (myself included) chimes in.

SolidWorks discussion forums serve as a place where you can

- ✔ Discuss the design, drafting, programming, and administration of SolidWorks CAD systems and SolidWorks-related products.

- ✔ Share ideas, information, and specific experiences regarding the use of SolidWorks and SolidWorks-related products.

- ✔ Discuss third-party add-on products for SolidWorks.

- ✔ Discuss enhancements in SolidWorks and SolidWorks-related products.

- ✔ Educate and inform others about the strengths, weaknesses, and general use of SolidWorks and SolidWorks-related products.

Discussion forums are broken down into functional groups, such as parts, assemblies, drawings, installation, and sketching, for example. This structure makes it easier to ask questions of the right people.

You can find SolidWorks discussion forums in the Support section of the SolidWorks Web site: `www.solidworks.com/pages/services/Community.html`, or click the Discussion Forum link in the SolidWorks task pane.

Take the CSWP Test

If you aspire to become the SolidWorks superuser in your office, consider taking the test! The Certified SolidWorks Professional (CSWP) program provides a standard measure of SolidWorks competency. CSWP recognizes the most qualified and advanced SolidWorks professionals. Certification is a way to get recognition from your company and your peers. Now no one will ever again doubt your advanced knowledge.

The way to become a CSWP is to take a test, which is offered through participating SolidWorks VARs. (Check the SolidWorks Web site.) The test has two parts, in which you

- ✔ Answer a series of written questions that test your expertise in the different areas of SolidWorks.

- ✔ Create a design in SolidWorks.

For more information, visit www.solidworks.com/pages/services/Training/CSWP.html.

Really, what's the point of getting certified? Basically, it's like putting four stars across the top of your résumé. Certification acknowledges your skill level in SolidWorks. When companies look for new employees or consultants, they look for a CSWP. What's more, employers can use certification to train more advanced users. Employers most likely will have more confidence in the skills of someone who has passed CSWP certification.

Document Your CAD Standards

One of the best ways to ensure productivity in SolidWorks for you and your staff (if you have one) is to create a CAD standard book. Your CAD standard doesn't have to be a tome — just a binder's worth of documentation on how you get your work done in SolidWorks. Documented CAD standards help new employees get up to speed fast and bring projects to completion more quickly.

A well-defined CAD standard should document how you begin new parts and drawings, which layers contain which information in a drawing, how you handle design revisions, and where and how you manage standard parts, for example. All these documents should be stored in a manual.

Defining a set of CAD standards can be, and should be, a simple process. Hold a couple of meetings with key SolidWorks users, or even bring up standards as a topic for an internal user group meeting. One way I have found to be effective in ensuring attendance at this type of meeting is to offer food. (Rarely does an engineer turn down free pizza to talk about CAD.)

After the standards have been defined, you need to determine how to share this information. An effective means is to create an HTML or PDF document (that no one can mess with) and place it on a network drive where everyone can reach it. I prefer HTML because it's displayed faster in a Web browser.

Here's a checklist of items to cover in your CAD standards:

- ✔ Data management, or how you create, store, and archive files
- ✔ Document templates
- ✔ SolidWorks settings
- ✔ Assembly structure
- ✔ Materials
- ✔ Standard parts

✔ Modeling practices, such as feature names and order and in-context references

✔ Drawing practices, such as standards notes, custom properties, and title blocks

Communicate Design Standards

Just as important as creating a set of CAD standards is communicating what they are and how they're used. You can communicate your design standards by adding standards review to your design review or checking process, holding internal user group meetings, or conducting training classes on the standards. You may have a great set of nicely documented and detailed CAD standards, but what good are they if no one follows them?

The other advantage of this review is that the designers receive feedback so that they can incorporate it into current and subsequent designs.

Make sure that the standards are located where all the designers can get to the documents easily. Find a common location on the network and store the CAD standards there.

Manage SolidWorks Well

A CAD system plays a major role in how your organization designs its products. How well you manage and implement your CAD system has a large effect on your company's productivity and success. A key to this success is how well this technology is managed. So, what makes a good CAD manager in a SolidWorks environment, and why is that role important to your company?

Most companies have some form of CAD manager, whether formal or informal, full- or part-time. In a SolidWorks environment, a CAD manager is usually responsible for these tasks:

✔ Implement SolidWorks

✔ Manage SolidWorks

✔ Manage CAD data

✔ Handle training

✔ Implement the CAD standards

✔ Communicate among team members

If you're a CAD manager, your goal should be twofold:

✔ Find ways to increase your company's efficiency and effectiveness in using SolidWorks software. Small productivity gains in these areas can yield significant gains in productivity in the long term, especially when multiplied across all the CAD users in your organization.

✔ Lower your organization's total cost of ownership (TCO) in regard to using SolidWorks.

Chapter 16

Ten Ways to Extend and Reuse Your Design Information

*T*he fun never ends when you design in 3D, even after your product design is complete. You'll be pleased to know that literally dozens of other applications developed by SolidWorks and other companies enable you to reuse and show off your designs in many ways. These methods include add-in and downstream applications.

A SolidWorks *add-in* is a separate program that works inside SolidWorks. An add-in shows up on the SolidWorks main menu, so it looks like it's part of SolidWorks. One example is SolidWorks Routing, which builds and documents electrical cables in your assembly files. Another is PhotoWorks, which creates photorealistic images of parts and assemblies. Analysis, simulation, and manufacturing programs are considered *downstream applications.* The down stream programs I cover in this chapter work directly off the SolidWorks model, so data translation is never an issue.

In this chapter, I introduce you to ten add-ins and downstream applications. Keep in mind that my purpose is simply to make you aware of these programs, not to explain the details of how each program works.

SolidWorks add-in applications are available for purchase separately or as part of a SolidWorks package. Check with your SolidWorks reseller to see what's available. After you installed an add-in program, open SolidWorks and choose Tools⇨Add-Ins to run the program inside SolidWorks.

Show Off Your Model with Microsoft OLE

The next time you want to add zest to a PowerPoint presentation, color to a report, or "oomph" to a ho-hum presentation, include a SolidWorks design. Your audience member can gain an instant understanding of the benefits of your two-seated lawnmower if you simply show them the actual model.

You can add a SolidWorks model to a presentation or document by using *object linking and embedding* (OLE) or by including an image of the model.

OLE technology lets you embed or link an object from another program into a Microsoft document. When you *embed* an object, it's like including a copy of the real thing in the document. The embedded object has no link to the original. In contrast, a *link* is connected to its original and is updated whenever the original document is updated.

To access an OLE embedded or linked SolidWorks document, simply double-click the link or the object in your Microsoft Office file. As long as you have the SolidWorks program installed, the SolidWorks document opens. If the object is a SolidWorks model, you can spin the model around, show different views, or make changes as desired. (See Chapter 14 for more about working with OLE and SolidWorks.)

Another way to include a SolidWorks model in a report or presentation or even in a Web page is to include an image file of the model. One way to create an image is by using a Windows screen capture. To capture the current window on your screen, press Alt+Print Screen, which places the image on the Clipboard. Open an application such as Microsoft Word and choose Edit⇨Paste.

Another option is to save your SolidWorks model as a JPEG, TIFF, or PDF file. These options are available in the SolidWorks Save As dialog box. (Simply choose File⇨Save As to reach this dialog box.)

When you start working with graphical formats, you find that some fit your needs better than others. JPEG and GIF are generally safe bets. TIFF and BMP create larger files. My personal favorite is PNG. It's a small-size format that allows you to resize images without losing much quality.

Share Models with SolidWorks 3D Instant Website

If you want to create as little work as possible for the receiver, SolidWorks 3D Instant Website is a great way to send someone a SolidWorks design. In just one mouse click, this SolidWorks add-in allows you to publish a Web page of your SolidWorks document on a local intranet or — if you don't have an intranet or Web server to use — on a SolidWorks-hosted Web site. The Web page is based on a template and a style that you can customize with limited HTML programming experience.

By sending an e-mail with a link to the Web page, you can share SolidWorks models or drawings with anyone without requiring them to manually install any viewers or CAD software. An automatic wizard installs the necessary viewing software for them.

Here's an example of how this add-on can work. Say that your company makes high-efficiency fan blades, and your suppliers are located around the country. Sending a link to a Web page of your design makes it easy for all your suppliers to inspect your fans (they can rotate, zoom, and pan 3D models) and add comments, for example. They also can print documents from the Web page.

To start the 3D Instant Website Wizard, open your SolidWorks document and choose Tools⇨3D Instant Website.

Spice Up Model Images with PhotoWorks

A 3D model of a toaster looks just like, well, a 3D model of a toaster. If you really want to sell someone your design idea, show them how the toaster looks sitting on a kitchen counter. PhotoWorks, a SolidWorks add-in, allows you to create photorealistic images of your SolidWorks model in the model's natural (or unnatural) environment.

PhotoWorks lets you specify model surface properties, such as color, texture, reflectance, and transparency. You can also place the model in the setting you want, as I did with my toaster, shown in Figure 16-1. Although I could have made my toaster purple, given it the texture of brushed aluminum, and set it inside a log cabin, I chose something more mainstream instead.

Figure 16-1:
You can use
PhotoWorks
to specify
color,
texture,
and even
setting.

Photorealistic images lend impact to presentations and proposals and allow you to present design concepts quickly. Rendering an image in PhotoWorks is much easier than creating a physical prototype of the product and then hiring an expensive photographer to shoot it.

Simulate Movement with SolidWorks Motion Studies

What better way to demonstrate your SolidWorks assembly than to show how it moves? SolidWorks motion studies generate AVI movies of your SolidWorks part or assembly that play on any Windows-based computer. Motion studies show a viewer how a product is assembled and how it functions. In conjunction with PhotoWorks, motion studies can produce photorealistic animations complete with lights, shadows, materials, and reflections.

Suppose that you want to impress a group of potential customers with your design of a water filter that moves like a jellyfish around a swimming pool, sucking up debris with its mechanical tentacles. You can create AVI files that show how your product operates. This way, prospects can see how the pool filter moves and watch its filtering mechanisms.

In motion studies, a wizard walks you through the process of recording a fly-around, an exploded view, or a collapsed view animation. After you create the basic animation, you can edit or delete animation steps or play the animation a frame at a time using the MotionManager. The Motion Study tab is at the bottom of the graphics area. Click the tab to view the Animation Feature Manager and a timeline that shows the steps in the animation.

To open an add-in product, choose Tools⇨Add-ins and select the check box next to the add-in you want to use.

Share Design Info with PDMWorks Workgroup

If, during a large design project, you need to give folks outside your design team access to your SolidWorks data, you may find PDMWorks Workgroup a handy add-in.

This add-in extends access to the design information stored in your PDMWorks database. PDMWorks is the product data management (PDM) software that works with SolidWorks. (You can read more about PDM software in Chapter 13.)

PDMWorks Workgroup has two functions:

- **Application Program Interface (API):** Automate mundane PDMWorks functions to tailor PDMWorks to the specific needs of your organization.

- **Event Triggers:** Automate the execution of a task per a specific PDMWorks event. For example, you can set it up so that when PDMWorks releases a drawing, PDM Workgroup creates a PDF file of the drawing and sends the PDF to design team members by e-mail to notify them that the drawing is available for use.

Test a Design with COSMOSWorks Analysis

As a designer, you may be asked to do upfront *finite element analysis (FEA)* on your models. FEA shows you how your model holds up under real-world conditions. The results of analysis allow you to make better decisions about the types of material to use, the geometry of parts, and the interaction of the parts in an assembly. Analysis software helps to improve the quality and function of your design and to lower the cost of making it.

COSMOSWorks is a suite of four FEA programs that integrate tightly with SolidWorks and run directly on your SolidWorks model. COSMOSXpress comes standard with SolidWorks. The three other COSMOSWorks bundles are sold as add-ins and work on both parts and assemblies:

- ✔ **COSMOSXpress:** An analysis wizard that comes standard with SolidWorks and allows you to do upfront analysis on parts, as shown in Figure 16-2

- ✔ **COSMOSWorks Designer:** Performs stress, displacement, thermal stress, and contact analyses on parts and assemblies

- ✔ **COSMOSWorks Professional:** Adds frequency and buckling, heat transfer, and drop-testing

- ✔ **COSMOSWorks Advanced Professional:** Goes even further with capabilities to analyze beams and trusses, perform nonlinear stress analysis, and study fatigue and dynamic response

Figure 16-2: COSMOS-Xpress steps you through the process of analyzing a part.

Check Out Models' Moves with COSMOSMotion

Whereas COSMOSWorks (see the preceding section) tells you whether a part or an assembly will break, COSMOSMotion allows you to understand the mechanical motion of your assemblies. This SolidWorks add-in considers joints and linkages and the actual forces that occur during motion so that you can detect problem areas, such as collisions between parts. COSMOSMotion enables you to size motors, determine power consumption, lay out linkages, develop cams, understand gear drives, and size springs and dampers.

Included in the COSMOSMotion software are tools to simulate displacement, velocity, acceleration, linear and torsion spring and dampers, joints (created from assembly mates), and additional constraints to define how the components in an assembly interact with one another.

The assembly shown in Figure 16-3 illustrates how you can size motors and actuators on a design based on the COSMOSMotion results. The graphical output helps identify key areas and values for the analysis.

Figure 16-3: Use COSMOS-Motion to determine the size and kilowatts of the motor you need for the job.

Automate Tasks with the API and Macros

The SolidWorks *application programming interface* (API) helps you record macros even if you don't have much programming experience. *Macros* are small custom applications that automate a series of steps for a mundane task in SolidWorks. For example, if you export designs for machine tooling, you can create a macro that provides one-button export with all the options set inside the macro.

Macros are also a good way to maintain compliance with company standards. You can create a macro which ensures that specific settings are properly set and that a document complies with all the settings. You can even save macros in the SolidWorks Design Library to share with other design team members. (To find out more about the Design Library, see Chapter 13.)

When you record a macro in SolidWorks, the SolidWorks API creates a file that contains a record of all the commands (mouse clicks, menu choices, and keystrokes) that take place from the time you start recording to when you stop. The commands are stored in the Microsoft Visual Basic program language. SolidWorks sets some limitations on what you can record in a macro, but most of the basic functions are automatic. SolidWorks saves macros with the .swp extension. You can edit the files by using the Visual Basic Editor, so you need a basic understanding of Visual Basic.

The commands to record a macro are on the Macro toolbar, shown in Figure 16-4. To access the Macro toolbar, choose Tools⇨Macro.

Figure 16-4:
The Macro toolbar holds commands to run, stop, record, create and edit macros.

✔ **Run Macro:** Opens the Run Macro dialog box. In the dialog box, browse for the macro you want to run and click OK.

✔ **Stop Macro:** Stops the recording of the macro and opens the Save As dialog box. Enter the name of the new macro in the dialog box and click Save. The .swp extension is automatically added to the filename.

✔ **Record/Pause Macro:** Pauses the recording of a macro. Click again to begin re-recording.

✔ **New Macro:** Creates a new macro. Begin entering the steps you want to record. Click Stop Macro to save the file.

✔ **Edit Macro:** Allows you to edit or debug a macro that you already recorded. Click the Edit Macro button and browse to the macro to edit. The Microsoft Visual Basic Editor appears. Edit the macro and close the editor.

For additional reference, the SolidWorks API support site, at www. solidworks.com/pages/services/APISupport.html, has a wealth of API examples, downloads, and tips.

Note that many of the Visual Basic application examples on the API-support Web site have the .bas file extension. To use one of these sample files, you need to import it into VBA. To do so, create a new macro and import the file by choosing Import File from the Microsoft Visual Basic File menu.

Schedule the Intensive Work with SolidWorks Task Scheduler

Labor-intensive tasks — such as batch importing, exporting, and plotting — can gobble up hours, if not days. Even though these jobs don't require excessive brain power, they still tie up your mind and computer. But now you can automate these processes. Task Scheduler, a software utility included in the SolidWorks Office and Office Professional packages, puts your system to work while you're off in the Bahamas. It lets you run resource-intensive processes overnight or on weekends (times when the computer is normally idle), freeing you to focus on more creative projects.

Scheduling a task in Task Scheduler takes minutes. The program is a separate utility, so you access it either through Windows program files or a shortcut on the desktop. After Task Scheduler is up and running, here's how you can schedule a project:

1. **On the Task Scheduler screen, click the task you want from the list on the left side of the screen (see Figure 16-5).**

   Options include Print Files, Create Drawings, and Import and Export Files. You can even run custom scripts.

   Depending on the task, the program may ask you for more information.

2. **Provide the necessary information.**

   If you select Print Files, for example, Task Scheduler asks you to enter the paper size, number of copies, and the printer you want to print on.

3. **Select the files you want to run the task on by clicking Add File or Add Folder (see Figure 16-6).**

4. **Select the frequency (once, daily, weekly, or monthly), start time, and start date for the task.**

5. **Click Finish to close the Task Scheduler dialog box.**

   The task is now scheduled to run at the scheduled time and date.

Figure 16-5:
You can select the task you want to run from a list in the SolidWorks Task Scheduler.

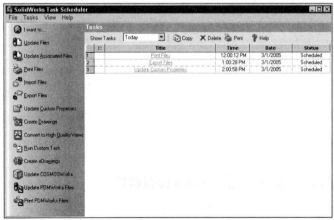

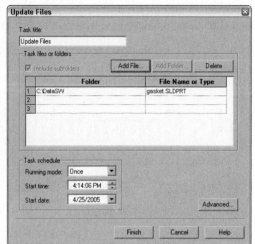

Figure 16-6:
Select the files or folders on which you want to run the task in the SolidWorks Task Scheduler Update Files dialog box.

SolidWorks Task Scheduler runs tasks at any time, even when you're logged off the computer. The Microsoft Windows service that runs the SolidWorks Task Scheduler is swBOEngine.exe, and it starts automatically whenever SolidWorks Task Scheduler is installed. When you restart the computer, the service appears in the Windows Start program group, and you simply click it to start the service. To remove the automatic activation of this service, remove SolidWorks Task Scheduler from the Windows Start program group.

Find Various Manufacturing Software

The final stage in product development is to send your SolidWorks design to the manufacturer to have the part or assembly made.

Manufacturers use *computer-aided manufacturing* (CAM) *software* to create parts using a variety of manufacturing methods (stamped, machined, turned, cast, and forged, for example). Some of these manufacturing methods use specialized software for the different processes, but in most cases they can take information directly from your SolidWorks design.

For more information on SolidWorks CAM software partners, click the Partners section of the SolidWorks Web site at www.solidworks.com.

Chapter 17

Ten Resources for the SolidWorks Community

· ·

In This Chapter

▶ Getting familiar with the six groups that make up the SolidWorks community

▶ Getting to know the SolidWorks Web site

▶ Meeting like minds at a SolidWorks user group

▶ Searching for CAD models of standard parts

▶ Becoming a certified SolidWorks know-it-all

· ·

A s a SolidWorks user, you can relax, knowing that you never have to go it alone. You can find plenty of places (most of them on the Internet) to meet up with other users, locate training and tech support, and get info on SolidWorks upgrades and add-on products.

In this chapter, you discover ten resources that are available from the SolidWorks community. Each element is a useful resource or reference as you begin or continue your journey with SolidWorks.

SolidWorks and COSMOS User Groups

One of the best ways to find out more about SolidWorks is to network with other users, which you can do by joining a user group. If you can't find a user group in your area, you can always start one. These groups are beneficial because they give you an opportunity to swap stories and share software experiences with other users.

User groups are a key component of the SolidWorks community. Figure 17-1 shows how the user groups have links to each of the other major areas of the SolidWorks community.

Figure 17-1:
The
SolidWorks
community
offers a
cornucopia
of
resources.

You can find user groups for SolidWorks and for COSMOSWorks, the finite element analysis (FEA) program that works inside SolidWorks. These user groups have local chapters all over the world. SolidWorks also hosts regional events and SolidWorks World, an annual international user group convention that changes location each year.

To find a group or to discover how to start one, go to www.swugn.org.

It's all about community

The SolidWorks community is composed of six groups that work together and complement one another:

- ✔ **Solution partners:** Companies that offer hardware and software products certified to work with SolidWorks software

- ✔ **SolidWorks Corporation:** The company that develops the software

- ✔ **SolidWorks resellers:** Organizations, sometimes called value added resellers or VARs,

that sell SolidWorks products and provide training and technical support

- ✔ **The SolidWorks manufacturing network:** A network of manufacturers that accept your native SolidWorks files to build parts with

- ✔ **Educational institutions:** Schools that include SolidWorks in their curricula

- ✔ **User groups:** Groups of SolidWorks users who meet to discuss SolidWorks and its products

The SolidWorks Web Site

To get the latest on SolidWorks, your first stop should be the SolidWorks Web site (`www.solidworks.com`), shown in Figure 17-2.

The site has six main sections, which you can access by using the menu bar at the top:

- ✔ **Products:** Offers information on SolidWorks products, which include CAD, analysis, and data management software.

- ✔ **Services:** Divided into the categories Support, Subscription Services, Training and Certification, and Services and Consulting Partners. The later section "The SolidWorks Customer Portal" covers the Support (technical support) category in more detail. Training and Certification offers information on software courses available at SolidWorks training centers and on how to become a certified SolidWorks know-it-all. (Read the upcoming section "Certified SolidWorks Professional Program.") Subscription Services shows you all the benefits of maintaining your license subscription. Services and Consulting Partners provides a searchable index of SolidWorks partner companies that offer products and services that can help your organization.

- ✔ **Customer Successes:** Includes links to customer success stories categorized by industry and by SolidWorks add-on.

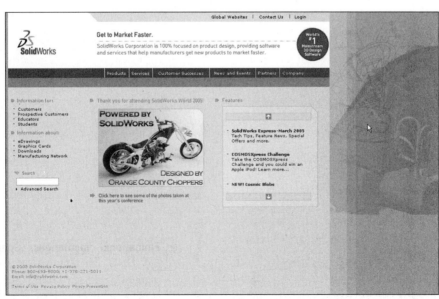

Figure 17-2:
The SolidWorks Web site offers information on products, services, partners, news and events, and success stories.

✔ **News and Events:** Offers the lowdown on what's happening in SolidWorks. This category includes press releases, seminars, trade show schedules, and user group meetings and has a link to the *SolidWorks Express* newsletter.

✔ **Partners:** Includes information on SolidWorks solution partners and the manufacturing network. (For more on the latter, see the "SolidWorks Manufacturing Network" section, later in this chapter.)

✔ **Company:** Lists the latest information on SolidWorks the company, such as who's running the show, directions to the office, and a list of internal employment opportunities (in case you're looking for a job).

The SolidWorks Express Newsletter

The *SolidWorks Express* online newsletter for SolidWorks customers arrives every two weeks (and sometimes more often). Each issue features technical tips, news on the latest happenings at SolidWorks, and real customer stories.

You can subscribe for free at `www.solidworks.com/swexpress`. To sign up for e-mail notification for new issues, click Subscribe at the top of the current issue of *SolidWorks Express* and complete the form. After you sign up, an e-mail notifies you that a new edition of the newsletter is available, and you can click the URL that takes you to the site.

The SolidWorks Customer Portal

One of the most important resources for SolidWorks users is technical support. Everyone needs a hand now and again. Look on the SolidWorks customer portal to find online technical support, software to download, and a slew of additional resources. To access the customer portal, you need to purchase an annual maintenance contract (about $1,200 for SolidWorks). Don't have one? Talk to your local reseller and have someone explain the features, benefits, and costs of the subscription service program.

Access the customer portal support section at `https://customer center.solidworks.com` (see Figure 17-3).

The support section includes this information:

✔ Links to download the latest version or service pack for SolidWorks software, including COSMOSWorks, PDMWorks, and eDrawings

✔ The latest news and technical bulletins

Figure 17-3:
The
SolidWorks
Customer
Portal offers
a myriad of
technical
and
community
information
for
subscription
service
customers.

✔ Sign-up forms to receive alerts, by e-mail, about new postings in the Support section of the Web site, the *SolidWorks Express* online newsletter, and other announcements from SolidWorks

✔ The ability to search for technical information and technical tips and knowledge base solutions

✔ Access to customer experience programs, which allow you to try out prerelease versions of software so that SolidWorks can get your opinions on its products and services

✔ Links to a wealth of reference documents (including the References and Guides section, which has installation, best practices, and other useful technical information)

✔ Information on system requirements and graphics card drivers that you need in order to properly operate SolidWorks software

✔ Online Webcasts and archives of previous Webcasts

✔ Numerous links to other community pages, including the *SolidWorks Express* newsletter, online discussion forums, user groups, the manufacturing network, 3D ContentCentral, the CSWP program, SolidWorks customer experience programs, and a page of links to other CAD industry Web sites

The Certified SolidWorks Professional Program

Another resource is the Certified SolidWorks Professional (CSWP) program. A *CSWP* is a person who knows SolidWorks like the back of his hand. But not just anyone can become a CSWP. You have to first pass a test, which is given at an authorized testing center, such as a reseller office. Being a CSWP entitles you to member-only privileges, including a special logo that you can put on your business card and invitations to exclusive CSWP-only events.

What's more (this is the best part), your name is put on a searchable certified professional directory on the SolidWorks Web site. If anyone in your area needs to hire someone who's quick on her feet with SolidWorks, he may give you a call.

From a company perspective, having a CSWP in the office is an advantage. You become the office guru, someone that other SolidWorks users can look up to and go to for software support. The certification enables you to help your company identify qualified new hires, consultants, or contractors that understand SolidWorks.

For more information on this resource, visit the CSWP section of the SolidWorks Web site at www.solidworks.com/pages/services/training/CSWP.html.

3D ContentCentral

Often, designs call for standard parts. Modeling those parts from scratch is a waste of time. 3D ContentCentral (www.3dcontentcentral.com) is a free Web site by SolidWorks that offers millions of supplier-certified and user-contributed part models in a number of different formats that you can download and drop into your SolidWorks designs.

The site has two sections:

- **Supplier Certified Parts:** Contains standard part models certified by the vendor to be accurate
- **User Library:** Lets designers upload CAD models to share with other users

To get started using 3D ContentCentral, all you need to do is register with the site and create an account. The process takes about a minute. After you're onboard, 3D ContentCentral makes searching for standard components easy. After you find what you need, you can download the model and request a quote from the vendor. Some online catalogs allow you to configure parts to your unique specifications.

The SolidWorks Manufacturing Network

When you need to work with a vendor or a manufacturer, it's a heck of a lot easier if the company can just accept your native SolidWorks data. Otherwise, you end up hassling with intermediary exchange formats, such as STEP and IGES, which can add extra steps to the process and put your data at risk.

If you need to find a company that will take your data "straight up," check the SolidWorks manufacturing network. This free online directory of contract engineering, CNC (computer numerical controls) machining, mold making, industrial design, machine design, rapid prototyping, and other types of companies accepts native SolidWorks files. When you work with a company in the manufacturing network, there's no stressing over file transfer issues.

Use the manufacturing network Web site (see the URL at the end of this section) to search for a designer, manufacturer, or supplier by name or by area of expertise, such as industrial design, metal stamping, rapid prototyping, or even reverse engineering.

If your organization provides services to the SolidWorks community, consider joining the manufacturing network yourself. Sign-up is free, and you get a free listing on the manufacturing network Web site.

For more information on this SolidWorks community resource, visit `www.solidworks.com/pages/partners/mfgnetwork.html`.

SolidWorks Solution Partners

One strength of SolidWorks is its Solution Partner program. *Solution partners* are companies that develop best-in-class software and hardware that work with SolidWorks software. Look for logos on products to identify these certification levels:

- **Research Associate:** A company that has the intent or is in the process of developing a product for the SolidWorks market.

✔ **Solution Partner:** A company that has successfully released a SolidWorks-compatible product and has a minimum of two SolidWorks customers.

✔ **Certified Gold Product:** A software product that carries the Certified Gold logo and is directly integrated with SolidWorks. Certified Gold products are designed to work well with SolidWorks.

✔ **Certified CAM Product:** A best-in-class computer-aided manufacturing or CNC machine software that works well with SolidWorks geometry.

For more information on this SolidWorks community resource, visit www.solidworks.com/pages/partners/partners.html.

SolidWorks Resellers

When you're ready to purchase SolidWorks, you can go to your local SolidWorks value-added reseller (VAR). SolidWorks has hundreds of VARs throughout the world. You can find one near you on the SolidWorks Web site by going to www.solidworks.com/pages/company/solidworksofficeworldwide.html, where you can find out who to contact for a current list of VARs in your area.

VARs do more than push a product. They offer a number of other services, including product demonstrations, technical support, and training programs. Among the clever and entertaining training courses they offer are night classes, lunch-and-learn workshops, and SolidWorks test drives. Check with your local VAR to see what it has to offer.

The SolidWorks Educational Community

If you're in college, keep your eyes peeled for SolidWorks in the classroom. SolidWorks develops a special educational edition of its software for use in high schools, colleges, and universities. Students who learn with SolidWorks get practical training and real experience. The Education Edition also comes with a teacher's guide, curriculum ideas, courseware, and sample part files.

Maybe you're not a student. You're thinking "What does this have to do with me?" If you're about to hire an intern or college graduate, post your ad at colleges and universities that offer SolidWorks in their curriculums. Because students from these schools are ready to start designing tomorrow, you don't have to spend heaps of money to train them.

For more information, visit the SolidWorks educational Web site at www.solidworks.com/pages/products/edu. Also available on the Web site are a list of events and associations and a newsletter for the educational community.

Appendix

About the CD

In This Appendix

▶ Discovering your system requirements

▶ Using the CD

▶ Finding out what's on the CD

▶ Troubleshooting

*T*his CD contains demos on how SolidWorks works, information about add-on solutions for SolidWorks, and examples of how other companies use SolidWorks within different industries. The CD runs on its own, so all you need to do is stick it in the CD drive.

System Requirements

Make sure that your computer meets the minimum system requirements shown in the following list; if your computer doesn't match up to most of these requirements, you may have problems using the software and files on the CD:

- ✔ A PC with a Pentium or faster processor
- ✔ Microsoft Windows Vista or Windows XP Professional
- ✔ At least 512MB of total RAM installed on your computer
- ✔ A CD-ROM drive
- ✔ A sound card for PCs
- ✔ A monitor capable of displaying at least 256 colors or grayscale
- ✔ A Flash-compatible Web browser
- ✔ A pointing device (mouse)

If you need more information on the basics, check out these books published by Wiley Publishing, Inc.: *PCs For Dummies,* by Dan Gookin, or *Windows XP For Dummies,* 2nd Edition, or *Windows Vista For Dummies,* both by Andy Rathbone.

Using the CD

To run the Interactive Tour CD, follow these steps.

1. **Insert the CD into your computer's CD-ROM drive.**

   The CD's introduction page appears. You see links to interviews discussing the focus, innovation, and use of SolidWorks.

   Note: The interface doesn't launch if you have Autorun disabled. In that case, choose Start⇨Run. In the dialog box that appears, type ***D:\start.exe.*** (Replace *D* with the proper letter if your CD-ROM drive uses a different letter. If you don't know the letter, see how your CD-ROM drive is listed under My Computer.) Click OK.

2. **Click the Start Tour button in the lower-left corner of the main page to continue.**

   The product demo section appears on the left side of the screen.

3. **Select which area to review by clicking the Product Demos, Add-On Solutions, or Case Studies tab at the top of the window.**

   After you select a tab, the menu on the left of the window changes to reflect the selected area.

4. **Click the topic category to view.**

   For example, when you click Drawing Creation within the product demos, the demos Create Drawings, Revise Drawings, and Revision Tables appear.

5. **Click the specific topic to view.**

   The main screen changes to show the selected demo, solution, or case study.

6. **Click the View button within the main window.**

   The View button says View Demo for product demos, View Add-On Info for add-on solutions, and View Video for case studies.

7. **To exit the tour, choose File⇨Exit.**

What You Find on the CD

I organized the following sections by category to provide a summary of the software and other goodies on the CD. If you need help with installing the items provided on the CD, refer to the installation instructions in the preceding section.

Shareware programs are fully functional, free, trial versions of copyrighted programs. If you like particular programs, register with their authors for a nominal fee and receive licenses, enhanced versions, and technical support.

Freeware programs are free, copyrighted games, applications, and utilities. You can copy them to as many PCs as you like — for free — but they offer no technical support.

GNU software is governed by its own license, which is included inside the folder of the GNU software. There are no restrictions on the distribution of GNU software. See the GNU license at the root of the CD for more details.

Trial, demo, or *evaluation* versions of software are usually limited by either time or functionality (and therefore might not let you save a project after you create it).

Product Demos tab

The Product Demos tab has links to demonstrations of SolidWorks features and functions. These video demonstrations show you how to use many of the features within SolidWorks.

The Product Demos tab is divided into different categories, such as Time-Saving Innovations, Drawing Creation, Part Modeling, Assembly Design, Product Data Management, Design Communications, and CAD Productivity. The links appear on the left side of the window.

Add-on Solutions tab

One strength of SolidWorks is the breadth and quality of the solution partners that add functionality and extend the reach of SolidWorks into other areas, such as electronic design, computer-aided manufacturing, and optical design.

The Add-on Solutions tab has links and references for a wide variety of SolidWorks add-on products divided into different categories, including Analysis, Communication, Component Libraries, Data Management, Design, Manufacturing, and Mold Making.

Case Studies tab

One way to discover more about SolidWorks is to see how other companies use and apply SolidWorks in their design environments. The Case Studies tab has industry-segmented case studies of SolidWorks customers.

Sales and Support tab

If you want more information about SolidWorks, the Sales and Support tab displays contact information for SolidWorks offices worldwide.

Troubleshooting

This CD is self contained and self running, so it doesn't need to be installed on your computer.

If the CD doesn't work properly, the two likeliest problems are that you don't have the CD set up to play Macromedia Flash within your browser or the CD doesn't autoplay the tour application.

If you see an error message, such as `Not enough memory` or `Setup cannot continue`, try one or more of the following suggestions and then try using the software again:

- ✔ **Make sure that you have a Flash-compatible Web browser.** Current Web browsers come with the ability to play Flash content. You can also visit the Macromedia Flash Player Download Web site at `www.adobe.com/shockwave/download/download.cgi?P1_Prod_Version=ShockwaveFlash` for more details.

- ✔ **Close all running programs.** The more programs you have running, the less memory is available to other programs. Installation programs typically update files and programs, so if you keep other programs running, the installation may not work properly.

✔ **Try running the application on another computer.** This is a simple way to see whether the problem is just a setup issue on your computer. If the CD runs fine on another computer, you may have a CD driver or Flash compatibility issue.

✔ **Reboot your computer.** Restart your computer and see whether the problem clears up.

If you still have trouble with the CD, please call the Customer Care phone number: (800) 762-2974. Outside the United States, call 1 (317) 572-3994. You can also contact Customer Service by visiting our Web site at www.wiley.com/techsupport. Wiley Publishing, Inc. provides technical support only for installation and other general quality control items; for technical support on the applications themselves, consult the program's vendor or author.

To place additional orders or to request information about other Wiley products, please call (877) 762-2974.

Index

• C •

• E •

• G •

• H •

• I •

• Q •

• W •

Notes

Notes

Notes

BUSINESS, CAREERS & PERSONAL FINANCE

0-7645-9847-3

0-7645-2431-3

Also available:

- Business Plans Kit For Dummies
  0-7645-9794-9
- Economics For Dummies
  0-7645-5726-2
- Grant Writing For Dummies
  0-7645-8416-2
- Home Buying For Dummies
  0-7645-5331-3
- Managing For Dummies
  0-7645-1771-6
- Marketing For Dummies
  0-7645-5600-2

- Personal Finance For Dummies
  0-7645-2590-5*
- Resumes For Dummies
  0-7645-5471-9
- Selling For Dummies
  0-7645-5363-1
- Six Sigma For Dummies
  0-7645-6798-5
- Small Business Kit For Dummies
  0-7645-5984-2
- Starting an eBay Business For Dummies
  0-7645-6924-4
- Your Dream Career For Dummies
  0-7645-9795-7

HOME & BUSINESS COMPUTER BASICS

0-470-05432-8

0-471-75421-8

Also available:

- Cleaning Windows Vista For Dummies
  0-471-78293-9
- Excel 2007 For Dummies
  0-470-03737-7
- Mac OS X Tiger For Dummies
  0-7645-7675-5
- MacBook For Dummies
  0-470-04859-X
- Macs For Dummies
  0-470-04849-2
- Office 2007 For Dummies
  0-470-00923-3

- Outlook 2007 For Dummies
  0-470-03830-6
- PCs For Dummies
  0-7645-8958-X
- Salesforce.com For Dummies
  0-470-04893-X
- Upgrading & Fixing Laptops For Dummies
  0-7645-8959-8
- Word 2007 For Dummies
  0-470-03658-3
- Quicken 2007 For Dummies
  0-470-04600-7

FOOD, HOME, GARDEN, HOBBIES, MUSIC & PETS

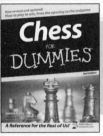

0-7645-8404-9

0-7645-9904-6

Also available:

- Candy Making For Dummies
  0-7645-9734-5
- Card Games For Dummies
  0-7645-9910-0
- Crocheting For Dummies
  0-7645-4151-X
- Dog Training For Dummies
  0-7645-8418-9
- Healthy Carb Cookbook For Dummies
  0-7645-8476-6
- Home Maintenance For Dummies
  0-7645-5215-5

- Horses For Dummies
  0-7645-9797-3
- Jewelry Making & Beading For Dummies
  0-7645-2571-9
- Orchids For Dummies
  0-7645-6759-4
- Puppies For Dummies
  0-7645-5255-4
- Rock Guitar For Dummies
  0-7645-5356-9
- Sewing For Dummies
  0-7645-6847-7
- Singing For Dummies
  0-7645-2475-5

INTERNET & DIGITAL MEDIA

0-470-04529-9

0-470-04894-8

Also available:

- Blogging For Dummies
  0-471-77084-1
- Digital Photography For Dummies
  0-7645-9802-3
- Digital Photography All-in-One Desk Reference For Dummies
  0-470-03743-1
- Digital SLR Cameras and Photography For Dummies
  0-7645-9803-1
- eBay Business All-in-One Desk Reference For Dummies
  0-7645-8438-3
- HDTV For Dummies
  0-470-09673-X

- Home Entertainment PCs For Dummies
  0-470-05523-5
- MySpace For Dummies
  0-470-09529-6
- Search Engine Optimization For Dummies
  0-471-97998-8
- Skype For Dummies
  0-470-04891-3
- The Internet For Dummies
  0-7645-8996-2
- Wiring Your Digital Home For Dummies
  0-471-91830-X

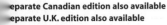

* Separate Canadian edition also available
† Separate U.K. edition also available

Available wherever books are sold. For more information or to order direct: U.S. customers visit www.dummies.com or call 1-877-762-2974.
U.K. customers visit www.wileyeurope.com or call 0800 243407. Canadian customers visit www.wiley.ca or call 1-800-567-4797.

SPORTS, FITNESS, PARENTING, RELIGION & SPIRITUALITY

0-471-76871-5

0-7645-7841-3

Also available:
- Catholicism For Dummies
  0-7645-5391-7
- Exercise Balls For Dummies
  0-7645-5623-1
- Fitness For Dummies
  0-7645-7851-0
- Football For Dummies
  0-7645-3936-1
- Judaism For Dummies
  0-7645-5299-6
- Potty Training For Dummies
  0-7645-5417-4
- Buddhism For Dummies
  0-7645-5359-3

- Pregnancy For Dummies
  0-7645-4483-7 †
- Ten Minute Tone-Ups For Dummies
  0-7645-7207-5
- NASCAR For Dummies
  0-7645-7681-X
- Religion For Dummies
  0-7645-5264-3
- Soccer For Dummies
  0-7645-5229-5
- Women in the Bible For Dummies
  0-7645-8475-8

TRAVEL

0-7645-7749-2

0-7645-6945-7

Also available:
- Alaska For Dummies
  0-7645-7746-8
- Cruise Vacations For Dummies
  0-7645-6941-4
- England For Dummies
  0-7645-4276-1
- Europe For Dummies
  0-7645-7529-5
- Germany For Dummies
  0-7645-7823-5
- Hawaii For Dummies
  0-7645-7402-7

- Italy For Dummies
  0-7645-7386-1
- Las Vegas For Dummies
  0-7645-7382-9
- London For Dummies
  0-7645-4277-X
- Paris For Dummies
  0-7645-7630-5
- RV Vacations For Dummies
  0-7645-4442-X
- Walt Disney World & Orlando
  For Dummies
  0-7645-9660-8

GRAPHICS, DESIGN & WEB DEVELOPMENT

0-7645-8815-X

0-7645-9571-7

Also available:
- 3D Game Animation For Dummies
  0-7645-8789-7
- AutoCAD 2006 For Dummies
  0-7645-8925-3
- Building a Web Site For Dummies
  0-7645-7144-3
- Creating Web Pages For Dummies
  0-470-08030-2
- Creating Web Pages All-in-One Desk
  Reference For Dummies
  0-7645-4345-8
- Dreamweaver 8 For Dummies
  0-7645-9649-7

- InDesign CS2 For Dummies
  0-7645-9572-5
- Macromedia Flash 8 For Dummies
  0-7645-9691-8
- Photoshop CS2 and Digital
  Photography For Dummies
  0-7645-9580-6
- Photoshop Elements 4 For Dummies
  0-471-77483-9
- Syndicating Web Sites with RSS Feeds
  For Dummies
  0-7645-8848-6
- Yahoo! SiteBuilder For Dummies
  0-7645-9800-7

NETWORKING, SECURITY, PROGRAMMING & DATABASES

0-7645-7728-X

0-471-74940-0

Also available:
- Access 2007 For Dummies
  0-470-04612-0
- ASP.NET 2 For Dummies
  0-7645-7907-X
- C# 2005 For Dummies
  0-7645-9704-3
- Hacking For Dummies
  0-470-05235-X
- Hacking Wireless Networks
  For Dummies
  0-7645-9730-2
- Java For Dummies
  0-470-08716-1

- Microsoft SQL Server 2005 For Dummies
  0-7645-7755-7
- Networking All-in-One Desk Reference
  For Dummies
  0-7645-9939-9
- Preventing Identity Theft For Dummies
  0-7645-7336-5
- Telecom For Dummies
  0-471-77085-X
- Visual Studio 2005 All-in-One Desk
  Reference For Dummies
  0-7645-9775-2
- XML For Dummies
  0-7645-8845-1

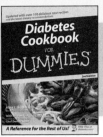

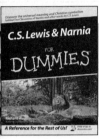